Business
Students
Focus on Ethics

THE LEARNED SOCIETY OF PRAXIOLOGY

PRAXIOLOGY:
The International Annual of Practical Philosophy and Methodology
Vol. 8

EDITOR-IN-CHIEF
Wojciech W. Gasparski
*The Institute of Philosophy and Sociology, Polish Academy of Sciences
Nowy Świat Str. 72, 00-330 Warsaw, Poland*
wgaspars@ifispan.waw.pl

Business Students Focus on Ethics

Praxiology:
The International Annual of Practical
Philosophy and Methodology
Volume 8

editors,
Leo V. Ryan
Wojciech W. Gasparski
Georges Enderle

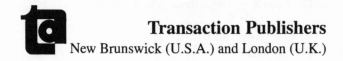

Transaction Publishers
New Brunswick (U.S.A.) and London (U.K.)

Copyright © 2000 by Transaction Publishers, New Brunswick, New Jersey, U.S.A.

All rights reserved under International and Pan-American Copyright Conventions. No part of this book may be reproduced or transmitted in any form or by any means, electronic or mechanical, including photocopy, recording, or any information storage and retrieval system, without prior permission in writing from the publisher. All inquiries should be addressed to Transaction Publishers, Rutgers—The State University, 35 Berrue Circle, Piscataway, New Jersey 08854-8042.

Preparation of this volume was partly supported by the Committee for Scientific Research (Komitet Badań Naukowych), Poland

This book is printed on acid-free paper that meets the American National Standard for Permanence of Paper for Printed Library Materials.

Library of Congress Catalog Number: 00-042599
ISBN: 0-7658-0037-3
Printed in the United States of America

Library of Congress Cataloging-in-Publication Data

Business students focus on ethics / edited by Leo V. Ryan, Wojciech W.
    Gasparski and Georges Enderle in cooperation with Christopher J. Moon.
        p. cm.—(Praxiology: the international annual of practical philoso-
    phy and methodology; vol. 8)
    Includes bibliographical references and index.
        ISBN 0-7658-0037-3 (cloth : alk. paper)
        I. Ryan, Leo V. II. Gasparski, Wojciech. III. Enderle, Georges.
    IV. Praxiology (New Bruswick, N.J.); vol. 8.

HF5387 .B885 2000
174' .4—dc21   00-042599

Contents

PART THREE: Ethical Issues in the Health Care

PART FOUR: Corporate Case Studies

Editorial

Wojciech W. Gasparski
Research Group for Ethics
in the Economy & Business
Institute of Philosophy and Sociology
Polish Academy of Sciences
Warsaw, Poland

Human action is characterized by praxiological and ethical dimensions. The praxiological ones are *effectiveness* and *efficiency*, while the ethical one is *ethicality*, so the approach based on these characteristics is known as the "triple E" approach. Human action in business, as approached from the "triple E" perspective, has been extensively overviewed by eminent scholars in one of the previous volume in the *Praxiology* series[1]. This volume, dealing also with human action in business, is composed of student's – business students – contributions. Some of them have been influenced by writings of the scholars who contributed the previous book, some of them by other educators and professionals but all of them are sensitive and conscious of how important moral competence is for those who fight for increased effectiveness and greater efficiency. This message was recently confirmed at the Research Conference on "Building Moral Competence in Organizations, in Business Schools and in Public Sector Institutions" organizedby the European Business Ethics Network (EBEN). [2]

Even those who, like Bill Gates, try to encourage business people to do their businesses at the "speed of thought", use praxiological arguments not without some ethical flavor:

> Streamlining administrative and internal business processes is an important way to improve the overall efficiency of your employees. Giving knowledge workers good internal tools also sends them a subtle but important message. Companies talk about rewarding initiative and keeping workers focused on business. When employees see a company eliminate bottlenecks and time-draining routine administrative chores from their workdays, they know that the company values their time-and wants them to use it profitably. It's easy to measure when you make your factory workers more efficient. It's hard to measure when you make your knowledge workers more effective, but it's just common sense that knowledge workers who are not distracted or burdened by routine matters will do better work. The benefit to customers is that your employees spend less time shuffling papers and more time on customer needs.[3]

The ethical fragrance stems from happiness of employees, customers and other stakeholders perhaps. Writes the quoted author:

> I recommend the following approach to integrating customer complaints and wish lists into product and service development.
>
> 1. Focus on your most unhappy customers.
>
> 2. Use technology to gather rich information on their unhappy experiences with your product and to find out what they want you to put into the product.
>
> 3. Use technology to drive the news to the right people in a hurry.
>
> If you do these three things, you'll turn those draining bad news experiences into an exhilarating process of improving your product or service. Unhappy customers are always a concern. They're also your greatest opportunity. Adopting a learning posture rather than a negative defensive posture can make customer complaints your best source of significant quality improvements. Adopting the right technology will give you the power to capture and convert companies into better products and services fast.[4]

We gradually observe a shift from a pure two dimensional (effectiveness and efficiency) analysis of human action in business to the three dimensional, i.e. taking into account ethicality as well. However, the shift is shyly masked under different 'nicknames' in the shift. Although the words 'ethics' or 'ethicality' are not present in the subject indexes of many business books *ethics* and *ethicality* are discussed implicitly in almost all of them. A good example of such books is the recent book by George Soros the number one investor and philanthropist. Writes he:

> My critique of the global capitalist system falls under two main headings. One concerns the defects of the market mechanism. Here I am talking primarily about the instabilities built into financial markets. The other concerns the deficiencies of what I have to call, for lack of better name, the nonmarket sector. By this I mean primarily the failure of politics and the erosion of moral values on both the national and the international level. [...]

Individual decision making as expressed through the market mechanism is much more efficient (a praxiological argument – my comment W.W.G.) than collective decision making as practiced in politics. This is particularly true in the international arena. The disenchantment with politics has fed market fundamentalism and the rise of market fundamentalism has, in turn, contributed to the failure of politics. One of the great defects of the global capitalist system is that it has allowed the market mechanism and the profit motive to penetrate into fields of activity where they do not properly belong.

[…] When I speak of the nonmarket sector, I mean the collective interests of society, of the social values that do not find expression in markets. There are people who question whether such collective interests exist at all. Society, they maintain, consists of individuals, and their interests are best expressed by their decisions as market participants. For instance, if they feel philanthropic they can express it by giving money away. In this way, everything can be reduced to monetary values.

It hardly needs saying that this view is false. There are things we can decide individually; there are other things that can only be dealt with collectively. As a market participant, I try to maximize my profits. As a citizen, I am concerned about social values: peace, justice, freedom, or whatever (ethical argument – my comment W.W.G.). I cannot give expression to those values as a market participant. Let us suppose that the rules that govern financial markets ought to be changed. I cannot change them unilaterally. If I impose the rules on myself but not on the others, it would effect my own performance in the market but it would have no effect on what happens in the markets because no single participant is supposed to be able to influence the outcome. […] The promotion of self-interest to a moral principle has corrupted politics and the failure of politics has become the strongest argument in favour of giving markets an ever freer reign.

[…] The global capitalist system is a distorted form of open society. Open society is based on the recognition that our understanding is imperfect and our actions have unintended consequences. All our institutional arrangements are liable to be flawed and just because we find them wanting we should not abandon them. Rather we should create institutions with error-correcting mechanisms built in. These mechanisms include both markets and democracy. But neither will work unless we are aware of our fallibility and willing to recognize our mistakes.[5]

Is this a replica of a century old *fin de siècle* that so many authors try now to suggest a new *Jugendstil* relevant for the 21st century? Or have we finally become aware of some of the whys and wherefores in the failure of social systems design.[6] I think that the contributors of this volume seem to be conscious of what they must take into account for their careers as 21st century managers, for their warnings are addressed not only to external stakeholders but also to themselves, and to their generation.

The Editorial in Volume 5 concluded with a reference to collaborative efforts and with a dedication of the volume *Human Action in Busi-*

ness: Praxiological and Ethical Dimensions to the First World Congress of Business, Economics and Ethics organized on July 25–28, 1996 in Tokyo, Japan, by the International Society of Business, Economics and Ethics (ISBEE). By fortuitous circumstances, this volume, *Business Students focus on Ethics* appears in time to be dedicated to two significant and related international conferences. It is a pleasure to dedicate this volume to the Second World Congress of Business, Economics and Ethics organization on July 19–23, 2000 in Sao Paulo, Brazil by ISBEE and the EBEN'2000 (European Business Ethics Network) Conference organization on September 2000 in Cambridge, U.K.

Notes

1. W. W. Gasparski, L. V. Ryan, eds., 1996, *Human Action in Business: Praxiological and Ethical Dimensions*, Transaction Publishers, New Brunswick (USA)–London (UK).
2. June 18–20, 1999, Sandvika n. Oslo, Norway.
3. B. Gates with C. Hemingway, 1999, *Business @ the Speed of Thought: Using a Digital Nervous System*, Penguin Books, London, pp. 59–60.
4. Ibid., p. 186.
5. G. Soros, 1998, *The Crisis of Global Capitalism: Open Society Endangered*, Little, Brown a. Co., London, pp. xxiii–xxix.
6. W. W. Gasparski, 1994, Some Whys and Wherefores in the Failure of Social Systems Design, *Systems Practice*, Vol. 7:6, pp. 687–697.

Introduction

Leo V. Ryan, C.S.V.
DePaul University
Chicago, IL U.S.A.

Business Students Focus on Ethics (Volume 8) should be considered a complimentary and companion volume to *Human Action in Business* (Volume 5). The development of the "Triple E" (Efficiency, Effectiveness and Ethics) in Volume 5 provides the theoretical framework for this volume. Twenty-five MA and MBA students from seven countries in Europe, North and South America, and the Pacific Rim have interpreted the theory, together with their respective international perspectives, to form the applied business ethics framework for this volume.

The use of "students" is intentional. The title describes their academic status at the time they undertook the preparation of the essays which comprise this volume. While "students" enrolled in MA or MBA level courses in Business Ethics, they were simultaneously "Future Managers" since these essays were written near the end of their formal studies. All have since graduated. As their biographical entries reveal, they are all presently "managers."

This Volume seeks to achieve several objectives: (1) recognizing ethics as legitimate content in graduate level studies in business worldwide; (2) presenting the serious examination of specific ethical concerns by young managers; (3) reflecting on these concerns from across cultural and geographic borders; and (4) demonstrating the quality of their analysis and recommendations. Volume 8 extends the relationship between praxiology and ethics that has been an underlying theme through-out this series of International Annuals of Practical Philosophy and Methodology.

In Volume I, *Praxiologies and the Philosophy of Economics*, Professor Henry Hiz, University of Pennsylvania, wrote:

> Ethics ... is a property of action, particularly of social action... I would prefer to say that people may be moral, benevolent, magnanimous, noble, and reserve the term 'ethical' to actions... Morality is a personal quality, whereas ethics is a property of social activity that must be judged by its results (Hiz 1992:422–3).

Professor Arne Collen concluded Volume 3, *Design Systems: General Applications of Methodology Praxiology*, with an invitation to explore further the ethical domain of human actions.

> With increasing complexity comes new paradoxes and a natural shift in human responsiveness toward greater engagement in preparatory activities...
> Preparation fully considered is responsible, in that it includes a careful examination of preparatory actions in relation to consequences of direct actions. This examination must be necessarily methodological, praxiological and ethical (Collen 1995:463).

Volume 5 was devoted to extending the praxiological and ethical dialogue through scholarly contributions which further developed the relationships between the efficiency of human actions, their effectiveness in business and economic life, and the impact on the field of social action known as ethics.

The student papers published in this Volume were prepared in connection with their respective Master of Arts and their MBA level courses. All of the papers, except two, were completed in fulfillment of requirements in Business Ethics courses taught by the co-editors, Professor Dr. Georges Enderle in China and the U.S.A., or by Professor Dr. Wojciech W. Gasparski in Poland or by our collaborator, Christopher J. Moon in the U.K. Two special research papers, which eventually became the chapters by William W. Kirkley (New Zealand) and Dianne Flannery (U.S.A.), were recommended by Dr. John Donaldson (U.K.) and Dr. Marvin Brown (U.S.A.) respectively.

Professor Wojciech W. Gasparski is Head, Research Group for Ethics in the Economy and Business, Institute of Philosophy and Sociology, Polish Academy of Sciences, Warsaw. He is also Honorary President, Learned Society of Praxiology (Poland) and Editor-in-Chief of this series of International Annuals of Practical Philosophy and Methodology.

The six Polish essays in this Volume were selected by him from papers written for his M.A. seminar, "Business Ethics and Culture" by students at the American Study Center, University of Warsaw.

Professor Georges Enderle is the Arthur and Mary O'Neil Professor of International Business Ethics, University of Notre Dame, South Bend, Indiana. He was a co-founder of the European Business Ethics Network (EBEN) and current Vice President, the International Society of Business, Economics and Ethics (ISBEE). The Chinese essays were selected from papers written for his MBA course in Business Ethics at the China Europe International Business School (CEIBS), Shanghai, where he has been teaching since 1996. The North and South American essays were chosen from papers written for his MBA course in "International Business Ethics" at the University of Notre Dame, where he has been teaching since 1993.

The essays from the United Kingdom were recommended by Christopher J. Moon, our U.K. collaborator former Senior Lecturer, Business and Organizational Ethics, Anglia Business School, Cambridge and Danbury, U.K., who is Manager, Ethics and Responsible Business Practice, Arthur Andersen, London. He is also Secretary, EBEN-U.K. and member of the organizing committee for EBEN 2000 at Cambridge. His U.K. essays were selected from papers written for the MBA Modules in "Business Ethics" at the Management School, Imperial College, University of London, where he taught before his appointment at Anglia.

Drs. Donaldson and Brown each recommended one significant paper to be included in this collection of student essays.

Dr. John Donaldson is an Honorary Visiting Fellow, International Centre for Law, Management and Industrial Relations, University of Leicester. He served as the project supervisor for William W. Kirkley's MA/LLM dissertation from which his chapter is adapted.

Likewise, Dr. Marvin Brown who has extensive experience in organizational ethics and communications and corporate ethical decision making, teaches at The College of Professional Studies, University of San Francisco, and the California School of Professional Psychology in Orinda, California. At the later school he taught a "Seminar on Business Ethics" in which Diane Flannery was enrolled. His course inspired the topic of her chapter; Dr. Brown was also her dissertation director.

To better appreciate the various chapters which constitute this volume, it is important to understand the ethical perspective, teaching philosophy and the context in which these selections were originally pre-

pared as MA or MBA assignments. The section which follows describes
Professors Gasparski and Enderle and Mr. Moon's approaches to business ethics in their respective courses.

Professor Gasparski approaches Business Ethics from a Praxiological-
Systemic perspective. For him the notion of *business ethics* (BE) is used
in two contexts: philosophical and practical. In the philosophical context BE is a reflection on the *ethos*, that is a collection of virtues constituting *resourcefulness* (called *arete* by ancient Greeks) of business people. According to Aristotle there are *aretai dianoetikai* (like discernment,
acuteness, wisdom, presence of mind, and others based on reason and
having an intellectual character) and *aretai ethikai* (like braveness, justice, kindness, etc.). The term *virtue* belongs to the second group, i.e. to
the *resourcefulness* founded on character developed by customs and
habits and not by education. In the practical context BE is understood as
the norms and values present in the business life, that is as the ethos of
business itself.

Resourcefulness, then, is the meeting point for ethics and praxiology.
Ethics studies *aretai ethikai*. Praxiology studies *aretai dianoetikai*. Both
encourage people to perform resourceful actions, that is, actions which
are effective and efficient[1] ('double E') and aimed to achieve ethical
goals ('the third E') in moral ways. Professor Gasparski considers the
resourcefulness of human actions from a systemic view and defined by
the 'triple E,' as the common subject of praxiology and ethics, which
demands their interaction and cooperation. He quotes Professor Hiz that:
"Ethics must be practical. The issues involved are too important to waste
any effort" (Hiz 1992:429).

Because Professor Enderle has included essays from his students in
China, North and South America, we describe his methodology in more
detail. Professor Enderle taught graduate and postgraduate business and
economic ethics for over ten years in Switzerland, Germany, and Italy,
before he began teaching MBA students at the College of Business Administration in the University of Notre Dame, U.S.A. In Europe, his
students, enrolled from various disciplines i.e. management, economics, philosophy, and theology, all with some training and interest in grap-
pling with theoretical issues but personally lacking clearly articulated
professional career goals. In the U.S.A., most students pursuing the MBA
already have several years of business experience and resolutely focus
their studies towards relatively specific business careers. They expect
the required business ethics course to be very practical, even entertain-

ing, and quickly dismiss most theoretical considerations. They want practical advice for improving the ethical quality of their decision-making as future managers.

Professor Enderle found the teaching situation again different in China. Chinese students are on the average older than those in the U.S.A., have more years of business experience, possess a very practical sense but also have an interest in broader theoretical questions. What distinguishes Chinese MBA students from MBA students in Europe and North America is their cultural background, their confrontation with modernity and the challenges of a rapidly changing economy.

Considering these contrasting circumstances, Professor Enderle recognized that teaching business ethics must vary in terms of objectives, methodology, readings, and case studies. His *teaching philosophy* embodies a number of common features which he applies in various circumstances and cultural settings and his philosophy influences the way his students write their research papers.

Professor Enderle believes that *decision-making* and *taking action* should be at the core of teaching business ethics. For him, to describe and analyze the world is not enough, nor does it suffice to only raise the awareness of ethical values. Rather, students must be exposed regularly to questions concerning "what to do" and "what one should do," that is, to the very essence of ethics. Normally managers are under pressure to act. When faced with *concrete* questions of "what ought we to do?", managers cannot postpone the answer indefinitely. Therefore, he believes that business ethics should primarily struggle with problems of decision making and taking action.[2] The research papers of the Chinese students attempt to follow this "action-orientation."

Professor Enderle also believes that because decision-making and action are integral components of human nature, so human decision-making involves *a moral dimension*. His students are encouraged to understand the quality of this dimension, to make it explicit, to relate it to their own moral understanding, and to enter a dialogue of *ethical reasoning* (cf. Brown 1998). He accords a special respect for the *expertise and competencies* possessed by MBA students because of their respective business experiences, often far exceeding the knowledge of the business ethics teacher. The challenge of an integrated approach to business ethics is to recognize and integrate these competencies, rather than to ignore them and retreat to discussing ethical issues in relatively abstract terms.

His teaching experiences in Europe, the USA, and China confirm ethical problems in business to be especially complex, particularly in the international and Chinese contexts for which there are no clear-cut nor quick-fix solutions. Students must become aware of and understand these complexities in both business and ethical terms. Yet, they cannot content themselves only with this awareness and understanding. Action-oriented business ethics is more demanding because it seeks "good" decisions and actions in complex situations. Students are challenged to develop, with expertise and imagination, practical recommendations which help to solve complex problems.

With reference to the essays selected for this volume, students were provided with a number of specific instructions for writing their research papers. The objective was to study, in some depth, a specific topic in international business ethics. Students were free to choose any topic within the triangular area defined by a "business" side, an "international" side, and an "ethical" side. All three sides were required to be addressed in the paper. The approach embraces three steps: (1) Clearly identify the problem as it arises in practice. (2) Analyze the different dimensions of the problem, that is, the "business," "international," and "ethical" dimensions, from an interdisciplinary perspective (theoretical input). (3) On the basis of the analysis, recommendations to (help) solve the problem, identified in the first step, are developed (practice-orientation again).

Ideally speaking, throughout this three-step approach, the student advances on "two legs," that is, the "leg" of factual, descriptive, and analytical knowledge (in practice and theory) and the "leg" of ethical values and norms (in practice and theory). Integrating both perspectives is the challenge of any applied ethics, including business ethics.

The objectives of the Business Ethics MBA Modules at the Management School, Imperial College designed by Christopher J. Moon, his philosophy and teaching methodology approximate the understandings of Professor Gasparski and the approaches of Professor Enderle.

The objective of the MBA Modules at Imperial College was to discuss ethical considerations that impact business activities; to help managers approach ethical problems in an informed and skillful way; and to encourage policy development and effective practice. Dialogue was encouraged between course participants. Sessions were organized around formal input, case analysis, and an open forum for discussion. Sessions included various current issues and cases in Business Ethics, ethical theory as related to business practice, and a review of those practical considerations necessary to manage business ethics in the workplace.

Mr. Moon employs real cases presented for analysis, some video presentations and recommended readings. Students delivered presentations on agreed topics, especially related to their own organizational experiences. He believs that the MBA Modules should "be captivating, theoretically sound, and practical in outlook." The assessments for the modules were based on individually negotiated topics. Mr. Moon used specific criteria for preparing assignments which included: a thorough, factual review of the topic; identifying the ethical issues involved; highlighting the factors contributing to the alleged unethical conduct (as appropriate); evaluation of the organizational response (as appropriate); identifying the management issues in the case and recommending what could/should be done to prevent similar incidents occurring in the future.

The three essays selected by Mr. Moon for this volume are international in outlook but represent quite different areas of concern. These essays have been updated for this Volume but still retain their original MBA student mind set.

As for Dr. Donaldson's teaching philosophy, he sees business ethics as part of a broad set of philosophical and praxiological issues in business. These issues relate to *whose* values are to count, *how* they are put into practice and *by whom*. They are all seen as problematic, but capable of resolution. He sees such resolution as requiring a measure of agreement on criteria and processes for improvement.

Dr. Donaldson recommended the Kirkley paper on "The Role of Values in Organizational Transformation and Strategic Success" because of its clear, mature style and the importance of the topic which advocates the concept that how things are done is as important as the ends and draws its conclusions from "real life hands on" experience.

The approach of Dr. Marvin Brown to business ethics focuses on the development of responsible communication among an organization's various stakeholders. This approach assumes that an organization's life can be understood as an on-going conversation among various stakeholders, who together have possibilities for engaging in dialogue and developing more just and mature human communities.

In presenting these student essays to the broader public we offer these essays as representative of student concerns about a range of ethical issues facing our global society. These essays reveal the emphasis and insights influenced by the particular culture of the student authors together with issues of concern and importance to them. Several essays are prompted by personal experiences. These essays reflect ways in which graduate business students of different countries and cultures assess problems related to business, the economy and society. We believe that this volume of essays can serve as a model for similar exercises in other graduate level international business ethics courses.

We have arranged the essays into four inter-related groups. The first essays are concerned with a *Praxiological and Ethical Framework*. The initial chapters relate issues of human action from both the theory of human action (i.e. praxiological) and ethical dimensions. Business ethics in the title of this Volume refers to both the field of business ethics and to the title of courses for which these essays were written. Our ethical concern is for the rightness or wrongness of human action. In the study of business ethics we also seek to understand business institutions, practices and activities in the light of norms, values and the ethos of business itself.

The *Praxiological and Ethical Framework* papers truly capture the multi cultural multinational perspective of this volume. William W. Kirkley (New Zealand) explores values as the foundation for organizational transformation and strategic success. Krzysztof Klincewicz (Poland) examines the post industrial era of information technology, Toffler's "prosumer society" globalization and the new ways of communication in the marketplace. He compares the changing paradigms for business ethics between the industrial and post industrial eras where the focus is the customer and building trust. Diane Flannery (U.S.A.) examines the enlarged concept of corporate social responsibility and its different interpretations in the U.S. socio-economic political culture.

Four complimentary papers complete this initial section. Barbara Szyszka (Poland) and Agnieszka Ratajczyk (Poland) in separate papers examine general cultural and ethical aspects of American business in Poland. Barbara Szyszka, using interviews with American executives associated in Poland with Warsaw Marriott, Coca Cola and PepsiCo, and employing the framework of Geet Hofstede, studied their performance in the areas of corporate culture, social responsibility and managerial ethics. She concluded that in her study, the ethical dimensions of corporate culture and social responsibility received more attention than managerial ethics. Agnieszka Ratajczyk studied products and promotion materials predicated on trademarks as a "cultural symbol of

America." The American scene is contrasted with the Polish experience where trademarks are more traditional and often reflect the "national culture" not a "consumer culture." Her study compares and contrasts trademarks and explores ethical issues related to both counterfeiting and the misuse of trademarks.

Angela Xu and Julia Tiam (China) study the ethical issues of multilevel marketing (MLM), popularly known as "pyramid selling" introduced in China by Avon and later by Amway and Mary Kay Cosmetics. The authors examine "responsible" versus "fraudulent" multilevel marketing from the macro, meso and micro perspectives considering market relationships and responsibilities and conclude "China today is not ready for [MLM]." (The government has since outlawed pyramid sales schemes.)

Pablo Flores (Equador) defends the world's most renowned site of environmental diversity, the Amazon Rainforest, and marshals a persuasive call not for "normal ethics" but for a new system of "environmental ethics." His essay surveys the economic motivation of interested stakeholders, the relevant ethical analysis, sustainability and intergenerational responsibility for Rainforest preservation. He contends that economic development and environmental protection can be compatible, but only when environmental ethics and corporate responsibility unite.

In our second division four papers address *Social Issues*, specifically, *Compensation and Labor*. The first two essays address questions of compensation. Hannah Lu and George Cui (China) explore the issues related to fairness of various compensation arrangements between expatriate and local counterparts. Using a joint venture case, the authors examine the "same job, same pay" concept from the economic, Chinese social-cultural and ethical perspectives. They outline the management consequences of compromises which fail to incorporate honesty, fairness and open dialogue. Victor Trujillo (Venezuela), drawing on personal experience, explores the socio-economic and cultural questions of what constitutes "adequate" pay for both low skilled workers and highly educated employees in Third and Fourth World countries. Respecting both the corporate and employee perspectives and acknowledging the complexity of Venezuelan conditions, he appeals to concepts from Catholic Social teachings ("common good," "fair profit," "living wage"), the pronouncements Vatican II, Caux Roundtable Principles and ethics education as basis for negotiating "adequate" compensation agreements.

Two specific applications of the praxiological and ethical principles are reported in essays by Kevin Kreuter (U.S.A.) who examines the plight of North American migrant workers in American agriculture and child labor, specifically in the Brazilian orange industry, studied by Michelle Amestoy (U.S.A.) and Melisa Crosbie (U.S.A.). Kevin Kreuter, using a biographical approach, exposes the hardships of the migrant agricultural worker. Examining, first, the facts about the wages, housing, health and safety of migrant field laborers and, then, acknowledging that practices are "unfair, unjust and unethical" he concludes that the ethical responsibilities "fall upon many shoulders" (farmer, landlord, government, public) and the "true ethical issues involved" are increasingly difficult to assess and assign. He concludes his extended analysis with "plausible solutions."

Incensed and irate about what they read in the business press about child labor "exploitation" in Brazil "the world's leading orange juice supplier" Michelle Amestoy and Melissa Crosbie examined the Brazilian economy, political and legal structures, and described regional and worldwide child labor legislation (extensive), local Brazilian enforcement (minimal) and public pressure (increasing). Using basic ethical analysis, they offer recommendations for addressing the issue.

Health Care has emerged as a critical social issue worldwide. A third section of papers examine three *Ethical Issues in Health Care* from three different cultural perspectives. Elizabeth Klein (U.K.) writes on the commercialization of gene therapy. Yan Cuo (China) challenges the claims that health foods really promote improved health. Bozena Kochman (Poland) examines the ethical impact of advertising, marketing promotions and sale of addictive products (alcohol and cigarettes) in the United States and in her native Poland.

Elizabeth Klein offers the reader a scholarly, but highly readable, analysis of gene therapy, ethical issues surrounding research, therapy and especially the biomedical ethics of gene therapy and commercialization (i.e., patents, testing, outcomes which result in job discrimination, insurance refusal, social or prejudice). Her essay invites study, ethical analysis and debate before "gene therapy becomes a common occurrence" and we loose "the opportunity to influence the debate."

Only in 1997 was "health food" define to include both common foods and foods designed to regulate human physiological functionality but not curing diseases. Yan Cuo examines ethical issues of overly exaggerated health food advertisements which promote "mysterious active substances" while disguising their functions or potential threat to health, and the selling of small dosages with low active substance content at high prices. She challenges marketers, government and the public to learn which is a "food" and which is a "drug substitute" and to be responsive to their moral and legal obligations. Bozena Kochman presents facts and the praxiological and ethical framework for her discussion about the exploitation of addictive American-Polish cigarette advertising as well as the questionable marketing techniques, legal actions and ethical controversies involved in promoting alcoholic beverage sales in U.S.A. and Poland. She ends with an example of Polish legal and ethical constraints applied to Lancut Distillery.

No collection of business ethics essays would be complete without a series of specific *Corporate Case Studies*. The concluding six chapters in this volume examine specific ethical, social responsibility or value questions. The cases student chose to examine are relatively well known. They include: Alima-Gerber, national leader in baby food and one of the first examples of privatized capital in Poland (Agnieszka Szumska, Poland); the evaluation of Liberian Ship Registry measured against the Richard De George Guidelines for Moral Multinationals (Keven Kelleher and Kerry Ward, U.S.A.); another case examines those cultural characteristics, illustrated by American and Polish examples, which permit advertising to be called a "Manipulative Art" (Monika Dębicka, Poland); an "on-site" study of the Bangladesh Grameen (Banking for the Poor) Bank experiment; (Lawrence Pineda and John M. Walusis, U.S.A.); Ethical Issues and Contributing Factors in the Barring Bank Collapse (Sue Cooper, U.K.); the final case represents a 1999 updated report on Shell in Nigeria (Simon Bernstein, U.K.).

We now offer this volume for your study and reading pleasure. The twenty essays which comprise Volume 8 have been selected by the co-editors and collaborators from several hundred business ethics course assignments. We trust that your experience reading these choices will match the enthusiasm we experienced in selecting and publishing them in this Annual.

To quote Linda Trevino and Katherine Nelson:

> An understanding of ethics is critical to all of us because good ethics represents the very essence of civilized society. Ethics is the bedrock on which all our relationships are built; ... Ethics is not about the connections we have to other beings – we are all connected – rather it's about the quality of that connection. That's the real bottom line (Trevino & Nelson 1999:17–8).

Endnotes

1. As suggested by Tadeusz Kotarbinski, a founding father of Polish praxiology; Cf.: W. W. Gasparski, 1993, *A Philosophy of Practicality: A Treatise on the Philosophy of Tadeusz Kotarbinski*, Societas Philosophical Fennica, Helsinki.
2. For a discussion of this approach, see Enderle, G. 1993. *Handlungsorientierte Wirtschaftsethik. Grundlagen und Anwendungen.* [Action-oriented Business Ethics. Foundations and Applications.] Bern: Haupt; and Enderle, G. 1993. "What is Business Ethics?" In *Business Ethics: Japan and the Global Economy*, T. W. Dunfee and Y. Nagayasu (eds.). Dordrecht/Boston/London: Kluwer Academic Publishers, p. 133–150.

References

Brown, M. T. 1998. *The Ethical Process. A Strategy for Making Good Decisions.* Second edition. Upper Saddle River, NJ: Prentice Hall.

Collen, A. 1995. Introduction." In *Design Systems: General Application of Methodology. Praxiology* Vol. 3., ed. Arne Collen and Wojciech W. Gasparski. New Brunswick, N.J.: Transaction Publishers.

Hiz, H. 1992. Praxiology, Society and Ethics." In *Praxiologies and the Philosophy of Economics. Praxiology* Vol. 1, ed. J. Lee Auspitz, Wojciech W. Gasparski, Marek K. Mlicki, and Klemens Szaniawski. New Brunswick, N.J.: Transaction Publishers.

Trevino, L. K. & Nelson, K. A. 1999. *Managing Business Ethics: Straight Talk About How To Do It Right.* Second edition. New York: John Wiley and Sons, Inc.

PART ONE

Praxiological and Ethical Framework

Organizational Transformation and Strategic Success: The Role of Values

William W. Kirkley
Management Consultant
Auckland, New Zealand

1. Introduction

The CEO stared out from his corner office across the harbor, cluttered with racing yachts gathering at close quarters to start the Friday afternoon regatta. You could almost feel the sleek hulls quivering like so many leashed greyhounds waiting for the starter's gun. A puff of smoke from that launch, and they're off! The CEO moved forward in his leather chair in anticipation ... nothing happened! Yachts floundered, scattering in different directions as if in a slow motion action replay of some fast paced game. A sudden drop in wind and all those quivering vessels were lying dead in the water, sails flapping listlessly, no one going anywhere fast, or at all, for that matter. The CEO watched as sails came down, boats turned and made their way back to anchorage under motor power. There would be no further racing that day. The CEO turned away, the anticipation and excitement of watching racers carve their way through the swell, furiously tacking to gain an advantage over their opponents, giving way to sudden disappointment and uncharacteristic frustration. Where was the wind? Why didn't they wait for it to pick up again? Why did they give up so soon? What will happen next time? Who will come out the winner? Instead of some free entertainment, I'll have to face the rush hour traffic, what a waste of time, effort and energy, he thought.

And so it is with many organizational transformations. The enthusiasm of new corporate vision and the challenge of taking the business to higher levels of performance generates untold excitement out of the boardroom, but it somehow flounders when communicated to the masses who rarely greet it with the same embracing eagerness. Like our racing yachts, the punch goes out of the message, the wind drops and so many employees wander back to their desks either waiting for the axe to fall or, at the very least, uncertain of their future. It is hardly surprising then that so many transformations end in failure. The problem in many instances lies not in *what* the business wants to achieve strategically, but in *how* to achieve it. The essence of these failed initiatives lies predominantly in the area of commonly shared values. Either these values do not exist as a formal system in the organization, or, where they do exist, they are not recognized as a critical foundation of the business and are consequently paid lip service.

The examples related here are taken from New Zealand experience; however, management ideas are often transferred from other countries. Certain values tend to transcend international boundaries whilst others represent the unique cultural circumstances of a particular country. Some of these common values are explored from a local perspective.

J. Donaldson (1989) offers the view that central to business ethics is the systematic handling of organizational values. In evaluating action, acceptable values need to be promoted and shared. The process of promoting and sharing these values is as important as the content of those values. This paper seeks to explore the role and practical application of some widely discussed values in business i.e. *trust, empowerment* and *quality.* How these values are perceived and acted upon is of vital importance to the organizational transformation effort, and indeed, to sustained organizational success. As Aristotle put it, "the conclusion of an ethical argument is an action."

This paper also seeks to determine some of the primary causes for organizational transformation and to illustrate the critical role played by commonly shared values. It is postulated that the stronger the shared value-base in an organization, the better the chance of instituting successful transformation initiatives and the greater the chance of sustained strategic success. It is widely recognized in business and economics that cause and effect sequences can be difficult to isolate. Many variables, both from within and outside the organization, impinge on transformation efforts. Even well managed initiatives can fail to achieve strategic goals. However, it is possible in most cases to identify some common factors that contribute to overall strategic success. With organizational transformation fast becoming recognized as a strategy for gaining competitive advantage, it is vitally important that transformation capacity be embedded in the organizational value system. This enables the organization to achieve *sustained* strategic success.

2. The Impetus to Transform

In New Zealand, a survey of 173 organizations cites competition, profitability, client demands and technology as the main catalysts for transformation (KPMG[1] 1997). Most of this change is driven by external factors, the top five of which are listed below:
• Competition – 78.4%
• Increased requirements for profitability – 74.1%
• Customer demands – 73.9%
• Introduction of new technology – 66.5%
• Introduction of new services / products by competitors – 53.2%
Other reasons include ownership changes, sources of supply and international agreements. External factors play a significantly more important role for inducing transformation in organizations than internal issues.

From the same report, 71% of the companies surveyed reported only moderate success with their change projects. Six percent reported total failure to achieve strategic initiatives. A constant bombardment of literature suggests that over 80% of all change initiatives fail to achieve strategic goals. Why is this? Is there a misinterpretation of concepts? Is it perhaps a lack of understanding about organizational dynamics? Or is it that we simply do not know how to go about achieving transformation?

3. Organizational Transformation

Organizational Transformation (OT) can be defined as: "Profound, fundamental changes in thought and actions, which create irreversible discontinuity in the experience of a system" (KPMG 1997:12).

Let's examine this definition in more detail:

(a) *OT is profound* – words synonymous with 'profound' include 'deep', 'extreme', 'intense' and 'penetrating'. A system undergoing profound transformation will therefore have actions taking place that are radically altering its basic configuration. OT is intense, focused, and pervasive, influencing everything in that system.

(b) *OT fundamentally changes thoughts and actions* – businesses essentially comprise three elements, namely, processes, technology and people. Processes and technology are relatively easy to change in comparison to people. OT requires a core change in people's attitudes, values and behavior if it is to be successful. A significant number of people in the business need to come to a new appreciation of the future direction of the company and actively commit through their behavior to fulfilling those goals.

(c) *OT creates an irreversible discontinuity in the experience of the system* – a system generally undergoes incremental change in a fluid, continuous way with little or no disruption to its routine. It reaches a state of balance, which it can maintain with minor adjustments over a period of time. OT in a business systems context represents an almost abrupt stop. The system literally takes on a new strategic dimension and form in order to embrace an alternative direction from which it cannot return.

The essence of the above definition must be emphasized. For an organization to qualify its initiative under the heading of 'transformation', the majority of individuals in that organization must fundamentally alter their behavior and demonstrate an active commitment toward the future direction of the business. OT is about the emergence of a new belief system and necessarily involves re-framing, a fundamental and pervasive altering of the business context, which represents a discontinuous change in the organizations shared value system and culture.

Transformation is clearly not incremental change. Its realizable goal is a paradigm shift in organizational capability – a resocialization so thorough, that employees feel they are working for a different company, a leap in a company's ability to meet or exceed industry benchmarks, a jump in bottom line results.

The words 'change' and 'transformation' are often used synonymously. Transformation, in and of itself, entails a considerable amount of *radical* change. However, not all change is transformation and it is important to make this distinction. Three types of change have been identified as those most frequently implemented by organizations.

1. *Improving Operations*. The goal of improving operations is to achieve a quantum improvement in the organization's efficiency either through cost reductions, quality, service improvements, reducing development or service cycle times. The most common tools used to do this are Business Process Re-engineering (BPR), organizational restructuring and redefining performance outcomes. Change in this context cannot be referred to as organizational transformation as there has been no radical redefinition of the business, merely the processes within it.

2. *Strategic Improvement*. This is a process of changing an organization's strategy and seeks to regain a sustainable competitive advantage by redefining business objectives, generating new competencies and using them to better address market opportunities. Various methods are used to generate improvements from within the organization. Formal reviews and debating strategic alternatives throughout the organization enable management to obtain useful input and build shared commitment to future action. For some firms, however, strategic improvements take place against a backdrop of changing technology, aggressive competition, shifting customer demands and new market opportunities, all of which require swift action on behalf of management. Compared to improving operations, strategic improvements take longer and carry substantial risk as there is no guarantee that the new strategy or competencies will succeed. In and of itself, this also, cannot be construed as transformation as it seeks only to re-align the business and its capabilities around its original strategic objectives.

3. *Organizational Self-renewal*. Self-renewal creates abilities within the organization to anticipate and cope with change so those strategic and operational gaps do not develop. Self-renewal demands particular types of behavior, such as, facing reality, setting high performance standards and being accountable for results, by large numbers of managers and employees. To enable these changes organizations find it necessary to strip away bureaucracy, de-layer structures and provide mechanisms for speedy decision making. Many of the techniques mentioned above, such as BPR, are used as tactics in an overall transformation strategy. Programs that introduce quality systems and provide for policies regarding continuous improvement are fairly typical of this approach. Self-renewal, because of its emphasis on actual behaviors, comes closest to the definition of the essence of transformation. Self-renewal further suggests that the organization has the long-term capacity, in terms of skill and knowledge, to constantly regenerate itself. Hence, organizations

characterized by this inherent capacity will undergo successively less disruptive transformations and achieve sustainable strategic advantage.

Successful transformation follows a carefully planned critical path. Neglecting to take cognizance of each step in the process increases the risk of failure in the initiative. An analysis of the role values play in this process will indicate why, in most cases, New Zealand organizations achieve only marginal success in their transformation initiatives.

4. The Critical Role of Values

Despite the body of knowledge and widespread evidence of change applications, New Zealand business continues to struggle with the actual implementation of transformation initiatives. Constant competitive pressure often forces organizations to attempt any measure and consequently sacrifice longer-term goals for short-term expediency. This short-term focus is underpinned by several factors present in the economy.

- There is a significant reduction in reliance on managerial authority as evidenced by short-term employment contracts.
- Formal work rules and narrow divisions of work are giving way instead to increasing individual empowerment and wider task responsibilities.
- The traditional hierarchical structure is being dismantled in favor of self-directed work teams responsible for whole processes that, in turn require significant training to cope with multiple tasks.
- Accountability for results is being driven down the organization to the operational level and teams now perform many of the typically specialized management roles such as marketing, human resources, budgeting and operations within their specific sphere of influence.

So, whilst senior executives understand and appreciate the need to transform and become more responsive, the longer-term capacity of the organization to change and bring about sustainable strategic success is frequently sacrificed for short-term bottom line results. Every time the organization faces some form of serious threat it reinvents its capacity to deal with these events without building the system's immunity.

Two fundamentally flawed assumptions appear to prevail in these circumstances. First, that it is through business-wide orientation programs, mission statements, 'cultural realignment' programs, training courses, quality assurance policies and new remuneration systems that organizations are transformed. Second, it is assumed that by altering the organizational structure and systems it will automatically result in a change of employee behavior.

One of the greatest obstacles to OT is the suggestion that it is perpetuated by a series of change programs. This perspective of transformation is fallacious in the sense that it supports the belief that, one has to alter the knowledge and attitudes of individuals. Organizational Transformation is about changing the nature of, and way in which *business is being conducted*, not changing specific individual behavior. OT is not something you 'do' to people, rather it is something that you 'do' to the business, *the results of which are reflected in people's behavior*. People change their behavior when they understand, accept and commit to the new direction of the business. Instead of trying to influence individual behavior through elaborate change programs as if employees were the problem, attention should first be given to the issues impeding strategic progress in the business.

To avoid the potential pitfalls and high-risk profile of programmatic transformation, companies should concentrate instead on re-establishing a commitment to shared values, reorganizing employee roles, responsibilities and cross-functional relationships to solve specific business problems.

The success of a transformation initiative hinges on the following three inter-related factors:

• Commitment – a significant number of employees in the transformed organization must display behavior consistent with strategic success. This requires high levels of individual commitment to the effort and a belief in the fundamental value system of the organization.

• Cooperation – competitive advantage is secured through greater cooperation between departments who jointly act on issues such as cost, quality and innovation. Teamwork is especially important if an organization is to achieve the type and form of agility required to survive in an ever-changing environment. Teamwork achieves maximum success when strong relationships of trust and cooperation are established through shared values.

• Competence – people throughout the organization will be required to broaden their skill base and develop an appreciation of the wider challenges facing the business. Problem solving and interpersonal skills are critical for individuals operating in a team environment. Competence also refers to the ability of the organization to constantly adapt to changing circumstances without having to reinvent itself. The values of the organization should be so strongly adhered to that all it may have to do is temporarily alter its course before continuing down the path of its strategic vision. Threats in the environment therefore represent minor obstacles to organizations with the inherent capacity to regularly transform.

The absence of any of the above elements will significantly reduce the potential success of the transformation initiative.

5. Developing Shared Values

Values describe the path to the successful achievement of vision and in essence explain how the organization intends achieving it. Developing values jointly between management and other employees enhances commitment to the transformation effort and reduces the potential for resistance. This is the crux of OT.

At a personal level,

> A true and universally acceptable 'value' is one that produces behavior that is beneficial both to the practitioner and to those on whom it is practiced (Eyre and Eyre 1993).

A fundamentally held individual value is therefore a common principle that is acknowledged by others as being mutually acceptable, positive and the essence of a sound relationship. Although beyond the scope of this paper, I would suggest that it is possible to determine the fundamental value system of most cultures and how they compare with others. I would surmise that it would also be possible to establish which values run as a common thread through many diverse cultures. Organizations function because of the relationships that develop in them. Hence, if many different cultures congregate in an organization to produce a result, it can be assumed that those relationships will be based on some common value base.

Core organizational values are little different from the above. They are

> the organizations essential and enduring tenets – a small set of general guiding principles; not to be confused with specific culture or operating practices; not to be compromised for financial gain or short-term expediency (Collins and Porras 1996).

If we accept that organizations are collections of individuals seeking to achieve some common purpose, then their success will be driven largely by their ability to relate and cooperate with one another. As such, successful action must be built on a foundation of shared principles.

Sustained success is based on a shared value system that endures over a long period of time.

The importance of values cannot be overemphasized. Thomas J. Watson, Jr., former IBM CEO commented in the following way;

> I believe the real difference between success and failure in a corporation can very often be traced to the question of how well the organization brings out the energies and talents of its people. What does it do to help these people find common cause with each other? … And how can it sustain this common cause and sense of direction through the many changes, which will take place from one generation to another? … [I think the answer lies] in the power of what we call beliefs [values] and the appeal these beliefs have for its people. …
> I believe that the most important single factor in corporate success is faithful adherence to those beliefs … Beliefs must always come before policies, practices and goals. The latter must always be altered if they are seen to violate fundamental beliefs (Collins and Porras 1996).

Values are what we strive to uphold to ensure that our actions are perceived as just and fair. They focus on principles that will enable continuous improvement in people relationships and performance. Trust is a value, for example, both at an individual and an organizational level.

A problem arises, however, where the individual holds a fundamental value to which the organization merely pays 'lip service'. Under these circumstances it is difficult for the individual to align their commitment to the organization. An example is an organization's management publicly espousing the fact that 'People are our greatest asset', whilst in reality acting inconsistently with that statement.

A professional services firm with whom I was associated encountered such a breakdown at the expense of their entire transformation initiative. It was quickly apparent from a series of change sensitization workshops that very few individuals even knew what the corporate values were. As organizations grow older and reach maturity they begin to display the symptoms of a condition known as 'Organizational Drift' (Pascale et al. 1997).

Increasing complexity of structure, policy and procedure often drives people to carve out niches for themselves and to begin identifying narrowly with their department, profession or function instead of the organization as a whole. It is at this point that corporate values, no matter how noble or outstanding, are sacrificed for short-term cultural expediency. This condition has plagued many large corporate organizations such as Ford, Sears, IBM and GM to name but a few. In this case several factors were present to demonstrate that the organization was well in to 'organizational drift'. The tax group, for example, stuck mainly to themselves in a work and social context. Clearly they had their own subculture that made it difficult if not impossible for outsiders to penetrate. Their reaction to the restructure was to defend their existing position at all costs and challenge at every turn the pragmatism of the new organization. For most other individuals the only driving force to recognition, promotion and increased earnings was achieving chargeable hours.

Pascale et al. (1997) use a medical analogy by checking certain so called 'vital signs' to determine how well an organization is aligned to its strategic intent and the influence of culture on its performance. One of these relates to 'identity' that is do employees identify with the organization as a whole or very narrowly with their profession, department or team? Identity in this case ran typically from the individual's profession first then to their particular discipline. People would introduce themselves by referring to their job title and their profession first before anything else. In extremely rare cases the name of the firm would be mentioned at introduction or in casual conversation.

The values of the organization had been sacrificed in favor of the chase for chargeable hours. Culture, and not organizational values, are more important to the firm at the present time. Whether the organization can be realigned with its original strategic intent is doubtful given the current degree of decline. Other professional services firms are experiencing less of an economic downturn and some are actually increasing their resources to cope with new market demands. So, while external factors have had a significant impact in this case, this organization's response has been one more closely related to panic and crisis. It has failed to realign itself with key corporate values and has simply continued to decline in performance.

A deep belief in client focus, integrity, professionalism and trust would have been reflected in people's behavior. Instead this is an environment where the individuals behavior is tuned in to using whatever means possible to generate chargeable hours and rank distrust of particularly management and the Partners.

By contrast, a light engineering firm studied along the same dimension, revealed radically different results and the atmosphere generated by people in the organization reflected this. The most critical of all values in this company is trust. Employees trust their executive coaches implicitly to lead the company forward and to do everything possible to sustain a superior competitive position in international markets. Operators and support personnel trust their team leaders to provide them with up to date information, materials, tools, guidance and training that enables them to perform optimally throughout their processes. Above all, the reliance on a high performance team based structure can only be achieved if individual members trust one another. Where additional resources are required for example, the members of that team do the recruiting, interviewing and selecting of suitably qualified and oriented personnel.

A second value contributing to the company's success has been the level of *empowerment* it has given to its employees. Teams are accountable for their budgets, recruitment and discipline, work scheduling, output targets and everything else that impacts on their process. Training has provided expertise in each of the teams enabling them to look after their machinery and maintain it to optimum standards. Production is consequently kept at peak, wastage is virtually non-existent, conflict in and between the teams is remote and quality output is guaranteed. One team leader offered the following comment;

> We're in control of our destiny. We don't see much of a gap between the executive coaches and ourselves. If someone is encountering a problem within the team we help analyze what they are doing and assist them in making any defined changes. When a member comes to me and asks what should be done about a particular issue I always ask 'What do you think should be done?' That's true empowerment.

A third key value is *quality*, the attitude toward quality is almost fanatical. Teams will not accept sub-standard products from within their own ranks nor from outside suppliers.

If we assess the values environment according to Pascale et al. (1997), as with the previous case, we discover a totally opposite view with regard to identity, to the professional services firm. While employees in the firm are team structured the elimination of barriers has enabled them to identify with the larger organization. It is always with pride that they refer to themselves as a globally competitive organization, who are perceived as leaders in their particular technology.

Allowing employees to participate in the process of values formulation generates a unique excitement because it has grown out of their own analysis of real business problems. Personal commitment is enhanced when individuals participate in developing systems, policies and procedures that give affect to personally held values.

6. Embedding Transformational Capacity into Values

The key to sustaining strategic advantage through transformation is to embed the capacity in the value system of the organization through formal policies, systems, structures and developing competencies. It is important to mention here that the capacity to transform the organization must exist independently of any one individual. This capacity must consequently be owned by the organization. Few organizations demonstrate how well they have done this better than 3M. This unique work environment has been carefully nurtured over many years by instilling values that create and sustain a level of energy and innovation competitors have found difficult to replicate.

Trust is fundamental to 3M's success. Without mutual trust through all levels of the organization they would have little success in upholding their reputation for innovation. There is recognition that individuals will make mistakes but because it happens in a supportive and trusting environment, there is inherent faith in the individual to learn from the experience and grow.

An organization experiences successful transformation when it has to provide an environment where people are forced to think, act and interact differently. Strategic success in transformation occurs when the organization has internalized a set of values and disciplines that will not evaporate once the business encounters positive results. The degree to which an organization can imbed those values critical to its long-term success into its structure, systems and policies, greatly enhances its chances of overcoming future obstacles.

7. Conclusions

KPMG's 1997 Change Management report concludes that the most widely implemented transformations of the last five years were new strategic visions and plans, restructuring, changes in senior management, large technology installations and major quality management projects. 82% of the companies surveyed report that their transformation initiatives were either successful or highly successful. These findings run contrary to global experience where in the United States, for example, 85% of re-engineering projects reportedly fail to achieve their objectives and over 50% of restructuring initiatives do not achieve their projected cost saving targets. Are New Zealand businesses being overly optimistic or do they have a maligned view of organizational transformation? My belief is that it is the latter.

In order for organizational transformation to be successful we need to look carefully at the organization's strategic goals and their employees' behavior. First, strategic goals are hardly likely to have been achieved within a twelve-month time frame, although it is possible to achieve some immediate cost savings in the short-term. The first initial positive effects of an organizational transformation initiative are usually only likely to be seen eighteen to twenty-four months after the transformation has taken place.

Second, successful transformation requires a core change in people's attitudes, values and behavior. A significant number of employees need to come to a new and deep appreciation for the direction in which the business is moving and be excited about the possibilities. Unfortunately, New Zealand businesses' transformation track record leans significantly toward a 'slash and burn' mentality, sacrificing core organizational values for short-term expediency. Instead of building commitment and enthusiasm for strategic goals, it is often simply easier to cut people out of the system. The consequences of this approach are apparent throughout New Zealand business. People have not only developed a significant distrust of management but have also developed a rather self-centered attitude by looking out for themselves. This merely enhances the 'us/them' syndrome and reinforces the dim outlook for successful transformations.

A shared value system is the glue that bonds employees together in pursuit of a common goal. Without the system or 'glue', strategy, focus and commitment either do not exist or are so fragmented that internal conflict result, which could ultimately destroy the enterprise. Shared values provide a framework from which to operate throughout corporate life. Taking Maslow's hierarchy of needs and the self-actualization model, individuals need to identify with one another through a system of shared beliefs that enhance support and commonality of purpose. Corporate values underpin successful business performance particularly if they expressed and lived in behavioral terms others can see.

An organization that drifts away from its core value system courts its own demise. Employees begin to disbelieve the organization and its goals. When organizations say one thing and actually do the opposite, employees begin to distrust and the organization's leadership lose credibility. Hot on the heels is a diminishing commitment to the organization's strategy and goals, increasing internal conflict, flight of expertise and reduced business performance.

The essence of any corporate value system must necessarily lie in the concept of trust. Marris (1974:15–8) suggests that the success of organizational transformation is directly related to the level of trust engendered in the individual and in groups. Where trust is high, transformation is more successful and managed more effectively. Where it is low, communication and cooperation suffer and there is an increasing tendency to resort to power and coercion. Handy (1985:327–30) in addition, mentions that the more control used in the transformation by management, the less trust employees will have for the process. This is particularly critical if the object of transformation is to create an entirely different structure based on self-directed teams of individuals. Employees have to trust not only one another but also their leadership before they can commit to organizational strategy and transformation. Where this is weak, or coercive power is used, commitment will be notional.

There is a view that transformation is actually an easy affair and that it deals with all the 'warm, fuzzy stuff' like values. Just how powerful is a shared value system and what consequences does it hold for the transforming organization? When the structure or processes change in an organization, they often reflect different values, which may be a consequence of different cultural pressures. An Asian company, for example, taking over a New Zealand company will bring different cultural values to the takeover. Values are important because they are concerned with prioritizing what we want and will condition our expectations. If we accept for the moment that our values are correct then we will expect them to be fulfilled and this increases the chance for conflict or coercion. Leaders in transformation or those in authority who take no cognizance of values will find the path to transformation extremely difficult to negotiate. The risk of failure is also greatly enhanced particularly in instances where new technology is being introduced and there is no active input from those human beings that the changes affect the most.

To achieve sustained strategic success it is critical that new behaviors and the values underpinning them become deeply embedded in the fabric of the organization. Many organizations fail to achieve this. Every time a new issue confronts them, new blood is required and the same repetitive rejuvenation cycle is implemented with the same risks of success or failure. There are a number of reasons for this.

Firstly, because vision, values, and their interpretation are largely conceptual to start with, it takes time to build not only commitment but also to see them reflected in individual behavior. When managers change things, whether processes or technology, they expect to see immediate results. Effective transformation requires conceptual understanding and where this is absent, managers' flounder with no basis to motivate others.

Second, the capabilities for transforming a business as opposed to improving its performance are quite different. This lack of understanding is amply demonstrated by several NZ organizations and the way they approach the exercise. Employees are simply expected to get on with the task of transforming the organization with little or no tangible understanding or commitment to new strategic directions. Without training, development, resources, systems, practices, clear goals and adequate reward there is little incentive for individuals to disrupt their routine. Since there is no recognition of the specific requirements to bring about successful transformation, there is no reinforcing action to embed them in the organizations core capability.

A third major reason for failure to achieve sustained success relates to the relationship between payback and investment. Initial investment in a transformation exercise is significantly large enough for leaders to question when they can expect a return. Building commitment to the vision and shared value system are long-term activities and the pay-off occurs some way down the transformation track. So while commitment and behavior are critical to sustained transformation success, they do little to bolster current business performance. Organizations with a short-term view who offer managers incentives for immediate results are therefore doing little to build future change capacity and skills into their business.

Endnotes

1. Klynveld, Peat, Marwick, Goerdler.

References

Adams, J. D. 1984. *Transforming Work: A Collection of Organizational Transformation Readings*. Alexandria, Virginia, U.S.A.: Miles River Press.
Collins, J.C., Porras, J. I. 1996. *Built to Last: Successful Habits of Visionary Companies*. London: Century Ltd.
Donaldson, J. 1989. *Key Issues in Business Ethics*. London: Academic Press.
Eyre, R., Eyre, L. 1993. *Teaching Your Children Values*. London: BCA.
Handy, C. 1985. *Understanding Organizations*. London: Penguin Books Ltd.
KPMG Change Management. Report, 1997.
Marris, P. 1974. *Loss and Change*. London: Institute for Community Studies, Routledge and Kegan Paul.
Pascale, R., Millemann, M., Gioja, L. 1997. "Changing the Way We Change." *Harvard Business Review* (November–December).

Postindustrial Business Ethics

Krzysztof Klincewicz
Collegium Invisibile
Warsaw, Poland

1. Introduction

.We experience significant changes in the social and economic environment, related to the transformation into postindustrial society. This new society is characterized by the dominant role of information technology, which changes private and professional lives. The business world reflects the social structure, adjusting activities to new social requirements. This paper will present the postindustrial environment of economic activities, especially changes in the area of market exchange. The analysis of new business tendencies will then induce reflections concerning corresponding alterations in the normative content of postindustrial business ethics.

2. Information Economy

Alvin Toffler (1980) divided the history of Western civilization into three periods, following significant social and economic changes, or 'waves'. The first historical period was related to self-production, and the second one – to production for exchange, which introduced industrialization and wide-spread markets. The guidelines for business activities after the Second Wave were: standardization, specialization, synchronization, concentration, maximization and centralization (Toffler 1980:46–56). Nowadays, we experience what Toffler (1980) described as the Third Wave – a transformation into the postindustrial society.

The classical theory of postindustrialism is based on three assumptions (Castells 1996:203):

1. the source of productivity and growth lies in the generation of knowledge;
2. economies undergo shifts from production of goods to delivery of services and therefore we observe the demise of manufacturing;
3. importance of occupation with a high information and knowledge content increases.

The bases of economies are changing. In the postindustrial society, labor theory of value is replaced by 'knowledge theory of value' (Kumar 1995:12), stating that knowledge is the critical factor for creation of economic value. The classical approach to the manufacturing process, described as 'fordism', and based on a strong division of labor, mass production of standardized products and automation of assembly lines (Murray 1992:270), has transformed into 'postfordism', based on 'flexible specialization', enabling economic and profitable production of small batches of goods, and using modern information technology (Kumar 1995:43). The newest technologies, supporting teamwork and knowledge management, promote organizational decentralization – which is an obvious contradiction to the traditional concept of management, described as 'taylorism', where only the first line managers possessed sufficient knowledge and competencies to make decisions affecting the work of other organizational members.

The new class of so-called knowledge workers, college educated employees, replaces the dichotomy between blue and white collars. The role of blue collar workers is taken over by machines, and the authority of white collar workers vanishes when faced with decentralization of knowledge and decision making. According to Hage and Powers (1992), one of the main indicators, showing whether a sector entered the postindustrial era, is the high proportion of labor force that is professional when compared with only technical specialists (Hage and Powers 1992:46).

Information seems to be similar to other goods, when considering its market exchange. However, as Kenneth Arrow (1962:616) pointed it out, "there is a fundamental paradox in the determination of demand for information: its value for the purchaser is not known until he has the information, but then he has in effect acquired it without cost." Purchasing information is therefore a matter of high risk, and as such differs from other market transactions. As Hodgson (1988) suggests, the trade of information is not a 'pure' contract – "there will always, for instance, be a degree of trust on behalf of the buyer that the information will be worth its price" (Hodgson 1988:163).

Business activities focus on knowledge and information more than on automation or technology. In the new world, more attention is being paid to people, their needs and capabilities. The transforming object of economic transactions – information instead of commodities – defines also conditions of exchange – non-contractual elements, such as trust, play an increasing role, and incorporating business ethics issues into the everyday business life.

3. Prosumer Society

A significant characteristic of the postindustrial society is the changing role of consumers. In the new economy, consumers are becoming active (Tapscott 1996:229), as opposed to passive being only victims of advertising influence as in the past. Mass production disappears, as the new, college-educated consumer demands customization, quality and innovation instead of standardized product offers (Hage and Powers 1992:58). We live in 'prosumer society' ('prosumption' refers to the production for purposes of own consumption; Toffler 1980:273), where people seek out individualized products and services (Hage and Powers 1992:59), and the gap between consumers and producers blurs: consumers are deeply involved in the manufacturing process, and mass production is replaced by customization (Tapscott 1996:62).

> They [customers] can, for example, enter a new car showroom and configure an automobile on the computer screen from a series of choices. Chrysler can produce special-order vehicles in sixteen days. The customer creates the specs and sets in motion the manufacture of a specific, customized vehicle. In the old economy, viewers watched the evening network news. In the new economy, a television viewer will design a customized news broadcast by highlighting the top ten topics of interest and specifying preferred news sources, editorial commentators, and graphic styles. Moreover, that same viewer will be able to watch that broadcast whenever time permits or the need arises (Tapscott 1996:62).

Postindustrialism is therefore the time of heterogeneity – we are faced with difference and customization of offers in order to suit the sophisticated needs of single customers. The relationship between consumers and products undergoes corresponding changes:

> No longer do people attempt to define themselves through the products they consume, best exemplified by the wanton excess and spectacle of the last decade. Instead, people define themselves in relation to the products that are ever-present in their everyday lives – they make meaning and significance of the multiple interdependencies between themselves, others, and name-brand products. After branding comes placing: no longer do products have their own aura, manufactured through a brashly cynical, cleverly crafted marketing campaign, and aimed at some narrowly-defined demographic. Placing is about the relationship between a product and an individual: it's at once unique and intimate (Steadman 1996).

We do not deal with intrusive advertising any more – people shape the meanings themselves; products and commercials live their own lives, due to consumer reactions. We notice the increasing power of consumers, their wishes and needs, and the importance of heterogeneity and communication between customers and producers. As revealed in a survey of American companies, conducted by McKinsey researchers almost two decades ago, "the excellent companies tend to be more driven by close-to-the-customer attributes than by either technology or cost" (Peters and Waterman 1982:186). Nowadays, this is not only the matter of excellence, but everyday practice.

4. Relationships Instead of Markets

The interpersonal dimensions of relationships between customers and producers make us witness to the abundance of classical market forms in economic life. "Markets and hierarchies are being largely supplanted by network structures" (Hage and Powers 1992:181), because the assumption of any market was its impersonal character, anonymity of both sides of transaction. We rediscover nowadays the importance of non-contractual elements in each economic transaction, shaping the actual relationships between buyers and sellers.

Social processes are not solely based on contracts. Non-contractual elements are present in all kinds of relationship – from marriage to the previously mentioned exchange of information, where the central position of trust has been stressed. The notion of exchange is an insufficient explanation of many business activities, for example of corporate charity. A suggested economic interpretation of charity as non-altruistic maximization of expected returns by increasing loyalty of customers cannot offer any criteria for assessing or predicting behavior of economic agents due to the too broad concept of profit maximization (Hodgson 1988:77).

Hodgson (1988) presents two typical examples of economic exchanges, established in other ways than through the market. The first example is a habitually renewed contract to supply a good or service to a regular client, where the buyer is committed to the same supplier ignoring the market mechanism. The second case concerns unique, highly customized products – a kind of market exchange occurs only at the very beginning of the process, enabling contact between two parties. Those two cases accurately depict current strategic trends: strives for building long-term relationships and providing individual, customized solutions. "A relationship includes much more than exchanges, and if a trusting relationship between two or several business partners exists, exchanges should inevitably occur from time to time" (Grönroos 1996:8).

The current trends in marketing theory emphasize the need for a long-term approach to customers: building and maintaining relationships instead of concentrating on single transactions, which can be profitable only in short-run. This concept is sometimes defined as 'relationship marketing', whose task is "to identify and establish, maintain, and enhance relationships with customers and other stakeholders, at a profit, so that the objectives of all parties involved are met, and that this is done by a mutual exchange and fulfillment of promises" (Grönroos 1996:7). Relationship replaces exchange, but economic agents have their long-term objectives in mind – therefore, non-contractual elements of the process such as trust, cohesion and solidarity, are in a way consistent with instrumental, non-altruistic considerations (Hodgson 1988:170). "We learn from experience in what sort of situation we can normally place our trust, and by becoming familiar with them we begin to act habitually once trust is established. Although trusting in its most meaningful sense is conscious and deliberative, it is also important in that its repeated endorsement by perceived events and symbols gives rise to habit and routine" (Hodgson 1988:166).

What is called 'market' in economic theory, can nowadays be found only in financial markets (dealing not with commodities, but financial instruments). As Alvin Toffler (1980:283–284) points out,

> the human race has been busy constructing a worldwide exchange network – a market – for at least 10,000 years. In the past 300 years, ever since the Sec-

ond Wave began, this process has roared forward at very high speed. Second Wave civilization 'marketized' the world. Today – at the very moment when prosuming begins to rise again – this process is coming to an end (Toffler 1980:283–284).

5. Global Standards

Another important trend in the postindustrial economy is its globalization. This phenomenon is, however, interpreted differently from its past applications. In the past, we experienced global advertising campaigns and global product offers; nowadays we speak of globalization of standards and ways of doing business. The common strategical principle states: think globally, act locally (Kotler 1997:XXXIII;: on the global level, companies set standards for conducting local business activities, which include among others moral imperatives for managers.

John Naisbitt (1994) emphasizes that the globalization of business activities involves a transfer of certain moral norms, and the emergence of global ethical standards, for example the abundance of bribery in politics. It happens even in countries, where the same activities have previously been accepted. Public opinion observes reactions to bribery in other countries, and shares these common views and moral norms.

> Why are the Japanese people now expressing outrage at what Westerners would consider unethical behavior? Because they have witnessed the downfall of politicians around the globe for similar infractions. And because they intuitively understand that to be citizens of the global community they will have to adapt their behavior to new standards. Observes Thomas W Whitson, a partner and auditor at KPMG Peat Marwick in Tokyo, 'If morality is important to do business in the United States, then I think they would go along with it – not because it's right, but because it's good business' (Naisbitt 1994:153).

The above described phenomena, among others, globalization of ethical standards, relationship development, importance of trust, may suggest that a limited number of ethical concepts have been incorporated into business practice solely due to instrumental reasons. It will however be suggested, that this is rather matter of a changing model of business, regarding company as a social system, focusing on customer needs and environment, with no place left for the classical economic motivation towards profit maximization.

6. Perspectives for Business Ethics

The postindustrial changes have created a new paradigm of business activities, where the focus of companies is customer, not only profit (although relationships with customers should be profitable).

The changing role of consumers (activity, or even prosumption) shaped a new way of communication in the market place. The communication in the industrial era could be described as a monologue, where the producer was spreading information (or misinformation) about his offer, using above the line promotion, such as advertising. Customers were anonymous, and seemed to be somehow homogeneous, which justified mass production of commodities. The postindustrial model is based on a dialogue, listening to customers needs. Customers are no longer anonymous; they are personally known due to interpersonal relationships between buyers and sellers (or rather: problem solvers).

Ethical benefits, which result from relationship approaches replacing the exchange model, are obvious. In the exchange model, companies did not really care for customers in terms of attempts to understand their actual needs. In most cases, the so-called Golden Rule was employed – treating others the way we would like to be treated. However, as Milton J. Bennett (1979) convincingly presented, if there should be a proper criterion for interpersonal relations and communication of the Golden Rule's kind, it should state: "Do unto others as they themselves would have done unto them." (Bennett 1979:422). This emphasizes differences in perception and difficulties related to understanding the real needs of other people without learning those people and the context in which they live. In market exchanges, no-one paid attention to understanding of other people – sellers employed sympathy, "the imaginative placing of ourselves in another person's position" (Bennett 1979:411) instead of empathy, "the imaginative intellectual and emotional participation in another person's experience. ... In empathy, we 'participate' rather than 'place', and we are concerned with 'experience' rather than 'position'." (Bennett 1979:418).

In case of a single exchange transaction, we are inclined to assume human similarity by the psychological mechanism of projection, referring to our own experiences, values and emotions. Only developing close relationships enables people to understand and satisfy the real needs of other people – by accepting the difference and heterogeneity. As in the example, provided by Block (1990:70), "the personal link reduces the likelihood of a shipment of inferior parts or increases the reliability of promises of prompt delivery." The personal character of relationships between economic agents resolves many previously difficult problems of business ethics.

The second sphere of business ethics is related to human resources management and internal organizational issues. Similarly, the changing approach to communication gives a solution to several ethical problems. The industrial era can be associated with Erving Goffman's (1959) concept of impression management, an assumption that everyone attempts to project an inaccurate impression of himself to others in order to influence them. The postindustrial society disregards this approach, moving towards a more open and honest communication (Hage and Powers 1992:101). So we experience a shift in approach to customers, employ-

FIGURE 1

Industrial and postindustrial eras
– changing paradigms for business ethics

	Industrial era	Postindustrial era
Focus of the company	Profit	Customer
Model of business relations	Market exchange Contract	Relationship marketing Trust
Model of human relations	Social roles	Interpersonal relationships
Mode of production	Mass production of commodities	Service offering and customization
Role of consumers	Passive	Active (prosumption)
Perceived character of consumers	Homogeneity and anonymity	Heterogeneity
Approach to consumers	Sympathy or manipulation	Empathy
Model of communication with consumers	Monologue (advertising)	Dialogue (direct marketing)
Character of communication	'Impression management'	Openness and honesty

ees, and in the whole sphere of professional lives. No longer can our work be defined in terms of organizational roles. The gap between occupation and home life blurs; we act in the same way in the office and at home – "most social bonds are losing some of their role properties and gaining more of the properties of interpersonal relationships" (Hage and Powers 1992:161).

Open and honest communication is based on trust – the most important non-contractual element, accompanying economic transactions. Summarizing the work of a feminist philosopher Annette Baier, who writes on importance of trust in interpersonal relationships and ethics, Rosemarie Tong (1993:176) states:

> The essence of trust is 'reliance' on another person's 'good will', knowing far well that the other person's 'good will' is not absolutely dependable. My spouse can betray me; my friends can desert me; my partner can abandon me; my colleagues can undermine me; and so on. Realizing that trust entails risks, we must ask ourselves why we willingly make ourselves vulnerable. ... We need to trust others because we are not self-sufficient.

Trust is the key concept, moving postindustrial business ethics towards other spheres of ethics, especially an ethics of interpersonal relationships. Business ethics can no longer be only a kind of applied ethics, as its connections with all spheres of our social and personal lives require the more holistic approach to problems of business activities. It is an integral part of ethics – defined rather not as set of principles, moral laws, concepts of justice or responsibility, but as a matter of everyday life, emotion, interpersonal relations and dependencies. The suggested solution is a pragmatic one – based on the actual cultural context, tastes and feelings. This cultural approach is different from what mainstream economics offers with the universal notion of economic man, but it differs significantly also from praxiological ideals, which focus on the solely subjective character of human action.

Robert H. Frank (1988:781) raises the problem, which has been extensively discussed also by business ethicists: the relationship between instrumental and ethical norms.

> Moral philosophers have invested great effort trying to show that honesty is the best policy. Yet none has argued persuasively that a person will do better by not cheating when it is certain he will not be caught. The reason is simply he will *not* do better. There is a perfectly coherent reason, however, why a rational, selfish agent might choose to have a conscience. And once possessed of a conscience, it will be his *emotions*, not any rational calculation, that prevents him from cheating.

The postindustrial economy poses ethical threats to its participants, which cannot be analyzed by the use of the traditional methodology. An example is the critical issue of privacy. The networked economy enables and supports collecting personal data from consumers, which creates new problems, resulting from the 'Copernican turn in privacy' (Masuda 1981:114). The confidential character of commonly collected data puts everyone at high risk, e.g. taking unfair advantage of consumers could cause severe social damages. In the past, problems of privacy were mainly attributed to marketing research problems. Today personal data are involved in all stages of the marketing process, and a customer often cannot avoid disclosing them; he can only hope that the details would not be misused. Trust becomes the essential category, as the only answer to surrounding risks and doubts – trust creates an ethical climate, which cannot be established only by the implementation of rules or principles.

Postindustrial business ethics focuses on interpersonal relations and culture. It is consistent with current management theories such as the concept of relationship marketing. It shifts towards 'personal' approaches to ethics, stressing the importance of trust, heterogeneity and honest direct communication. The term 'business ethics' may still sound like an oxymoron for managers, but they have already incorporated most of its contents into their activities. Despite this seemingly idealistic picture, there are new challenges for postindustrial business ethics, such as the rising problem of privacy, or bribery, which has gained new dimensions, and the question, where are the limit of marketing activities, targeted at a single customer, still remains unanswered.

References

Arrow, K. 1962. "Economic Welfare and the Allocation of Resources for Invention." In *The Rate and Direction of Inventive Activity: Economic and Social Factors.* Princeton: National Bureau of Economic Research, Princeton University Press.

Bennett, M. J. 1979. "Overcoming the Golden Rule: Sympathy and Empathy." In *Communication Yearbook 3. An Annual Review Published by the International Communication Association,* ed. Dan Nimmo. New Brunswick, New Jersey: Transaction Books.

Block, F. 1990. *Postindustrial Possibilities. A Critique of Economic Discourse.* Berkeley, Los Angeles and Oxford: University of California Press.

Castells, M. 1996. *The Rise of Network Society.* Oxford and Malden, Massahusetts: Blackwell Publishers.

Frank, R. H. 1988. "Passions Within Reason: The Strategic Role of the Emotions." In *Applied Behavioral Economics. Volume II,* ed. Shlomo Maital. Brighton, Sussex; Wheatsheaf Books.

Goffman, E. 1959. *The Presentation of Self in Everyday Life*. New York; Doubleday Anchor Books.

Grönroos, Ch. 1996. "Relationship Marketing: Strategic and Tactical Implications." *Management Decision* 34/3: 5–14.

Hage, J. and Powers, Ch. H. 1992. *Post-Industrial Lives. Roles and Relationships in the 21st Century*. Newbury Park, London and New Delhi: SAGE Publications.

Hodgson, G. M. 1988. *Economics and Institutions. A Manifesto for a Modern Institutional Economics*. Cambridge and Oxford: Polity Press, Basil Blackwell.

Kotler, P. 1997. *Marketing Management. Analysis, Planning, Implementation, and Control*. Upple Saddle River, New Yersey: Prentice Hall International.

Kumar, K. 1995. *From Post-Industrial to Post-Modern Society. New Theories of the Contemporary World*. Oxford, Cambridge: Blackwell Publishers.

Masuda, Y. 1981. *The Information Society as Post-Industrial Society*. Washington: World Future Society.

Murray, R. 1992. "Fordism and Post-Fordism." In *The Post-Modern Reader*, ed. Charler Jenkins. London and New York: Academy Editions and St Martin's Press.

Naisbitt, J. 1994. *Global Paradox. The Bigger the World Economy, the More Powerful Its Smallest Players*. London: Nicholas Brealey Publishing.

Peters, T. J. and Waterman, R.H. 1982. *In Search of Excellence. Lessons from America's Best-Run Companies*. New York: Harper & Row Publishers.

Steadman, C. 1996. *Placing. Press Release*. San Francisco. http://www.placing.com/pr.html

Tapscott, D. 1996. *The Digital Economy. Promise and Peril in the Age of Networked Intelligence*. New York: McGraw-Hill.

Toffler, A. 1980. *The Third Wave*. Toronto, New York and London: Bantam Books.

Tong, R. 1993. *Feminine and Feminist Ethics*. Belmont, California: Wadsworth Publishing Company.

Understanding Different Interpretations of Corporate Social Responsibility in the United States

Diane Flannery
California School of Professional Psychology
Alameda, Calf. (USA)

1. Introduction

In recent years a new generation of American corporations has evolved, both large and small, national and global, that firmly defines themselves as socially responsible businesses, with a double bottom line, whereby the companies' success is measured both by its financial and social performance. These corporations are successfully integrating traditional business functions with aggressive and far reaching social goals. The companies are redefining the notion of corporate social responsibility and are raising important questions about the capacity of business to serve multiple roles in society. Years ago the number of American companies that would define themselves this way was relatively small. Recently, in the field of professional practice, there has been an explosion of interest in this issue. Business for Social Responsibility (BSR), a membership organization that promotes responsible business practice, has grown tremendously. Today, BSR has over 800 member companies that represent over 2.75 million employees and well over $ 400 billion in annual revenues: a major evolution from its humble grassroots beginnings.

Corporations in United States have different interpretations about what constitutes a company's social responsibility. Beyond adhering to legal obligations, the discretionary options available to a company regarding „doing good" for society are endless. Corporations are questioning the neoclassical view that the primary function of business is the production of goods or services and making a profit for its shareholders. Many contemporary corporations are pushing the definition and the scope of social responsibility. Companies are successfully weaving their social agendas into their main business. This integration of social issues into business functions provides a unique opportunity to understand how corporations interpret their responsibility.

In an attempt to examine the activity going on in the field of professional practice, this author proposes three distinct modes of understanding how a company interprets, builds and shapes its social identity and expresses its social responsibility through its main business functions. The three modes include: (1) its corporate values and business practices, (2) its marketing strategies and (3) its product or service. While some companies approach their social objectives through only one dominate mode, such as its product or service, other companies weave social concepts through all three. This author is not advocating one mode over the other. Rather this writer proposes a framework which identifies where companies are focusing their discretionary social efforts, a framework which leads to a more complete definition of this concept. The three modes are best illustrated by examining exemplary corporations that are well known for their social responsibility. The companies to be examined include: Levi Strauss, Ben & Jerry's Homemade Inc., The Body Shop, Wild Planet Toys, Working Assets and GAIA Bookstore.

2. Corporate Values and Business Practices

Corporate values and business practices can best be described as *how* a corporation does its business. Corporate values are an important construct when attempting to understand the social responsibility of a corporation. Values motivate people to act. Most behavior can be traced back to a particular set of values (Cavanagh 1990; Ravlin & Meglino 1987). Corporations develop standard business practices based on the company's values. For example, San Francisco based Levi Strauss & Company is the world's largest brand-name apparel manufacture. Started in the mid 1800s by Levi Strauss, the company now has more than 37,000 employees, operates in over 60 countries and generates $ 6.7 billion in annual sales. Levi Strauss started as a dry goods business and quickly moved to making sturdy pants out of canvas for miners. Today, Levi Strauss manufactures lines of menswear, womenswear and childrenswear that include jackets, jeans, shirts, skirts, slacks and sportswear. The company currently holds 19% of the domestic jeans market with earnings over 6 billion dollars a year.

The Levi Strauss name is synonymous with corporate social responsibility. As a company, it has been very successful in conducting business in a way that truly reflects its values. Levi Strauss' social objectives are driven and dominated by its corporate values and business practices, rather than its product or marketing strategies. While the Levi Strauss product has an excellent reputation, it is not the primary means of the company accomplishing its social purpose. The company developed a strong commitment to ethical business practices stemming from its values. Levi Strauss has a long history of corporate social responsibility and leads the field with its corporate practices, such as the company's treatment of its employees, its ethics program, its sourcing guidelines and its diversity programs. While the Levi Strauss product is high quality and is reputable, one has to ask the question: Is the actual product any different from any other in the apparel industry? If you take away *how* this company does business, its product is no different from other apparel products except its policy of "social responsibility." The values and business practices of this company are the primary vehicle for promoting its social objectives.

The Levi Strauss mission statement, which clearly states this company's intention, reads as follows:

> The mission of Levi Strauss & Company is to sustain responsible commercial success as a global marketing company of branded apparel. We must balance goals of superior profitability and return on investment, leadership market positions, and superior products and services. We will conduct our business ethically and demonstrate leadership in satisfying our responsibilities to our communities and to society. Our work environment will be safe and productive and characterized by fair treatment, teamwork, open communications, personal accountability and opportunities for growth and development.

According to Levi Strauss' beliefs and values, corporations are responsible to behave ethically, create a fair and honest work environment for its employees and to give back to the communities in which the company does business. While manufacturing a quality product is a responsible action, the societal impact of this company's values and business practices far out weigh its product's social impact.

Levi Strauss also does not express its responsibility through social marketing strategies. Actually, Levi Strauss has been criticized for its lack of social awareness in some of the company's advertisements. Recently, the company ran a series of advertisements on large billboards for its blue jeans, which, in a light hearted manner, challenged some of its competitors. One of these ads depicted a group of tough looking male models asserting to the competitors: "Our models can beat up your models." While the ad was successful drawing attention to the company's product, it also drew criticism asserting the company was promoting violence to sell its product.

3. Marketing Strategies

Spurge et al. (1997:517) defines marketing strategies that incorporate social issues as: "using marketing techniques to influence and change people's attitude and behavior toward social problems." Ben & Jerry's Homemade Inc. and The Body Shop, also two corporations in the vanguard of socially responsibility, while driven by their values and business practices purposely use marketing techniques to promote social issues, rather than their products. Both Ben & Jerry's and The Body Shop uses their companies as platforms to influence and change people's perspective and behavior toward social issues.

Ben & Jerry's Homemade, Inc., located in Vermont, manufactures and sells super premium ice cream, frozen yogurt, ice cream novelties and sorbets. Sales for 1995 reached $ 155 million. The company is best known for its indulgent and whimsical ice cream flavors, made only with Vermont milk, and for carrying names such as Cherry Garcia, Chunky Monkey, Rainforest Crunch and Chocolate Chip Cookie Dough.

Ben Cohen and Jerry Greenfield, while building a top-quality ice cream manufacturing company, also built an equally strong social agenda and social image for their corporation. The company is as much known for its aggressive social and environmental programs as for its ice cream. "Ben & Jerry's is a company with a unique mission to do more that just make ice cream. It also strives to make a difference in the world. The company measures its success by how much it gives back to the community – locally, nationally, and internationally" (Laabs 1992:51). "Caring

Capitalism" is how Cohen describes the crux of his company's business philosophy. Cohen and Greenfield, themselves both products of the 1960s, have a unique perspective on the responsibility of business. They take a long-term social view, often at the expense of short-term financial gains. The Ben & Jerry's 1995 Annual Report summarizes the company's interpretation of its social responsibility:

> The easy part of describing our vision of caring capitalism to the world was to hold forth a picture of how commerce might be an innovative source of creative social problem-solving as well as an attractive source of profit. The hard part is making this picture come to life in a manner that is sustained by its continuing successes (Ben & Jerry's Annual Report 1995:2).

The social impact of this company derives from *how* it conducts its business and *how* it strategically combines the marketing of both its product and its social concerns. The Ben & Jerry's product in and of itself is not the vehicle for this company's expression of its social values. Interestingly, Ben & Jerry's has been challenged around its perceived "irresponsible product."

> I am mystified by how Ben & Jerry's is looked upon so favorably as a model for socially responsible businesses. Consider its product: Ben & Jerry's ice cream is loaded with sugar, fat and cholesterol. Its success is built on the poor eating habits practiced by many Americans in a country where heart disease is the number one killer. And now 'New Priorities' messages are to appear on the products' wrappers. Would Phillip Morris be applauded for printing a similar message on a pack of Marlboros? Would the Beef Industry Council draw praise for putting the message on packages of red meat? If Ben & Jerry's was really a socially responsible company, it would be selling grapes and bananas (Fowler 1993:4).

This commentary exemplifies the notion that companies can choose how they want to be responsible. Ben & Jerry's made a conscious choice to direct its social efforts into the environment, natural ingredients, company policies, strong values and aggressive social cause related marketing. The company deliberately did not develop or position its product to advance the social concerns of health and sound eating habits. Ben & Jerry's did make a commitment to the local economy, by having Vermont farmers supply all the milk for their ice cream. The company uses only natural ingredients. The company has taken a strong stand on Bovine Growth Hormone (rBGH), which many dairy farmers use to increase production, by only buying milk that is free of rBGH. Most of Ben & Jerry's social efforts do not directly relate to the company's product, but rather include far reaching social initiatives; from saving the rain forest, to world peace, to youth themes, to changing the way business is conducted.

The Body Shop, based in England, has a strong social and business presence in the United States. This company interprets its social reasonability in a similar way as Ben & Jerry's. The company, founded over 20 years ago by Anita and Gordon Roddick is now a multinational corporation with over 1,366 shops in 46 countries around the world, with one hundred sixty-two of these shops directly owned by The Body Shop. Annual retail sales reached $ 349 million at the end of 1995, with a reported worldwide 78 million customer transactions.

The Body Shop develops and manufactures natural beauty products that are sold exclusively through the company's catalogue and in its franchised shops. The company has built a corporate and product image which represents a major departure from the established marketing and advertising approaches in the cosmetic industry. The Body Shop, while selling skin and hair products, focuses most of its public visibility on its social efforts. The Body Shop strongly promotes the belief that business has a responsibility to the community and can be a powerful vehicle for social change. The Body Shop promotes an aggressive social agenda that includes a variety of causes, for example, saving the rain forest, banning ozone-depleting chemicals, sponsoring abandoned orphanages in Romania, campaigning to help political dissidents and petitioning to end French nuclear testing in the South Pacific. None of these causes have a direct link to its product.

The Body Shop reflects a company that has pushed the limits of business and its responsibility to the environment, the community and society. The Body Shop has become a leader in social education by using its business as a vehicle to disseminate educational materials to the community, locally, nationally, and internationally. It is often more about teaching the general public on complex social issues, than selling a product. The Body Shop appeals to people's values, concerns for social problems and desire to make a difference in the world.

> The Body Shop is perceived as a socially responsible company. It starts really with its founder Anita Roddick, who for the last ten years has been very active in social issues, whether it's the burning of the rain forest or getting people out to vote, or talking about HIV and AIDS. She started using the shops as a platform for putting out information for customers and the general public. So the public started to coming into shops and reading and hearing and knowing about issues (Aron 1996).

Working Assets provides another interesting example of a company using the mode of marketing strategies as an expression of its social responsibility. Working Assets, a privately held company, offers credit card, long distance and pager services, and internet access. While these services are not any more or less socially responsible than other credit card companies and telephone services, the feature of Working Assets that makes the company different is its unique commitment to social causes through its marketing efforts. Working Assets has taken discretionary philanthropy and woven it into its main business strategy. Working Assets developed its company as a platform for social change efforts. Its corporate mission includes active participation in building a world that is more just, humane and environmentally sustainable. The company seeks to accomplish its mission by providing customers with ways to be effective citizens and philanthropists. Working Assets designed an interactive process whereby the customer can be involved in social issues such as the environment, social justice, peace and human rights, all through Working Assets' services. During the first ten years of operations the company donated more than $ 7 million. In 1995 alone, Working Assets distributed $ 2.1 million to thirty-six nonprofit groups chosen by individual customers. In addition to its philanthropic program, Working Assets also provides its customers with updates on relevant social issues in its monthly bills, along with simple ways to speak out and lobby on political issues.

Some examples of Working Assets advertisements illustrate how this company interprets its social responsibility and takes bold social stands on often controversial issues:

> Phone your narrow minded, self righteous, abortion clinic picketing sister in Alabama and thank her for helping you support a women's right to choose (Working Assets advertisement, 1996).

> Give your conservative, Newt-Pushing Homophobic brother in Idaho a call and tell him how he's helping you defend the rights of gays and lesbians everywhere (Working Assets advertisement, 1996).

> Social change is our reason for being. Profit is simply a means to that end (Working Assets advertisement, 1995).

> Plastic with purpose (A Working Assets advertisement for its credit card, 1995).

> Help save rainforests, defend reproductive freedom and house the homeless while you save money on long distance calls (Working Assets advertisement, 1995).

Working Assets created its company to develop products for people to spend in a socially responsible manner. Working Assets, along with other companies that position themselves to market social causes have experienced its share of criticism and skepticism about its approach to business. Working Assets has been compared to AT&T, with the argument that AT&T has a good phone service, and it also has a significant philanthropic program, only it does not use its philanthropy as a marketing tool. Working Assets response to this argument states: There is a huge difference between us and AT&T. Our customers decide where the money goes. AT&T does not give 1% of its revenue. While they do give money, they are a 32 billion dollar company and they give a couple million away each year. Working Assets gives money whether it makes a profit or not. The approach Working Assets takes fully integrates its social objectives into its business goals and marketing functions (Scher 1996).

4. Product or Services

In comparing the approach to social responsibility taken by Levi Strauss, Ben & Jerry's The Body Shop, and Working Assets, Wild Planet Toys represents a company that uses its product to express its social mission and its corporate values. Wild Planet, launched in 1993 produces high-quality toys for children that are non-violent and non-sexist, a departure from the industry standard. The toy industry has been notorious for producing products for children that are gender specific and particularly focused on fun. Wild Planet's toys are gender neutral, encouraging both boys and girls to explore the world. While producing toys that are fun is important to Wild Planet, equally important is ensuring that the toys promote self-esteem in the youths who purchase the company's products. Wild Planet aims to help kids feel better about themselves through its toys. The company believes that encouraging creativity and exploration of the world results in a higher level of self-worth and accomplishment, which translates into higher self-esteem. Wild Planet's socially responsible efforts are embodied in its product. The product differs from other toy products in regard to social responsibility.

The Wild Planet mission statement reads:

> Wild Planet aims to play a leading role in bolstering the self-esteem of our children. We will accomplish this by providing a line of exciting, high quality toys that are as cool for kids as they are satisfying for parents. Producing these toys will result in more confident children of all ages, as well as outstanding profits for us and all our partners (Grossman 1996).

Wild Planet does not use the function of marketing to promote social issues. In fact, the company has been hesitant to advertise. The company's reluctance toward advertising recognizes that promotion of toys through advertising creates a need where it may not have priorly existed. The company interprets and expresses its social responsibility through its product. The company does not use the business function of marketing to reach its social objectives, although it very easily could if that was how it chose to approach its responsibility. Social activism through marketing efforts is not the choice of this company

Similar to Wild Planet Toys, GAIA Bookstore and Community Center approaches its social responsibility through its product. As a small community based business, GAIA has survived the recent wave of large-chain bookstores that are literally opening around them. GAIA does annual sales of approximately $ 500,000. The company has been named "Best Specialty Bookstore" in the *East Bay Express* for the last three years. The company derives its social objectives from its product and corporate values and business practices. GAIA, an independently-owned bookstore located in Berkeley, California sells only books that promote community, sustainability and spiritual traditions. GAIA will not sell a book that the owners believe does not promote responsibility. GAIA also operates with a strong set of business practices that reflect its values. The product defines how this company understands its social responsibility. "We carefully select books. We don't carry books on crime. We don't carry books that are damaging to women. We have very select criteria for what kind of books we sell" (Wynne 1996).

5. Conclusion

All six companies make use of their corporate values and business practices to express the company's social commitment. In addition, The Body Shop, Ben & Jerry's and Working Assets engage in social marketing strategies that build and shape these companies' social identities. Wild Planet Toys and GAIA Bookstore are good examples of companies that use their products as the source of their social responsibility.

These case examples illustrate companies that do not regard their businesses as first and foremost economic institutions, with discretionary social efforts attached. Rather they view their businesses as institutions which afford equal economic and social responsibilities to their stakeholders. For example, these companies clearly state their social

FIGURE 1

Predominant Mode of Social Responsibility

Corporation	Social efforts: Product or service	Social Efforts: Values and Business practices	Social Efforts: Marketing strategies
Levi Strauss		The values and business practices are the **dominate mode** for its social responsibility	
The Body Shop		The values and business practices are a means of social expression	The social marketing strategies are the **dominate mode** for its responsibility
Ben & Jerry's		The values and business practices are a means of social expression	The social marketing strategies are the **dominate mode** for its responsibility
Working Assets		The values and business practices are a means of social expression	The social marketing strategies are the **dominate mode** for its responsibility
Wild Planet Toys	The product is the **dominate mode** for its responsibility	The values and business practices are a means of social expression	
GAIA Bookstore	The product is the **dominate mode** for its responsibility	The values and business practices are a means of social expression	

intentions and economic goals in the companies' mission statements, and give equal importance to both perspectives. Levi Strauss, over decades, has successfully integrated its values with its business functions, and has demonstrated this through its corporate behavior. Furthermore, Ben & Jerry's and The Body Shop's measurement of success is based on their social efforts as well as meeting their profitability goals. Working Assets has created a business that donates a predetermined amount of money whether the company makes a profit or not. Wild Planet Toys will not produce a toy that does not meet specific social standards set by the company, and GAIA bookstore will only sell books that the company deems socially responsible. These are not examples of grafted on social efforts, but rather social endeavors that are integrated into the company's main business functions, either through its corporate values and business practices, marketing strategies or its product or service.

The six companies used as examples in this discussion interpret and approach their understanding of social responsibility from very different perspectives, making corporate social responsibility a concept that is not easily defined. This complexity of definition and theory building is widely discussed in the academic literature (Swanson 1995; Wood 1991). It has become increasing complex to define social responsibility. At the same time corporations are aggressively promoting their commitments to social action. The mass media reveals many companies promoting both a product or service and a compelling social cause.

This development raises the timely and important issue of how to evaluate the claims businesses are making concerning their socially responsible efforts. Viewing a corporation's interpretation of its discretionary responsibility through the three modes of: corporate values and business practices, marketing strategies and product or service provides a useful framework that helps characterize the concept of corporate social responsibility.

This framework offers three advantages: First, when examining how different companies define corporate social responsibility, very different interpretations exist and out of these differences come a better understanding of what constitutes a complete assessment of corporate social responsibility. Is a company socially responsible if it only markets social issues? Does there need to be a social commitment made in all three areas to constitute social responsibility? If a tobacco company embraces socially responsible values and business practices, uses its company to promote social issues through its marketing efforts, is this acceptable? It makes sense if a company is going to declare itself "socially responsible" and trade on this image that the consumer can also expect a level of social performance in the company's business practices, marketing strategies and product or services.

Secondly, differentiating the options of how we understand social responsibility creates the opportunity to develop "best practices" for the field. How a company goes about positioning its product to advance social needs differs from how a company would develop responsible business practices or marketing strategies. Distinct ongoing management issues arise depending on the social goals of the company. For example, The Body Shop spoke out against testing cosmetics on animals and it was found that while The Body Shop does not test its products on animals, some of the ingredients the company purchases were tested on animals. This issue became a big problem for the company because it aggressively marketed itself as being against animal testing. This situation is by no means unique only to The Body Shop, but could happen to any company trying to weave social issues into its main business functions. By defining and examining the different ways a company can assert its responsibility, practices and strategies can be developed to assist company's in the successful management of its social objectives.

Finally, holding corporations accountable for their discretionary social efforts will be advanced by a better understanding of how companies view their responsibility. Contemporary corporations make far reaching statements concerning the impact they have on social problems. It is not unusual to purchase a product and be made to believe you are "saving the Rain forest", "ending world hunger" or simply making the world a more just and humane place to live. While these are noble endeavors, how does one know if the Rainforest is saved or the world is a better place? If the options open to a company for practicing social responsibility are clearly defined it becomes much easier to hold businesses accountable for the social claims they make.

References

Aron, L. 1996. Personal Interview (September 27).
Ben & Jerry's 1995 Annual Report. 1995. South Burlington, Vt.
Cavanagh, G. F. 1990. *American Business Values*. Englewood Cliffs, NJ: Prentice Hall.
Fowler, E. J. 1993. "Ben & Jerry's as Bad Guys." *Business Ethics* 4 (May/June).
Grossman, D. 1996. Personal Interview (September 16).

Laabs, J. J. 1992. "Ben & Jerry's Caring Capitalism." *Personnel Journal* 50–57 (November).

Ravlin, E. C. & Meglino, B. M. 1987. "Issues in Work Values Measurement." In *Research in Corporate Social Performance and Policy, Vol. 9*, eds. W. C. Frederick and L. E. Preston. Greenwich, CT: JAI Press, 153–83.

Scher, L. 1996. Personal Interview (October 29).

Spurge, L., Spivak, K. M. & Hamermesh, R. G. 1997. *Knowledge Exchange Business Encyclopedia.* Santa Monica, Ca: Knowledge Exchange.

Swanson, D. L. 1995. "Addressing a Theoretical Problem by Reorienting the Corporate Social Performance Model." *Academy of Management Review* 20 (1):43-64.

Wood, D. J. 1991. "Corporate Social Performance Revisited." *Academy of Management Review* 16:691–782.

Wynne, P. 1996. Personal Interview (October 11).

Basic Ethical Aspects
of American Companies Operating in Poland

Barbara Szyszka
American Studies Center
University of Warsaw
Warsaw, Poland

1. Introduction

Corporate culture, social responsibility and managerial ethics are important aspects of the operation of The Coca-Cola Company, PepsiCo, IBM Corporation and Marriott Corporation both in the U.S. and in Poland. The studied companies' managers recognize that not only praxiological components of the "Triple E", that is Effectiveness and Efficiency, but also Ethics are necessary to insure success in business. The four companies pretend to be regarded as conforming to ethical standards and being socially responsible.

2. Corporate Culture

Every company develops its own way of conducting business, dealing with customers and partners, treating employees, communicating and solving conflicts that distinguishes it from other companies. It is called *corporate culture*. Geert Hofstede (1994:18) defines culture as "software of the mind" and corporate culture as "collective programming of the mind" of members of an organization, the specific way the people in the company have learnt to think, feel and act. Corporate culture is also the special climate or atmosphere in the company. It is about how things get done in an organization as opposed to how they do not. It involves some beliefs and values that are shared by majority of people in the company. Culture is to the organization what personality and character are to individual. The studied companies have been striving to build their corporate cultures on moral principles, which allows them to achieve their goals in an ethical manner.

2.1. Value Systems

Strong corporate culture founded on sound values and ethical principles is a key to long term success. Value is a belief that a specific way of behavior or end state of existence is preferable and appropriate to fulfill organization's aims. It is what the company views important for the successful operation and long term profitability.

The manager has to be careful about how business is done, otherwise the company's *reputation* is at risk. Reputation quite often comes form intangibles like the way the company treats its employees, the strength of its management team, quality of product or service and involvement in community affairs. Companies care about their reputation partly for financial reasons. Recent studies reveal that financial performance correlates strongly with reputation. In 1995 and 1996 The Coca-Cola Company occupied the first position on the list of the most admired American companies, in a survey conducted by Fortune at the same time being the top wealth creator for its shareholders. Coke's CEO Roberto Goizueta believes that employees with integrity are the ones that build the company's reputation (Fisher 1996:25).

Another common value for American companies operating in Poland is the *welfare* and *satisfaction* from work of the employees. A satisfied employee works better producing higher quality product or service. The Warsaw Marriott Hotel conducts Associate Opinion Survey every year which measures employees' satisfaction from working for the corporation. Workers are encouraged to express opinions about their supervisors, cooperation, problems they encounter etc.

All the companies I studied pay special attention to trainings and development of an employee. They give the workers an opportunity to improve their skills. PepsiCo Restaurants International in Poland plans to train 70% of its employees this year. Trainings are connected with improving the quality of service or special kinds of promotion. Managers of restaurants undergo three months BMT (Best Management Training). IBM Polska offers a variety of trainings including both professional and language courses. It is usually the supervisor's or general manager's decision who is going to take part in the training, but sometimes it is an employee initiative.

Customer satisfaction & high quality of product and service are common values shared by American companies in Poland. In every PepsiCo office there is a note "Remember, the customer is our boss." Consumer satisfaction is the lifeblood of The Coca-Cola Company. Every employee recognizes and fulfills his responsibility to enhance quality and image, which are synonymous with customer satisfaction. Employees are committed to quality that is not a destination but a way of life.

Creativity is highly valued by the companies studied. IBM appreciates creative ideas of its employees and its managers respond to all comments received in suggestion boxes.

The Warsaw Marriott Hotel encourages creativity, as well. There are special quality idea boxes where employees can put their ideas written down on paper. Quality Improvement team chaired by the General Manager meets once a week, reads and evaluates the ideas. If the team decides that the idea is worthwhile, then employee gets a note that it has been accepted. The ideas should meet the following criteria of:
- improving working conditions and associate satisfaction,
- increasing hotel sales, profits and reducing costs,
- improving quality of service and guest satisfaction.

Employee's creativity is always rewarded with a certificate, a small gift, for example mug or a bottle of wine. If the idea leads to cost reduction, then the person receives 5% of the amount of money saved by the hotel.

An important cultural aspect of the companies in which my research was conducted is *growth*. Coca-Cola Poland has six bottling plants and 2000 workers. The company is expanding and continually hires new employees. PepsiCo sees growth as an essential part of its corporate culture, the primary reason for growth being not financial but spiritual, since it produces a winning spirit. It creates a vital, enthusiastic atmosphere in the corporation where people see genuine personal opportunity. They take bigger chances and work harder and smarter (Calloway 1995:1). Presently, with 480,000 people worldwide including 3,000 in Poland, PepsiCo is the third largest corporate employer. PepsiCo Restaurants: Pizza Hut, KFC and Taco Bell are the largest worldwide restaurant system. They have got 28,000 units. Poland is the most important market for PepsiCo restaurants in Eastern Europe and new units are going to be opened in this country in the next few years in addition to the fifty-one already existing restaurants.

Brand and trademark are important values in all the companies I studied. Coca-Cola's brand is considered the most valuable and best known in the world. It is recognized by 94% of people all over the world. The power and prestige of Coca-Cola were exemplified in 1988 when three independent studies conducted by Landor&Associates confirmed Coca-Cola as the best known and most admired trademark in the world (The Chronicle of the Coca-Cola Company). Executives at Atlanta office say that if the place was obliterated off the earth, they could go to the bank and borrow $100 million and rebuild Coca-Cola in a matter of months, just on the strength of the brand (Morris 1996). Employees are proud to be able to work for the company that sells one of the most famous and admired products and speak of the brand with respect.

2.2. Communication

Communication takes the form of information and advice and not only decisions issued by supervisors. Managers of the Warsaw Marriott Hotel openly discuss new ideas with employees, and consult their decisions with them, since employees are regarded as the best judges. Communication is not only vertical (superior – subordinate) but it goes in all directions: horizontally, top-down and bottom-up. At IBM Polska there is "breakfast with the boss" once a week when everybody can come and talk to the boss on informal basis. Also once a week at the Marriott Hotel there are meetings of General Manager, HR manager and representatives of a given department. The most often discussed issues concern unfair treatment of employees by managers, supervisor's inability to manage and difficulties in cooperation within the department. At PepsiCo and IBM offices they use e-mail, so communication is constant and in all possible directions.

All the representatives I spoke with agree that communication is enhanced by informality. People are on first name basis in all the companies I studied. It is not only in relations between employees but also in relations superior subordinate. Although the Polish culture is much more formal than American culture, Poles had no difficulties in adopting to this custom, in fact they accepted it enthusiastically. Majority of staff of Coca-Cola Poland, PepsiCo and IBM are young people, very open to changes and new ideas. It is slightly different at Marriott, which has employees at the age of nineteen and fifty, and the youngest workers sometimes use a more official way of addressing their older colleagues.

Two languages are spoken in these companies, Polish and English; Polish being used in every day contacts between employees and English used in contacts with top management and the corporation.

Fluency in English is required from all office workers and basic knowledge of the language from other employees. It is due to the fact that general managers are usually American and some positions in the senior executive staff are also occupied by Americans or corporate employees form international structures. All the companies I visited have been present in Poland for less than ten years. Initially, their senior management staff were American. Gradually, however, they were being replaced by Polish managers. Presently, the number of expatriates, that is individuals who are not Polish citizens, but have been assigned to work in Poland has decreased. In the Warsaw Marriott Hotel the number of expatriates has decreased from forty when the corporation started doing business in Poland ten years ago to eight in 1997. The corporation chose the parent company option that is often used at early stages of internationalization when there is a major need to transport various aspects of parent company particularly technological expertise to the subsidiary (Bartol and Martin 1991:762). Expatriate managers were more knowledgeable than local employees about the latest technological developments of the parent company, but in the course of time the local managers were trained and they were able to take on the positions once occupied by the employees from international structures.

2.3. Celebrations and Ceremonies

Celebration, ceremonies and rituals reinforce the feeling of unity and identity of the employees with the company, they make them feel like a big family, they are also a way of articulating the company's culture.

At Coca-Cola they celebrate Christmas parties and they chose the employee of the year for the first time in the December 1996. All the employees of the region office took part in a secret voting. This was important both to the person chosen, who knew that was liked and respected, but also to employees who were free to speak and express opinions.

PepsiCo workers choose the nicest manager. Christmas parties and picnics are organized. Records of sales are celebrated and dinner with the boss is a common reward for outstanding performance.

At the Warsaw Marriott Hotel the employee of the year is chosen. There are generous rewards, e.g. the best manager goes on a trip to foreign country like in other companies, the choice is made by voting. There is a special program called Tender Love and Care. The corporation organizes balls for employees and lotteries with valuable prices. Workers celebrating birthdays get cards with greetings and signatures of the executive staff. Employees who have babies get presents usually some baby cosmetics. Newly wed couples spend a night in the Marriott Hotel room. Employees get presents from the corporation, for example last year they all got watches with the Marriott logo.

When asked about the culture of the companies, their representatives had some difficulty in describing it. Most probably because cultures have ephemeral qualities of flame or fog. We know they are there we know they are real but we can't grab hold of them or even describe them very well (Leavit 1986:23). However, they all agreed that the corporate cultures in their companies have been developing since the companies were founded and the process will continue as long as the firm exist. Culture is an important component of the company's operation, because it defines rules and norms of conduct that have to be respected by the employees.

3. Social Responsibility

Businesses exist to make profits but also to serve the society. Business and society enter a contract in return for the permission to do business, the society places certain obligations on the companies. The business is expected to benefit not only its creators and owners, but also those, who permitted it, which means society at large (Bowie 1979:87). Corporate officials have a responsibility that goes beyond serving the interest of the owners. To be socially responsible, the company has to improve the quality of life of society. Corporations are public institutions, so stricter legal and moral standards of responsibility can be required from them. Business receives the mandate from the society and therefore it has to respond quickly to its changing needs and expectations. It is no longer enough to satisfy economic needs, since people have become affluent. Now they expect companies to act in the public interest: give employment, respect human dignity, provide high quality goods and services, train unemployed, contribute to education and research foundations (Evans 1981:20).

3.1. Corporate Responsibility to Various Groups of Stakeholders

The business managers ought to recognize their responsibilities to various groups having a stake in the company's survival. The studied companies claim to be responsible to the following groups:

Customers, who want a safe and quality product at reasonable prices. Coke's CEO Roberto Goizueta maintains that the firm is going to emphasize product quality worldwide. For years business was built on the "Three A's" – Availability, Affordability and Acceptability. Now the company is striving for the "Three P's" – Pervasive penetration, the best Price and making Coca-Cola the Preferred beverage everywhere (The Coca-Cola Company Annal Report 1995).

PepsiCo prides itself in selling soft drinks, juices and snacks that appeal to all people in all places and of all incomes. PepsiCo attracts customers by delivering great food service and value, by making product news and expanding distribution. Products and services are tailored to local tastes to satisfy better the needs of customers all over the world.

The studied companies declare to take this responsibility because they know that inadequate appreciation of the duty to provide a safe and quality product may lead to product liability lawsuits, which every socially responsible firm should avoid, because they undermine company's good name.

Employees can expect good working conditions, safety at work and decent salaries, as well as chances of promotion for those who have deserved them. This duty arises from the respect to the worth and dignity of individuals who devote their energies to the business and who depend on the business for their economic well being. Even when crisis comes, the company ought to minimize the hardships imposed on employees like workforce reduction or plant closing by giving workers opportunities of retraining (Thompson and Stricland 1990:702). Although all the companies studied are good performers with strong position on the market, if they were forced to reduce the number of workers, the employees that were made redundant would relatively easily find new jobs because of high qualifications they have achieved through various trainings organized by their former employers. Marriott, Coca-Cola, PepsiCo and IBM, all being huge international corporations have a multicultural and multinational personnel and foster the international family concept which has been a part of their traditions. All employees have equal opportunities to grow, develop and advance within the company, and their progress depends on their abilities, ambitions and achievements.

Government wants the companies to operate legally and pay taxes, which all the studied companies do. They contribute significantly to Poland's economic growth by creating new opportunities for employment. Only a few members of their senior executive staff are foreigners. The rest of the personnel are Poles. Marriott, PepsiCo and Coca-Cola employ 1,100–3,000 people. The Coca-Cola Company takes pride in worldwide business that is always local. Company's bottling plants are operated by business people native to the nations in which they are located. Most supplies are bought from the local sources creating new supply industries within the local economies.

Creditors seek to receive the principal as well as interest on money loaned to the firm when it is due. They also want to be informed about the security of the loan. In return they will lend capital to the company in the future.

Suppliers want to be paid on time for the supplied materials and equipment, and to be treated fairly and receive adequate information about operations of the organization. This duty arises out of market relationship that exist between suppliers and the firm. They are partners and the quality of supplied materials affects the quality of production, but at the same time they are adversaries because suppliers want the highest prices for materials and equipment whereas the firm wants to buy at the cheapest possible price (Thompson and Stricland 1990:620).

The community in which the companies operate can expect them to behave like good citizens and exercise care in the impact their activities have on the environment and community, which all the firms involved in the study recognize, since they want to be accepted by members of the community.

The owners want financial returns on their investment, security as well as basic information about the organization's performance and activities, which they receive in the form of the annual report.

In the return for fulfilling the obligations toward stakeholders the company receives customer loyalty and satisfaction, employees time, talent and effort, government protection and willingness of suppliers to continue doing business with the company in the future.

3.2. Environment

The Coca-Cola Company and its bottlers have been at the forefront of helping solve environmental, litter and solid waste issues for more than 20 years. The managers realize that the company touches the lives of billions of people around the world and that its responsibility to them includes conducting business in ways that help preserve the environment. All of the packaging is recyclable. In 1990 just after fast food restaurant system McDonald's Corporation announced phaseout of styrofoam packaging from its hamburgers, both Coca-Cola and Pepsi announced that they would sell its products in plastic bottles made with recycled materials. These changes were made because of consumers concerns over degradation of the environment.

Coca-Cola supports numerous litter prevention organizations including the Center for Marine Conservation and Keep America Beautiful (Coke is a founding member of the latter). The company has been recycling thousands of pounds of waste annually. As a result it has donated more than $100,000 to charity.

The personnel of the Warsaw Marriott Hotel segregate waste placing paper and glass in special containers, which facilitates the recycling process. Guests are encouraged to use their towels for more than one day, if it is possible, to reduce the amount of detergents used in washing.

IBM uses recycled paper, its trademark is always made with ecological materials and employees are encouraged to pay special attention to the economical use of paper.

3.3. Corporate Philanthropy of the Studied American Companies

Coca-Cola, PepsiCo, Marriott and IBM have been voluntarily contributing to charitable and social responsibility causes.

In Poland Marriott and Coke are sponsors of the olimpic games for the disabled. Coca-Cola and IBM support various sporting events, also at the local level, for example marathon in Warsaw, basketball and tennis competitions. The Warsaw Marriott Hotel employees are encouraged to collect unnecessary things, for example clothes. Charitable organizations come and take the things and distribute them to the poorest.

All four companies give aid to orphanages and hospitals. IBM supports schools, museums and theaters donating both money and computers. Occasionally the firm helps individuals in need e.g. a blind university student, a talented child who would not be able to afford taking part in a music competition abroad without financial aid.

In December 1996 Coca-Cola donated money to orphanages all over Poland. Children in forty orphanages got gifts from the company. Additionally Coca-Cola offered financial aid to twenty houses to help organize winter holidays for children. Also last year, Coke cooperated with Polish Humanitarian Action donating money for the poorest children in the Bieszczady Mountains, in the south-east of Poland. Coca-Cola will always try to help children and give them a bit of joy. Coke's General Manager in Poland promises that those actions will be continued in the future.

The studied companies recognize their social responsibility mostly in the following three areas:
• corporate philanthropy,
• environmental protection,
• giving employment and fostering economic growth of the country in which they operate.

Coca-Cola believes that its real social responsibility is creating new employment opportunities. Hiring one employee causes employment growth by ten people in other firms cooperating with the company, for example suppliers or distributors. One of the firms producing Coke's signs for the company is expanding and making good profits, and before signing the contract with the company it was declining. Giving jobs to people in a country which has only a short experience in market economy and has not fully recovered from the economic transition means a lot. It is a much more important aspect of social responsibility, because it really solves problems for many people, whereas charitable donations will always be a drop in the ocean.

4. Managerial Ethics

A business manager is a person responsible for running a firm and performing the function of planning, controlling, organizing, staffing and motivating. He is responsible for making profits, however financial matters are not the only ones he is concerned with. The manager makes decisions that have impact on his subordinates, customers and community at large. Therefore he has to act responsibly, predict the consequences of his actions, respect the welfare of people who might be affected by a particular decision. Responsibility is an integral part of managerial ethics, which addresses the question how should a manager conduct himself so that organization's aims are achieved in a manner consistent with the principles of ethics, philosophy and mission of the firm (Rasmussen 1988). The managers ought to act effectively that is to be able to undertake and complete the task and efficiently that is to be able to complete the task in a timely and a cost efficient manner (Natale and Benton 1996:237), but they must not forget about ethics. They need to base their actions on solid values, ideals and principles. They need to consciously establish the beliefs and ideals to which they will hold and meet social expectations. The studied companies' managers aspire to be ethical in their dealings with the firms' stakeholders.

When I asked the representative of Coca-Cola Poland about the qualities of an ethical manager, he answered simply that the manager has to be a decent man, fully engaged in his work for the company, frank and honest. He sets an example for the employees, he affects the culture and behavior of employees. The IBM Polska representative adds to these qualities objectivism. Being calm, sober-minded, the ability to cope with unpredictable situations are critical features of a person managing personnel, which is usually a stressful activity. Being open, friendly and always ready to help are highly appreciated. Expertise is necessary. Although there is no manager who possesses all the knowledge of the world, an employee needs to be aware that there is someone who knows more and knows better.

Since the manager is more knowledgeable about the firm's operation, he ought to be willing to share his skills and expertise with his employees. At the Warsaw Marriott Hotel they say that the manager ought to be a good teacher and should be able to train another person to take over his position in the future. He must be modest, kind and helpful. He knows how to manage the personnel without using threats or force, and he can motivate and inspire the employees toward the achievement of organizational goals. The PepsiCo representative emphasized the ability to manage, to communicate the goals and strategy to his employees and to work in a group.

All the representatives I spoke with talked mostly about professional skills, certain features of character, but they either failed to mention ethical qualities or listed them on further positions. This might suggest that ethical qualities of a manager are not viewed as extremely important in the four companies. My analysis would have been more precise if I had been allowed to conduct a survey in which employees were supposed to point to the features of a good manager, among which there were personal qualities, professional skills and ethical qualities.

Likewise I was not able to conduct a survey in which employees were to answer questions concerning ethical dilemmas. These facts as well as unwillingness to share with me information about ethical codes, their implementation and unethical behavior of employees show that the studied companies are afraid that the results of my research could have revealed that not only do their employees act unethically but also that they get away with it.

It appears that in the ethical dimension corporate culture and social responsibility are important aspects in the operation of the studied companies, whereas managerial ethics receives much less attention.

References

Bartol, K. & Martin, D. 1991. *Management*. New York: McGraw Hill Inc.

Bowie, N. 1979. *Changing the Rules in T.Beauchamp & N.Bowie. Ethical Theory and Business*. Englewood Cliffs: Prentice Hall.

Calloway, W. 1995. "Letter from the Chairman in PepsiCo Inc." *1995 Annual Report*.

Evans, W. 1981. *Management Ethics. An Intercultural Perpective*. Boston: Martinus Nijhoff Publishing.

Fisher, A. 1996. "Corporate Reputations. Comebacks and Comeuppances." *Fortune Magazine* 4 March.

Hofstede, G. 1994. *Cultures and Organizations*. London: Harper Collins Publishers.

Leavitt, H.J. 1986. *Corporate Pathfinders*. New York: Pengiun Books.

Morris, B. 1996. "The Brand's the Thing." *Fortune Magazine* (4 March): 72–86.

Natale, M. & Benton, M.B. 1996. "Praxiology: Components of Managerial Actions in a Diverse Working Environment." In *Human Action in Business. Praxiological and Ethical Dimensions*. New Brunswick: Transaction Publishers.

Rasmussen, D. B. 1988. "Managerial Ethics." In *Commerce and Morality*, ed. T.R.Machan. New York: Rowman & Littlefield.

Thompson, A. & Strickland, A. 1990. *Strategic Management. Concepts and Cases*. BPI Irwin Homewood.

Ethical Issues in Multilevel Marketing

Angela Xu
Julia Tian
China Europe International
Business School (CEIBS)
Shanghai, China

"Never has any other form of marketing elicited such craze and adoration on one hand, while facing the awkward situation of being condemned on the other. This 'angel' and 'devil' 2-in-1 thing is multilevel marketing (MLM), or 'Pyramid selling' as it is usually called" (San Lian Life Weekly 1998).

1. Introduction to the Problem of Multilevel Marketing

1.1. The Situation

In November 1990, Avon Products, the U.S. cosmetics direct sale company, first brought MLM into China. The new concept then spread like wild fire through major cities like Guangzhou, Shanghai, Beijing, Shenyang, and thus through the whole country, bringing a second wave of craze following the first issuance of stocks in the late 1980s. Since then, about 518 MLM companies have registered in China, including Amway. However, the number of companies actually in operation is estimated to be at least 1,500, with individual sales persons of around 1.5 to 2 million, according to the *China Daily Business Weekly*, the government-owned newspaper.

Are those sales people getting rich? Most are not. Thousands of MLM sales persons end up with their golden dreams broken. More serious consequences have occurred: criminals have used MLM as an umbrella to set up sects and cults, spread superstition and carry out illegal activities, affecting the country's social stability (San Lian Life Weekly 1998). In seminars held by recruiters, messages like "what's the purpose for working with the Communist Party? Why are you still so poor? Join our MLM and it will bring you a fortune..." are expressed covertly or with religious zeal. Some fraudulent firms seize the opportunity to cheat millions out of the gullible. Many, unaware of consumer rights, are easily taken in, according to authorities. Those doing MLM sell smuggled, fake and low quality goods with inflated prices, harming the interests of consumers. For example, the retail price of an electric massage machine was supposed to be US$85, but some unsuspecting buyers were paying US$474 in the hope of being able to sell on at a profit. Some distributors have bought goods in bulk with life savings or money borrowed from their families and relatives. The prospect of making a fortune is so alluring that not a soul seems to care if there is a need or demand for the goods they sell. Some firms also evade taxes and seriously affect the work of the government and schools by inducing government and Communist party officials, teachers and soldiers to become involved. (Note: Law forbids these people to participate in the trade; San Lian Life Weekly 1998.) Although the State Administration for Industry and Commerce (SAIC) has criticized several times those illegal players, the effect has been minimal. As a result, many people call for putting an end to MLM.

1.2. What is MLM?

It seems there is no clear definition of MLM in dictionaries. An acceptable characterization might be the following: MLM is a type of business method in which the company does not sell its products through intermediary shops, but sells directly to consumers through MLM individual sales persons (distributors). It has three unique characteristics: closed organization, non-transparent transactions, and dispersed distributors (Jiefang Daily 1998a).

Is such a fad a normal phenomenon in the world? The answer is NO. Statistics of the world MLM Association show that among all MLM members, 85% bought products for their own consumption, only 15% intend to develop his/her own business through network building; while among the 15%, only 1% really make some achievements and choose MLM as a career. In the USA, the average annual income from MLM for 90% MLM members is no more than US$5,000, which is far from being a sufficient means of making a living (San Lian Life Weekly 1998). Amway and Mary-Kay, two giant players in MLM in China, commented that "we have been educating our members not to equate MLM to a short-cut toward getting rich!"

Then, what makes MLM so attractive in China, a less developed country? What lures people to join? Who should be responsible for the consequences? In the following section, we will look at the MLM structure and analyze in detail the whole situation on three levels, namely, the macro, meso and micro levels (Enderle 1993, Enderle and Tavis 1998).

2. Analysis

2.1. MLM Structure and How the System Works

Before making an in-depth analysis of this industry, it is crucial to gain insight into the structure of MLM and to understand its major distinction from other marketing strategies.

Take Amway (China) as an example. Registered in 1992, Amway has invested more than US$170 million in China. It sells a variety of household and personal care products and recorded retail sales of over US$178 million in 1996. It is the top MLM company in China. At present, (1998) there are more than 80,000 distributors in Amway. These distributors, forming a strong sales force for Amway, are independent contractors, not employees.

According to Amway's policy, a new distributor has to purchase a product kit, which costs around RMB 700 (or US$85). As a registered salesperson, his income comes from two sources: first, a 15% to 20% margin on his direct products sales; second, a 3% to 21% commission on the whole sales price of products purchased by his "down-lines" (people joined under his introduction). Compared with the former income, the latter is more incentive. This policy offers "first mover advantage" to those who enter earlier. Obviously, it encourages distributors to devote time recruiting and training their downlines. The reason is clear: as he moves higher and higher up the "pyramid," a distributor's income could increase at a geometrically expanding speed! For this reason, the MLM is also called "Pyramid sales."

As mentioned above, MLM has brought ideological confusion and serious consequences in society. So we ask: What is wrong with MLM? Who should be responsible for the consequences, the government, the companies or individuals? Should this issue be discussed from the legal or ethical perspective?

2.2. Macro-level: Responsibility of Government

At this level, the major issues are related to the political, economic and social-cultural systems. Within these systems, the role of government is of paramount importance because it is government's responsibility to establish and keep a well-ordered society with a well-designed legal framework, supported by a certain moral philosophy.

Although criticized in some media, most MLM companies can survive against negative public opinion because they have spent a lot of money to protect and insulate themselves through lobbying. In this sense, some local governments actually have acted as "up-lines" (the recruiters who introduce people to join) in MLM. To our knowledge, the following issues have not been seriously considered by government:

• How should the benefits and damages to society, resulting from MLM industries, be balanced? This is a dilemma faced by government. No doubt, this new industry in China has created some benefits to society, such as alleviating unemployment pressure, attracting foreign investment, increasing tax revenue and so on. On the other hand, through various pyramid schemes and an uncontrollable sales network, a number of unscrupulous people have engaged in a series of unethical and illegal activities, such as selling fake goods at inflated prices.

• How should a clear guidance in terms of laws and regulations for the MLM industry be designed? Government should determine how to maintain fair competition, sound profit, consumers' rights, and a healthy implication on society. However, this guidance can not fully determine business conducts. Thus, it leaves a certain space of freedom to corporations for ethical decision making. In China's current situation of development, the crucial question is whether the government has the ability to institute fair and reasonable guidance in order to set a boundary of such freedom to the new industry. If government can establish a set of concrete guidance, the further question is how to enforce and monitor the guidance's application. All the problems reflected in MLM obviously indicate that currently our government does not have enough experience and ability in creating and monitoring such rules and regulations.

• During the past two decades, Chinese government has made great efforts for economic reform. Unfortunately, the standard of moral conduct has been somewhat neglected. Worshiping money induces many people to admire blindly western life style. They dream to become overnight millionaires by fanatically selling "dreams" to their relatives, friends, neighbors, rather than by selling real products directly. The new rich person is regarded as hero who shows up in corporate magazines and meetings again and again.

These serious moral problems strongly call for the Chinese government to concentrate on not only material but also ethical and cultural progress in order to cope with these ethical challenges.

2.3. Meso-level: Responsibility of Companies

At the meso-level, we focus on corporate responsibility. No corporation exists in isolation, and it has to take on responsibilities toward its customers, employees, communities and stockholders. Although most legal MLM companies are operating within the realm of law, some ethical issues should be addressed here:

• Relationship with "contractors": To some extent, a distributor is not equal to a formal employee, but rather a so-called "contractor," or even "entrepreneur." However, the company can not ignore responsibility for training and controlling its distributors' network. This being said, we still wonder whether a company like Amway really has the power to carry out such responsibilities; think about its huge sales force: over 80,000 distributors in China. Further, has the company really provided benefits to these distributors, in both the economic and ideological sense?

Much evidence induces us to believe that most companies indeed downplay their roles for the purpose of making quick money at the expense of long-term benefit. Otherwise, they can certainly act better in ethical aspects. Most companies lack (re-)education programs for their distributors. Some companies even intentionally keep a rather loose sales network. Generally speaking, Amway is among the best companies within MLM industry. However, even in Amway, all the meetings for motivating people are held by distributors themselves, with no monitor from Amway. This "hot" meeting is the way the "dream" is planted and fertilized, and the quick construction of a pyramid under the "dream" creates large short-term profit for the company. This profit is gained at the cost of a lost corporate ethical standard, a freedom allowed within the law. The company can gain much more benefit in a short period, but it hurts its reputation and long-term well-being. The MLM system unquestionably provides companies with incentives consciously to give up the control of sales network and focus on short-run profit, without maximizing profit in the long term.

On the other hand, is the company fair to these distributors in different levels? The designed structure in the MLM gives each distributor an illusion: success is easy through geometric expansion, where you get ten to sponsor ten, and so on. This is usually shown as an expanding matrix with corresponding kickbacks at various levels. The problem here is one of common sense: At only three levels there would be 1,000 people. At six levels deep, there would be 1,000,000. But who supports these 1,000,000 people? What about the unfortunate "distributors" at the bottom? It is clear that this system cannot provide a fair treatment to those different distributors at different levels. Then, we shall ask the question: if the defects of the structure are so apparent, why does MLM continue to exist? Is the structure itself unethical? And, by carrying on such business, are those MLM companies ethical, no matter if they do it consciously or unconsciously?

• Relationship with customers: Due to relatively inexperienced sales people, it is impossible to expect that customers can get proper products and good service. Further, since China is a society favoring "Guan Xi" (relationships), the first sales target of those salespersons would be their relatives and friends. Under most circumstances, they are unable to reject purchasing the product even when they do not really need the product for the sake of face-saving. Is this fair to customers? When these companies designed this marketing system, did they seriously consider customers' rights, especially under Chinese traditional cultural background?

• Relationship with community: As stated above, the MLM industry brought along various moral problems to China. Although some people are joyfully staying in this industry, most cast aside the concept of MLM, and some even regard MLM distributors as greedy liars. Exaggerated claims, one-shot game cheating (a game in which there is no chance for revenge), poor products and high prices have led to an overwhelmingly negative public opinion. It even has corrupted public morals and created disturbance. This MLM system has undermined people's mutual trust, the consequences go far beyond what government and companies have originally anticipated.

Corporate responsibility includes respecting legal and socio-cultural standards of the society in which they operate. We think over-advocating "western life style" and "American dream" fails to show a respect for (and consideration toward) Chinese custom and cultural heritage (see Enderle and Tavis 1998). One of the reasons why MLM networks can be established in China so rapidly is that the system takes advantage of Chinese interpersonal relationship. In a sense, it hurts people's feeling and social custom.

2.4. Micro-level: Responsibilities of Individual Consumers

At this level, we attempt to answer the following questions: why can the MLM industry exist in foreign countries outside China without major social problems? Do we, as individual Chinese citizens, bear a moral responsibility for the bad consequences of MLM in China?

A story reported in newspapers can illustrate the above argument. When Amway announced that customers could return used goods if not fully satisfied, the result was perplexing. Many people purposely returned the used bottle just to take the benefit of Amway's policy! This well-intentioned policy soon became a headache and difficult to carry on. How can a company healthily grow along with such immature consumer conducts?

In addition, except for some innocent distributors, many others do not really believe in their products or the recruiting program. Why, then, do they enroll? It is greedy nature that impels them to motivate their close friends to buy products or become their downlines with exaggerated claims. Apparently, by this way, they make money only by misusing other's trust, certainly unethical conduct!

All these ugly conducts urge us, each Chinese person, to realize that it is time to make a self-criticism on moral behavior.

3. Recommendations and Remaining Concerns

3.1. On the Macro-level

The government should establish a complete supervision and control system. For example, MLM companies that apply for registration must increase their registered capital. This will help to judge whether the company is serious and committed toward doing business in China. And companies should establish and implement the "return of goods" system, so as to protect consumers' rights and enhance the quality control of the companies.

One *concern* remains: if these terms are actually included in rules and regulations, will they work out effectively? The answer is unclear. Amway is a legal player; it invested a great amount in China to show its commitment; it carries on strict return of goods system; yet unethical conducts still exist. For example, in so-called "proper training" meetings, the meaning of MLM is still twisted as being a "short-cut to getting rich" (China Business News 1998). If a legal company like Amway can not prevent such deals, can those "pirates"? Even if the regulations are written down, will companies voluntarily follow? If not, does the government have the capacity to oversee this industry? If not, do all relevant government bodies have the ability to handle extra crimes, sects and cults, superstitions outrising from malpractices? These problems are all very difficult for the government to solve.

The media should help to establish a healthy ethical environment. As the painful process of restructuring state industries leaves millions of people out of work and excluded from the nation's new-found prosperity, the gulf between rich and poor is widening, and fantasies of short-cuts to wealth are ever more appealing. In an immature market like China, the media's role is especially important in order to guide consumers' mentality in a healthy direction. As discussed above, the media should encourage fair play and getting rich through solid efforts rather than promoting speculations and bubbles.

3.2. On the Meso-level

Before entering the market, MLM companies should consider at least one thing: Will this marketing concept bring more benefit than harm to the host country? MLM is new in China, but not at all new in the world. In its history of nearly eighty years, MLM has been sued or condemned in a number of countries. Even Amway has incurred such troubles in its home country and Taiwan (China Business News 1998). Why? MLM companies should think twice about this question before rushing to their self-defense. Aren't there any fatal defects in MLM structure itself? The analysis above actually touched this point. "Our history shows we're a business of successful entrepreneurs who found a way to reach our goals and help others do the same" (Amway's Web Site). Does reality match this vision?

After entry, an MLM company should establish its own rules and regulations to control its business and individual sales persons. These rules shall include terms such as the following: enforce no initial fee; provide quality goods with reasonable prices; goods can be returned by both MLM sales persons and customers; pay taxes; do no exaggerated promotions; pay attention to training the sales persons. In training potential distributors, the company should stress that it is hard work that leads to success and that there are no easy pickings. Legal MLM firms, if loose in their management, have every possibility to become illegal ones. This is determined by MLM's three characteristics. Thus, the future of MLM is in the hands of MLM companies themselves. That is to say, the key for continuity is MLM companies' own quality, motives, styles and management. In this respect, it is MLM companies' responsibility, rather than the government's, to handle the issue.

Still, it remains a concern whether the above mentioned terms are actually at the control of MLM companies in today's China? What if the individual sales persons, out of mean motives, work against the company's rules, and the company lacks sufficient capacity to handle the widely dispersed individuals? This is highly possible, as discussed in our analysis in the previous section.

3.3. On the Micro-level

To a large extent, MLM depends on the establishment of networks. Due to China's collective culture in which people have long valued cooperation and close family relationships, the first level of a network usually involves those who are near to the distributor. However, before inviting them to an opening meeting, one should ask oneself, are you personally convinced that MLM is an ethical business practice? If the answer is not clearly positive, stop doing it. As the Golden Rule says "Do not do unto others what you don't want them to do unto you."

The majority of innocent people who were conned into MLM should realize that there is no easy way to make money. The wish to get rich is not to be criticized, but do not let the desire override common sense. In this respect, individuals shall acquire more knowledge through self-learning.

The *concern* here is that some people simply will not give up until the their heads hit the walls. This is partly due to ignorance and backwardness, which in turn explains why many poor people in the countryside also join the craze. Will such backwardness be eliminated within a few weeks or months? Most likely not. A Chinese proverb says "it takes ten years to grow a tree, it takes a hundred years to cultivate people."

4. Conclusion

Based on the above recommendations and concerns, our final conclusion is as follows: Rule out the MLM (or pyramid) scheme for the moment. China today is not ready for such a scheme, due to its weak regulatory system and a mass of consumers not sufficiently mature to avoid scams. The purpose is to protect the legal interests of consumers, market order and social stability.

A new ethical question might arise here: By so doing, is government doing something unethical toward legal enterprises who have committed a lot to China? Shouldn't the government consider the trade-off at the very beginning to avoid the whole thing happen? If the government really decides to rule out the MLM scheme, it should also think about the story again. We cannot elaborate on this topic here, though.

5. Epilogue

This article was finished on April 20. And just two days later, on April 22, 1998, pyramid sales schemes were outlawed in China. The State Council pointed out that such sales were not suited to national conditions and have done some serious harm. It announced that any business registered for pyramid sales before the State Council announcement must halt the practice before October 31. They should also register another form of business and cancel the original registration (Jiefang Daily 1998b). The SAIC reconfirmed that legally registered companies can remain in business by setting up as shops or regular distributors (Harding 1998b).

There are different reactions. Some commented that "to say all of this is illegal calls into question about China's commitment to consistency." "The U.S. Government would see the mainland's decision as a backward step and an overreaction" (South China Morning Post 1998). The official *China Daily* argues that "the act reflects government's role in a market economy as order establisher and keeper. In attacking such deeds, the main role is nobody's but the government."

The ban threatens to hurt some big international door-to-door distributors, such as Amway, Avon Products and Mary Kay Cosmetics. The U.S. government "started lobbying to have the ban lifted, or at least modified to allow these companies to continue operations" (Harding 1998a).

Amway reacted calmly, saying it "understand[s] that the government... is acting to prevent fraudulent pyramid scams" (South China Morning Post 1998), and it has decided to accept a proposal from the government side to switch to selling its goods through retail outlets only (Yau 1998). Amway has forty existing distribution centers, and these will be opened to the general public as shops.

However, it is not easy at all to switch to retail operations. Retail selling requires a different set of skills, so any switch would require considerable time before adaptation is possible. Moreover, nowhere else in the world does Amway operate in this way. The company is afraid that certain internal conflicts might result.

Despite the feelings of frustrations over the ban, the company stressed that "it had an unwavering commitment to the mainland market" (Yau 1998). In the mean time, it calls for the government to separate the "sheep" (legitimate manufactures) from the "goats" (the pirates).

Avon Products claims that its business operations are legal and that it has provided employment up to 2,300 staff with branches in seventy-five cities on the mainland. It says that it has a number of options on how to proceed (Kynge 1998b). Some of these might be to restructure sales to resemble more closely operations in Malaysia and Taiwan. In Malaysia, for example, Avon has "beauty boutiques" open to the public, but it also runs door-to-door sales representatives who pick up their goods at these boutiques. With big stakes in China, Avon hopes that "any changes to be made to its operations will be kept to a minimum" considering the network and channels to be built up from scratch (Yau 1998).

The ban dealt quite a blow to the millions of individual distributors hoping for riches. With hundreds to thousands of Yuan of stock on hand, these people swarmed into direct sales firms clamoring for their money back. Riots are reported in inner provinces such as Hunan where illegal MLM firms are rampant. Many of the people are unemployed and were lured by the promise of riches and then deceived. Riot police had to be called in to quell the angry protesters (Yau 1998a). However, at legitimate companies such as Amway, the compensation process is said to be "in order." The government will act as a judge in each case to help deal with complains and restore order. For millions of innocent people, this experience is a bitter lesson.

As Chinese, we welcome the decision because China really cannot afford to adopt MLM scheme; however, we hope the government will handle the matter in a prudent and proper way. What is even more important is to remember the painful lessons and put the MLM case into consideration for future policymaking.

References

Amway's Home Page. http://www.amway.con/ourstory.

China Business News. 1998. 7 April.

Enderle, G. 1993. "What Is Business Ethics?" In *Business Ethics: Japan and the Global Economy*, ed. T.W. Dunfee and Y. Nagayasu, 133–150. Dordrecht, Boston, London: Kluwer Academic Publishers.

Enderle, G., Tavis, L. A. 1998. "A Balanced Concept of the Firm and the Measurement of Its Long-term Planning and Performance." *Journal of Business Ethics* 17, 1129–44.

Harding, J., Kynge, J., Ridding, J. 1998. "Ban of Pyramid Schemes Sparks Rioting in China." *Financial Times* 1 May.

Harding, J. 1998a. "China's Pyramids of Unsold Foot Masseurs." *Financial Times* 2–3 May.

Harding, J. 1998b. "China Clamps Down on Direct Sales Schemes." *Financial Times* 11 May.

Jiefang Daily. 1998a. "Stop MLM Activities." 24 March.

Jiefang Daily. 1998b. "MLM Activities Are to Be Ruled Out." 22 April.

Kynge, J. 1998a. "U.S. to Press China on Direct Selling Ban." *Financial Times* 23 April.

Kynge, J. 1998b. "U.S. Direct Sales Groups in Fightback." *Financial Times* 29 April.

San Lian Life Weekly. 1998. "Put Money into Your Soul." Vol. 6.

Yau, W. 1998. "Sales Dreams Turns into Nightmare." *Hongkong Standard* 11 May.

South China Morning Post. 1998. "Mainland Bans Direct Marketing." 23 April.

American and Polish Trademarks:
The Culture and Ethics Behind Them

Agnieszka Ratajczyk-Zwierko
University of Warsaw,
Warsaw, Poland

1. Introduction

Looking at trademarks on various products and promotional materials one does not realize their tremendous impact on our life. This is because the role of trademarks is mostly abstract and symbolic and for that reason difficult to take in through the usual, practical reasoning. Therefore, the thorough understanding of what trademarks are and how they function requires a deep insight into their origin, the way they are created and protected, and the problems they face.

2. The Development of American and Polish Trademarks

Trademarks according to the resolutions of the Lanham Act and the Polish law on this subject are defined as:

> any word, symbol, or device, or any combination thereof adopted and used by a manufacturer or merchant to identify his goods and distinguish them from those manufactured or sold by others (Arens 1994:51).

While examining the mentioned definition, the first impression that comes forward is that trademarks are the creations of marketing and economics. However, this concept about trademarks is far from complete. The insight into the roots of the early American and Polish trademarks provides another dimension determined by the culture and tradition of both countries. The development and history of trademarks clearly suggest that trademarks are a cultural phenomenon as well.

2.1. Trademarks – the Cultural Symbols of America

The early American culture is frequently associated with the Wild West, immigrants, cowboys, Indians and the fights between them. At the time when cowboys used marks for branding animals nobody realized that these particular marks would give rise to the development of the present trademarks. The custom of branding animals originated because America, the land of dreams, was also the land of a very strong competition among cowboys often governed by very strict rules. Therefore, cowboys were forced to mark their animals in order to protect them from the possible theft. And these were the cowboys who were primary responsible for creating such terms as *brand* and *branding* (Drabik 1993:72).

It can be said that the cowboys' strive towards preserving their own property is a pattern behavior characteristic for the immigrant culture that was being shaped by the immigrants coming to America from different corners of the world and for various reasons, mostly to start their own new living there and to tear off the social and economic problems that they faced in their mother country. And they protected their property more than anything else in their lives since everything they had were the fruits of their own hard effort. The infinite possibilities offered by the 'new land' changed them into the present entrepreneurs looking for every opportunity in the environment and thus making their dreams into a reality (Altkorn 1994:28).

Therefore, the characteristic thing in the philosophy of American branding was that the owner of the brand was pursuing their goals as quickly as possible and in the simplest way possible. This is because the consumers focused on fulfilling their 'American dream' demanded simple and straightforward names of the products not to waste time guessing their application and origin. Therefore, the first American trademarks and iconic images included commonly understandable information about the features of the product and its source. What is more the trademark protection rules from that time allowed the companies to register both simple and descriptive trademarks such as Dial-a-Lash (eyeliner) or HandiWrap (food packages) (Altkorn 1996:28).

Inversely, the manufacturers marked their products to promote their goods and attract their loyalty to the particular company. In order to do so, they exposed themselves directly to the public by placing their marks on various kinds of sign boards, wrappers, boxes, and labels. Due to such extensive measures, the names of the patent medicines like Swaim's Panacea, Fanhstock's Vermifuge and Parry Davis' Vegetable Pain Killer soon became the most famous and recognizable names in the first half of the nineteenth century. Also the names of tobacco products were extremely popular specially names such as Smith's Plag and Brown and Black's Twist (Morgan 1986:10).

The lack of the homogeneous culture in the U.S. failed to produce the national symbols being the most important designates of the existing culture. However, in the course of the abrupt development and strong connections with the national culture, trademarks acquired the proprieties of the national symbols and the dignified representatives of the U.S. abroad. Therefore, the later overview of the American trademarks shows how they developed into the cultural symbols of America.

In examining the development of trademarks it is important to remember that trademarks first originate in the corporate culture of the companies which has a direct impact on their future image and prominence. In fact many American trademarks were created by the founders of the companies or by the people involved in that kind of business for many years. For example, the Coca-Cola trademark was invented in 1887 by Frank Robinson, the company's book-keeper who was experienced in calligraphy. Interestingly enough, the Coca-Cola trademark, which later grew into the American 'identity card', written in a style fashionable in 1887 combined with an exceptional taste and quality of the product is not perceived as out-dated now and successfully competes with the most modern trademarks and other drinks. This evidence indicates the symbolic proprieties of this trademark in surviving the passing of time and becoming the most recognizable trademark ever since (Morgan 1986:12).

Other examples of such trademarks comprise the Levi's jeans trademark assuring the customers with the permanent strength of this product, also the automobile trademarks such as Ford, Pontiac, Buick, Chevrolet are worth mentioning since they are not only perceived as high quality products but are also being associated with the ultimate power of the U.S.

All of the mentioned trademarks are a source of big profits for their companies and these marks attract a great deal of loyal and devoted customers. From this perspective trademarks constitute very important business tools. However, apart from being business tools, the American trademarks have placed themselves among the most important designates of the American culture. What is more, every customer abroad relies on the mentioned marks as everlasting symbols of high quality and credibility and properly associates them with the culture of the U.S. And this is the evidence of how important trademarks are for a given country and they represent not only the company and its product but also the images reflecting the culture and tradition of a particular country.

2.2. The Impact of History and Tradition on the Development of Polish Trademarks

Poland since the early times of its existence has been involved in battles and wars. Even at the time of peace Poland suffered the partitions from the neighboring countries in the course of which Poland lost its independence and completely disappeared from the map of the world. The World War II was destructive for most of the countries however even after the war Poland could not enjoy the economic stability since the assumptions of the communist system hindered every creativity and innovation. Fortunately, the attitude of Polishmen towards Polish tradition was so strong that they managed to preserve its national symbols even at the times when Poland lost its own identity as a country. Thus, the development of Polish trademarks is much more complicated than in the case of American trademarks since it was determined by the Polish tradition and the changing historical conditions (Boruc 1997:22).

The Polish medieval period was specially abundant with various battles and wars which shaped the image of a brave and heroic knight. And this period was primarily responsible for the origin of Polish trademarks which played an indispensable role for the medieval culture.

Thus, the ancestors of the present Polish trademarks were the armorial bearings and emblems used by the knights to distinguish themselves in the battle and mark their identity. Such emblems differentiated the most victorious fighters and gave signal to the enemies that they are the ones to be afraid of. Apart from the battles, the knight could become famous during knight contests. At the contest the knights differentiated themselves by means of their parchment rolls with the emblem on them. The function of verifying emblems and establishing their origin was fulfilled by the persons called heralds. The role of heralds gave rise to the later discipline called heraldry (Serwatowski 1997:79).

The heraldic emblems were also attached to the armor used by knights. The most important of the knight's armor was a sword which was a symbol of dignity and power. The fashion of naming swords originated from English and French legends about famous knights. The Polish kings also had their famous swords. For example, Polish king Bolesław Krzywousty fought with a sword called 'Żuraw' (in English 'Crane') and Bolesław Chrobry owned a legendary sword 'Szczerbiec' (in English 'Jagger') (Lewandowski 1992:15).

The creation of the noble society in the fourteenth century had a tremendous impact on the development of Polish trademarks. The membership in the noble society was based on the affiliations with the knightly ancestors. In Poland the noble emblems were the signs of identity and ownership in the political, societal, and family life. The emblems marked the buildings, the attributes of power, armor, carts, everyday life utensils like furniture, dishes, clothes, books, pens and were used for sealing the envelopes. The heraldic symbols also marked the ancestral flags during the elections, seyms, and wars and were owned by the royal, church, civilian, and military notables (Serwatowski 1997:79).

Although the existence of the noble status was replaced by the resolutions of the March Constitution in 1921, the tradition of using emblems has survived up till now. The Polish national emblem showing an eagle accompanies all prestigious events, meetings, conferences, international agreements, and treaties. The eagle is also visible every national banknote or coin. Moreover, emblems are used by the companies to create the desired image in the eyes of the customers and to promote luxurious and better quality products. In fact, emblems add light to the ordinary products since they associate them with the old traditions and customs (Turska 1993:21).

Surprisingly enough, the period of partitions in Poland strengthened the prestige and recognition of Polish trademarks. While preserving the Polish culture during this period, the Polishmen made effort to maintain the recognition of Polish trademarks. Being unable to fight the neighboring countries directly in war, the Polish companies competed with the German, Russian, and Austrian ones. The most recognizable trademarks from that time which acted as the economic and cultural symbols on the non-existing country were the trademarks of the Cegielski's company (a factory of agricultural machinery and tools in Poznań which competed with the best companies in Germany), the plant in Żyrardów – a town near Łódź dealing with the production of cotton material and stockings, and the famous Wedel company – a confectionery company set up in 1870 (Klonder 1997:40).

After gaining the independence Poland once again proved that Polish products are of a very good value and quality. The trademarks of the enamel utensil factories like Olkusz and Wulkan (in English 'Volcano') were known on several continents. Other famous companies were the soap and perfume companies from Warsaw: Fryderyk Puls and Ludwik Spiess & Son. It was also the first time in the history of Polish trademarks that the companies started to mark their products with the label 'Made in Poland' which presupposes about their significance (Klonder 1997:42).

The World War II was not favorable for Polish trademarks nevertheless many of them managed to regain their good position on the market. However, taking into account the damages made during the period of the communist system, it can be said that they were much more destructive than during the war. Due to the nationalization that took place at that time, most of the companies were forced to change their names and the monopoly-type business did not allow for the development of Polish trademarks. In fact, the only trademarks that could be considered as the dignified representatives of the national and the corporate culture was the swallow of Moda Polska (in English – Polish Fashion), the crane of LOT (Polish Airways), the snow-flake of Hortex (the producer of drinks and frozen food), and Polish 'Wyborowa' (the name of vodka) (Turska 1993:21).

As it can be seen, trademarks represent the values and beliefs cultivated in a given culture by commemorating the historical persons and events, the traditional customs, and the legendary heroes. Moreover, the very fact that trademarks were created by people being the members of this culture presupposes about their unique characteristics which can be visible by comparing the marks created by different and distinctive cultures. Thus, in comparing the American and Polish trademarks, it can be noticed that they are not only differentiated by the language, which is also a very important component of culture, but express the changing trends and tendencies prevailing in the culture of both countries.

3. What is the Role of Trademarks?

Trademarks have always played the function of reflecting the image of the company they represented. However, only recently they have been officially recognized as valuable elements of a company's corporate culture and the symbols of the national culture.

In fact, trademarks started to be treated by the companies with a greater respect mostly due to the fact that their monetary value is extremely high and the 'brand tax' put on the products is an important source of the companies' financial benefits and economic success. However, apart from the monetary value, trademarks have many other important advantages that cannot be forgotten (Morris 1996:74).

The outside expression of the company's culture on the market is its corporate image. The corporate image is, in other words, the personality of the company. It reflects what the company aspires to be and the way it wants to be perceived by the customers. Trademarks constitute an important part of the corporate image. Placed on products, leaflets, and promotional materials, trademarks play the same symbolic role as emblems and flags for the national culture. The symbolic meaning of trademarks has the ability to represent the company and its product, the area of the company's business, the tradition and values to which the company adheres, and commemorate its owners and designers. The graphics and lettering of trademarks indicate whether the company is modern with clear vision into the future or rather the one whose image focuses on preserving the traditional customs of the company and the way of making business by its first owners. Thus, trademarks play an important representative function acting as ambassadors of the company and its culture in relation to other companies, customers, and domestic and foreign markets. At the same time trademarks play a differentiating role by identifying the company from others existing on the market (Limański 1994:60).

The symbolic nature of trademarks has the power to attract the customers to a given company and its product. This is because a single name or logo is able to comprise all the necessary information about the product and its main features and at the same time transmit the corporate image and the company's mission. The ability of trademarks to create associations allows them to fulfil their communicative role by establishing a positive, emotional contact with the customers, gaining their loyalty and respect and convincing them that a particular product of this company is better than others. In result, the customers convinced about the quality of the product are likely to buy it repeatedly. Thus, the customers feel affiliated with the company and its mission and become a part of the company's culture (Limański 1994:61).

Among other functions, trademarks also play an important adverting role. They differentiate the company and its product among others existing on the market. In this respect, they facilitate the customers' buying behavior, especially in making their choices among products within the same product category. It is also true that the companies owning recognized and established trademarks do not have to spend big amounts of money on advertising their products and expressing the company's corporate image since at this point of the company's development the trademarks 'just advertise for themselves' (Limański 1994:61).

As it can be seen, trademarks have many functions that decide about their importance. Since trademarks are commonly exposed on different products, billboards, advertisements, they are mostly valued for their representative role. In the U.S. the status of trademarks has been established long ago and the strong and well-known trademarks are deeply connected not only with the corporate culture of their companies but some of them like Coca-Cola or Levi's are perceived as part of the national tradition. In Poland the role of trademarks has not been recognized up till now. Although Poland also has trademarks with long tradition like Wedel, it is only now that the Polish companies are starting to realize the role of trademarks as important elements of the company's culture and the symbols of the national customs and tradition.

4. Ethics Behind Trademarks

4.1. Counterfeiting as an Ethical Problem

The advantages and benefits resulting from owning well-known and established trademarks are accurately realized by the various kinds of counterfeiters and trademark infringers who make use of every possibility to enrich themselves by imitating trademarks of other companies. Despite the existence of strict penalties and fines for trademark infringement, the counterfeiters find more and more sophisticated methods in order to escape the law. For this reason, counterfeiting has become a growing problem both in the U.S. and in Poland (Waldbaum 1996:248).

From the legal point of view, counterfeiting means breaking the law by making use of someone else's trademark without permission. However, it is also an ethical problem, an issues of 'doing and not doing'. Making money out of someone else's property is considered an immoral deed both in American and Polish culture. From this perspective, it can be compared to stealing and in the literature on this subject this term is commonly called that way. Counterfeiting is also an unethical act with respect to the damages it makes to the companies, their culture, and tradition (Trompenaars 1993:130).

Counterfeiting can be considered an unethical act for a variety of reasons. First of all, counterfeiters diminish the value of trademarks by communicating a false massage to the customers and deceiving them that the fake comes from the original source. Moreover, the counterfeiters provide the customers with lower quality products than the original ones. In result, the customers after discovering that the product is of an inferior quality may shift their brand loyalty to other companies within the same product category. Inversely, the customers assured about the originality of the fake may unconsciously accept the lower quality of the counterfeited product and will start buying it regularly. In both cases, counterfeiting has a destructive effect on the companies since they lose of their greatest accomplishments that is loyal and devoted customers. Moreover, counterfeiting tarnishes the company's desired image since the counterfeited goods produced under the company's trademark are usually inconsistent with the demands and the expectations of the customers (Rubel 1994:8).

Apart from that, using products of other companies in the same style and manner is perceived in the same categories as stealing someone else's property. However, trademarks constitute more than just a sheer property for their owners. They are the symbols of the companies' corporate culture, reflect their image and constitute the primary and extremely valuable sources of information about the companies and their products. In this respect, trademarks attached to their owners have the same meaning as the names and surnames for people. For this reason, imitating products and services of other companies bears the same ethical implications as depriving a person of their own identity and distinctive traits of character (Rubel 1994:8).

Another ethical problem raise by counterfeiting is associated with food, cosmetics, or medical products in which the nutrition or chemical ingredients listed on the label do not reflect the real content of the package. Thus, the counterfeited products used by the customers diluted by the familiar trademark on the package might have a negative influence on their health. As a consequence, the original company does not only lose its goodwill and reputation but also acquires the image of the company that pursues unethical mission and goals (Alexander 1995:141).

Finally, the acts of counterfeiting diminish the monetary value of trademarks and in result cause financial damages for the companies. In extreme cases, counterfeiting may contribute to the bankruptcy of the whole business and destroy the company together with its all valuable assets (Rubel 1994:8).

Taking into account the mentioned arguments, it can be said that counterfeiting is perceived as unethical for at least two general reasons. One is that counterfeiting diminishes the recognition and reputation of the companies by offering the customers products of lower quality as compared with those coming from the original source. In result, the companies have to suffer the consequences for which they bear no responsibility whatsoever. The other reason is that the counterfeiters deceive the customers by giving them false information about the product and make them believe that the product is sold under the original trademark. And finally, from the religious point of view, 'giving false truth to someone' is a sinful act for which the sinner deserves a punishment.

4.2. 'Some Trademarks are too Scandalous to Register'   •

Trademarks in order to be protected have to be registered in the Patent and Trademark Office (PTO). In fact, the registration procedure is a very complicated process that double-checks every move of an applicant. Even after such strenuous effort the applicant may find the trademark rejected by the PTO. The point is that the registered trademark must be strong enough to resist both the passing of time and the attacks from various counterfeiters. Moreover, the registration procedure is intended to check whether the trademark does not violate the moral and ethical standards prevailing in a given country. Both the American and the Polish law does not permit the registration of a trademark which offends the religious feelings of the faithful, a sense of patriotism, and the generally accepted national values. Also, the law does not allow the registration of a trademark that is contradictory to the principles and norms governing the community life. However, the guidelines provided by the PTO in this area are, on the whole, vague and somewhat subjective. In some cases, the trademark evidently breaks the moral and ethical standards and the verdict prohibiting the registration of a trademark leaves no doubt to the decision-makers.

However, as it happens in resolving ethical problems, it is very difficult to make a definite decision whether a trademark offends the feelings of the general public or not (Podkański 1996:17). However, guidelines provided by the PTO in this area are on the whole vague and somewhat subjective. In some cases, the trademark evidently breaks the moral and thical standards and the verdict prohibiting the registration of such a trademark leaves no doubt to the decision makers. However, as it happens in resolving the ethical problems, it is very difficult to make a definite decision whether a trademark offends the feelings of the general public or not.

Thus, on one hand the U.S. Patent and Trademark Office rejected the registration of the name 'Big Pecker Band' on imprinted clothing and sportswear stating that the word 'pecker' has not only a vulgar, slang meaning but also bears other meanings that are definitely not abusive to the public. The Polish example comprises the name 'Chopin' used on vodka that was accepted by the board even in the presence of the strong objection of the Polish Minister of Culture and the name 'Sobieski' used on cigarettes that was rejected by the board because it might abuse the patriotic feelings of the Polish people (Barlik 1997:79).

Both American and Polish examples show how incompatible the decisions of the board can be. However, it is important to remember that although there is no direct solution in resolving ethical problems and such decisions are extremely difficult to make, the overly lenient verdict with respect to one trademark requires the board to accept a similar trademark no matter how ethical or unethical it might be.

4.3. The Misuse of Trademarks

The publications in the press suggest that counterfeiting is not the only problem facing the companies. The owners of the companies live in a constant fear that their trademarks might become generic one day. This issue seems to be more problematic than counterfeiting. As far as counterfeiting is concerned, the companies sue the infringer in court, eventually win the case and receive the repayment for the damages, but the trademark remains. In the course of genericide the companies may lose their trademark forever. Thus, from the perspective of the consequences resulting from the improper use of trademarks, the issue also acquires a moral and ethical dimension (Urbanek 1996:10).

It seems obvious that trademarks deserve to be treated with respect due to their immense role and functions. However, not everyone realizes that using trademarks in a casual, careless way is unethical. It is because due to such neglectful treatment, a trademark loses its identifying character and adopts the features of the product category. This danger refers especially to the famous trademarks used frequently by various people in their own manner in the result of which trademarks lost their distinctiveness and died of their users' negligence. Nowadays very few people remember that such products as aspirin, brassiere, cellophane, yo-yo, zipper, escalator, and linoleum used to be highly recognizable trademarks in the past until their frequent, careless use made them the victims of genericide. Such names will never fulfil their function as trademarks since they permanently lost their identifying features and they are no longer competitive with respect to other trademarks. In result, the once successful trademarks are nothing more then the ordinary names like apple, bread, butter, bicycle, and others (Urbanek 1996:10).

Trademark infringement, counterfeiting, and the misuse of trademarks have long before been recognized as breaking the legal norms and principles. However, for many people it is still difficult to understand those acts are also unethical and immoral. This is because the ethical problems are normally resolved with respect to humans, animals, or nature. Nevertheless, while looking closely at trademarks one can see that they also have human features. Trademarks have their image, a unique character, and communicate their massages directly to the customers' mind. They accompany most of our daily activities and are always eager to help us in making our buying decisions. Therefore, making harm to trademarks in exchange for the benefits that they offer is unethical and breaks the moral values accepted by both American and Polish society.

5. Means to Fight Trademark Infringement

The scope of the problem connected with trademark infringement is so great that the companies are very concerned about protecting their trademarks and desperately look for various means to fight trademark infringers and everyone who misuses their valuable assets.

5.1. Legal Proceedings

The most common means of fighting this problem both in the U.S. and in Poland are the legal proceedings. In comparing the American and Polish companies the conclusion is that using courts as a method for resolving the conflicts is also determined culturally. In the universalist culture of the U.S. the legal and moral norms were created to govern the life in the society and they can be applied to every committed offense and the personal obligations and relationships cannot decide whether the defendant is guilty or not. In the U.S. this approach is extremely visible which can be proved by the fact that the U.S. is considered to be the most litigious society in the world. Thus, trademark infringement is perceived in the same categories as other offences, for example stealing. Therefore, the American companies are very watchful in searching for the acts of breaking trademark law and are ready to initiate a legal action even in minor cases (Trompenaars 1993:36).

The Polish culture is on the whole difficult to define however as a Catholic country Poland seems to belong more to the particularist culture rather than the universalist one. Thus, for Polishmen the personal relationships, obligations, and unusual circumstances gain the upper hand over the law. Therefore, the number of lawsuits in Poland is much lower than in the U.S. Moreover, it also lies in Polish mentality that Polishmen simply do not like going to courts because of too much bureaucracy, the time-consuming procedures, and still weak legal basis in these matters (Zboralski 1996:245).

5.2. Creative Enforcement

The creative enforcement tactics proved to be effective in combating trademark infringement since they directly deal with the problem by finding the counterfeiters and depriving them of the infringed products. The creative enforcement methods, used widely in the U.S., include activities similar to the cunning tricks of the counterfeiters. For those purposes, the companies employ the groups of investigators acting as detectives looking for motifs that combine a number of separate events into a logical story. Using such tactics as raids on the counterfeiters, checking the phone messages, facsimiles, and other sources, the investigators provide the companies with a chance to catch the counterfeiters red-handed (Waldbaum 1996:251).

The companies are so concerned about protecting their trademarks that they frequently forget that they themselves cross the legal and ethical norms. In many cases they do not take into account that such raids and the seizure of the counterfeited goods without a special warrant violate the Fourth Amendment of the Bill of Rights. Furthermore, the ruling of the Fifth Amendment does not allow the investigators and the United States Marshals to ask the defendants for their correct name, address, or telephone number. Although the counterfeiters themselves break the law, they are still protected by the Bill of Rights. Therefore, the companies, acting in the name of law and ethics, should limit the scope of their activities not to be blamed themselves for crossing the legal and moral barriers (Waldbaum 1996:259).

5.3. The Proactive Action

As it has been mentioned before, the misuse of trademarks is even more complicated than counterfeiting since it deprives trademarks of their identity. Therefore, the companies use the proactive action in the form of educational campaign to make the public aware of the problem of counterfeiting before the actual offense is committed. In order to reach a great number of people, the companies put the advertisements in the press to educate the public how to properly use trademarks. On one hand, the press serves as aid in protecting the companies' trademarks. On the other hand, this is the press that contains the greatest number of mistakes on trademark usage. This is because, the journalists do not realize that their negligent use is extremely destructive for trademarks. However, the role of the journalists is to set an example for the public. Moreover, their persuasive power could have an impact on shaping the attitude towards trademarks. Therefore, the conclusion is that the actual dealing with this problem should start with educating the public about the legal and ethical aspects of using trademarks and it should be the first step before starting a real fight with trademark infringers (Bergerson 1994:12).

Summarizing, the issue of trademarks is in fact more complicated than it seems to be. And the undeniable truth is that trademarks are far more meaningful than the bare name or logo and their role for the national and the corporate culture is indispensable. Therefore, trademarks fully deserve to be treated with respect and the trademark infringement can be fully declared as an ethical problem. However, it is important that everyone is aware of those facts which can only be attained by the educational, legal, and creative action.

References

Alexander, M. J. 1995. "International Protection of Famous Trademarks in the United States." *INTA 1995 Annual Meeting*, 141–72. New York: International Trademark Association.

Altkorn, J. 1996. "Trzy podejścia do marki." *Marketing w Praktyce* (September–October): 27–30.

Arens, W. F. 1994. *Contemporary Advertising*. Boston: Irwin.

Barlik, E. 1997. "King size po polsku." *Businessman Magazine* (August): 78–9.

Boruc, M. A. 1997. "Marka-Markom-zaufać dziedzictwu, aby wygrać przyszłość." In *Rocznik 1996*, ed. Mirosław A. Boruc, 19–23. Warszawa: Instytut Marki Polskiej.

Drabik, M. 1993. "Magia marki." *Marketing* (September): 69–72.

Klonder, A. 1997. "Sławne towary ziem polskich." In *Rocznik 1996*, ed. Mirosław A. Boruc, 37–43. Warszawa: Instytut Marki Polskiej.

Lewandowski, A. 1992. *Współczesne polskie nazwy firmowe*. Zielona Góra.

Limański, A. 1994. *Marketingowe wyposażenie produktu*. Katowice: Akademia Ekonomiczna im. K.Adamieckiego.

Morgan, H. 1986. *Symbols of America*. New York: Steam Press.

Morris, B. 1996. "The Brand's the Thing." *Fortune Magazine* (4 March): 72–86.

Podkański, Z. 1996. "Spór o Chopina." *Rzeczpospolita* 30 September.

Rubel, E. A. 1994. "Trademarks and the Press: A Year in Review." *Editor & Publisher* 10 December: 6-8.

Serwatowski, W. 1997. "Heraldyka biznesu." In *Rocznik 1996*, ed. Mirosław A. Boruc, 77–83. Warszawa: Instytut Marki Polskiej.

Trompanaars, F. 1993. *Riding the Waves of Culture*. London: Nicholas Brealey Publishing.

Urbanek, G. 1996. "Marketingowe i prawne aspekty wyboru nazwy dla marki." *Marketing i Rynek* (March): 5–11.

Walbaum, M. 1996. "Weapons to Fight Counterfeiters: Creative Enforcement." *INTA 1996 Annual Meeting*, 248–62. New York: International Trademark Association.

Zboralski, M. 1996. *Nomen omen, czyli jak nazwać firmę i produkt*. Warszawa: Business Press.

Preservation of the Amazon Rainforest: The Importance of the Ethical Dimension

Pablo A. Flores
YPF Ecuador Inc.
Quito, Ecuador

1. Introduction

The Amazon rainforest in South America is one of the world's most renowned sites of environmental bio-diversity. According to the Rainforest Action Network (RAN 1999), a non-profit organization based in the U.S. with several international chapters, rainforests cover just 2 percent of the Earth's surface and are home to some 40 to 50 percent of all life forms on Earth. Many rainforest products such as coffee, rubber, and mahogany and other timbers have already been discovered and today take the form of readily available products which we take for granted in our daily lives. Still, many new medicines, foods, and fibers have yet to be discovered. Furthermore, the worldwide importance of the rainforest cannot be overstressed: the Amazon rainforest plays a vital role in the cooling of tropical regions and in stabilizing global temperatures. Destruction of this land increases the amounts of carbon dioxide in the atmosphere, heightening the harmful greenhouse effect for all human beings.

To some skeptical citizens it would appear that plenty of the forest remains. However, the impression of the rainforests being unlimited is incorrect, and the apparent infinity of the forest is a deceiving illusion.

Although we must acknowledge that there is disagreement about the exact rates at which the Amazon rainforests are being destroyed, scientists concede that all rainforest ecosystems will disappear by the year 2030 (RAN 1999). More troublesome is the fact that nearly all the primary rainforests in the world have already been destroyed. To put these statistics into perspective, global rates of destruction are as follows:

- 2.4 acres per second: equivalent to two U.S. football fields;
- 149 acres per minute;
- 214,000 acres per day: an area larger than New York City;
- 78 million acres per year: an area larger than Poland.

  (RAN 1999)

According to biologist Norman Myers, one of the world's leading authorities on the environment, current annual deforestation rates in Ecuador and Brazil reach 3,000 and 50,000 square kilometers per year, respectively (cited in RAN 1999). In some regions of the Amazon, huge areas of the forest are cut and pasture is being cultivated. In other sections, landless peasants are migrating into the forest and cutting it so they can plant food crops. Despite the fact that in many areas of the rainforest native Indian groups, such as the Ecuadorian Huaoranis, still practice farming methods that have sustained them for thousands of years, these practices are being replaced with other types of destructive methods.

2. The Amazon Rainforest as a Topic for International Business Ethics

Why was this topic chosen as a relevant issue in international business ethics? The answer to this question lies in my belief that the degradation of the Amazon rainforest represents a tangible example of the importance of incorporating both ethics and economics in the analysis of environmental problems. A new approach is required. Perhaps on 5 June 1997 the Seoul Declaration on Environmental Ethics, celebrating the 25th anniversary of the Stockholm Declaration and the 5th anniversary of the Rio Declaration, said it best: "We believe that in order to enhance the quality of life and to avoid wholesale ecological destruction, a deeper understanding of life and the formulation of a new system of environmental ethics is required."

The purpose of this research paper is thus to acknowledge the importance of developing a new framework of analysis that recognizes the interaction of business and economic principles with ethical standards so that the rainforest territory is effectively preserved. As a starting point, this paper will begin by identifying the different forces that motivate both the destruction and the preservation of rainforest land. This initial discussion is imperative so that the reader fully identifies the different stakeholders interacting in the Amazon rainforest region. The paper will then discuss the ethical dimension that is relevant in this analysis, and will include a discussion of sustainability and intergenerational responsibility. Finally, concluding remarks will incorporate policy proposals towards alleviating the degradation of this natural resource while addressing the role of ethics for the individual, multinational corporations, governments, and the international community at large.

3. Why Are the Amazonian Rainforests Being Cut?
Benefits Vs. Costs

For developing countries, demographic expansion and the pressure for cattle farming is enormous in many regions having territory in the Amazon basin. As a result of population growth, migration of landless peasants and jobless urban residents takes place into the Amazon. As one would expect, the economic incentive for the establishment of pastureland in the Amazon basin is certainly great. For example, it has been estimated that, in aggregate, cattle raising brings in $20 billion per year in revenues across all rainforest land (Hurst 1991).

In some cases, governments perceive the clearing of Amazon rainforest land as a political solution for overpopulation. In other instances, there appears to be the feeling in governments that the fleeing of citizens into sparsely populated Amazon border regions will help defend the territory against infringement by citizens of the neighboring country. This is especially clear in the Ecuadorian-Peruvian experience where governments of both nations have done nothing to detain the migration of citizens towards the eastern region of the Amazon rainforest – a region that has no official ownership and has been the subject of constant conflict and dispute.

Converted rainforest ecosystems also support production of food, fiber, and raw materials needed for exports. Countries with land in the Amazon need goods for export to increase their foreign exchange earnings and reduce their foreign debt. A typical cash crop, for example, involves tropical timber, which ranks among the leading exports of tropical forests. Myers (1992) indicates that tropical hardwoods represent more than $8 billion a year in revenues. To make matters worst, Rogene A. Buchholz (1993) argues that governments take the long-term benefits of their forests for granted, and negotiate logging rights too cheaply to exploit short-term benefits.

The development of third world countries' infrastructure also encourages the degradation of virgin rainforest land. Buchholz (1993) reports that many development projects have been financed by loans from the World Bank and other international lending agencies, but it was not until 1987 that the World Bank set up a department to formally review the environmental impact of the projects it was supporting. In Ecuador, during the mid 1970s when oil exploration and development was at its peak, the development of road networks through the Amazon was the first step in the large-scale development plan by both the national government and foreign oil companies. Areas in Ecuador were quickly populated, and governments thereafter emphasized the importance of building large-scale projects such as hydroelectric plants, dams, and other public utilities without considering the adverse impact these constructions had on the environment.

But just as there are reasons that explain the destruction of rainforest land, strong arguments in favor of conservation also exist. The most important arguments recognize the fact that many native groups are directly threatened by the depletion of land. These groups depend upon the forest to a large degree for both material well-being and perpetuation of spiritual values that have been passed on from generation to generation over hundred of years. RAN (1999) explains that indigenous people "eat wild game, use the plants for food and medicine, and may identify certain species as a sacred and essential part of their heritage. When these resources are destroyed, the people lose their homes, their food, and their very culture." Conflicts with developers of rainforest territory, and contact with diseases to which they have no resistance are also deadly by-products of deforestation.

Motives in favor of conservation also identify the fact that forest vegetation protects soil from the full force of tropical rainstorms; the vegetative cover on the soil surface of the rainforest is very rich in nutrients and safeguards the exposed earth from the impact of intense weather systems. Conservation of the rainforest will also reduce the levels of carbon dioxide released into the Earth's atmosphere and lessen the threat of expected worldwide decreases in rainfall, exacerbating desertification, global increases in temperature, and melting of polar ice with an inevitable rise in sea levels.

Tropical forest species too appear to be especially vulnerable to habitat alteration. Such species have habitat requirements that demand large areas of closed forest. If only a small niche of forest is affected, species can be lost entirely or become locally extinct. We must bear in mind that flora and fauna in the Amazonian region are more numerous and more varied than in other rainforests of the world. Myers (1992) notes that our scientific ignorance of tropical forests extends beyond the species that live there. In fact, our ignorance may be so profound that we have yet to devise a classification scheme of forest types that we can apply consistently from one region to another.

Finally, little as we may realize it, when we visit our local pharmacy for a medicinal product, there is roughly one chance in four that the product we purchase owes its origin, in some way or another, to plants and animals of tropical forests. Myers (1992) reports that many of the botanical materials found in the rainforest are being screened and developed in medicinal research laboratories of North America and Europe. Drugs used to treat leukemia, Hodgkin's disease, hypertension, arthritis, and birth control originated from rainforest plants. A cure to mortal diseases such as cancer and AIDS could eventually be discovered and developed with raw materials extracted from the Amazon rainforest.

4. Understanding the Importance
of Environmental Ethical Standards

The preceding arguments, supporting or discouraging the degradation of the Amazon rainforest, generally ignore any ethical implications. Because these policies fail to incorporate any ethical framework, it is my belief that this explains why many of today's policies tend to be short-lived and futile when dealing with the preservation of the Amazon rainforest.

We tend to be reactive in nature and deal with problems only after the damage has been done. To confirm this idea, we simply have to recall a few of the world's worst environmental accidents (e.g. Exxon Valdez, Chernobyl) to realize that we deal with the economic impact of environmental damage only when it is too late. The fact that just recently there has been a renewed interest towards more proactive policies and environmental regulations can be explained by the notion that "environmental ethics" is a relatively new field. The recent awareness of this field is explained by the historical remarks presented in the *Encyclopedia of Ethics* (Callicott 1992). According to the Encyclopedia, it was not until the 1970s, when Biomedical Ethics and Environmental Ethics came into being, that these issues began to be explored. The Encyclopedia makes an important point when it further explains that environmental ethics deserves special attention and should be perceived as a field on its own. The Encyclopedia contends that "normal ethics" is not enough when dealing with environmental issues. Specifically, most environmental ethicists fear that the application of normal ethics to environmental problems will only make matters worse since Western moral philosophy has been concerned almost exclusively with human action in relation to other human beings and has generally considered non-human natural entities to be mere means to human ends, not ends in themselves. Whether this contention is true or not is perhaps debatable, but what seems to be indisputable is that environmental ethics is an increasingly important field in today's world.

Authors such as Buchholz (1993) confirm that there is certainly a new non-human-centered approach to the environment which is sometimes referred to as the "naturalistic ethic." This approach holds that natural species have a right to exist regardless of whether or not they are useful to human beings. The flora and fauna of the rainforest should thus be considered in their own right apart from human interests.

The notion that economics and ethics can and should walk hand in hand is best explained with the principle of sustainable development. With this principle we should understand that the environment and economic activity are interdependent. Buchholz (1993) suggests that the traditional notion that policymakers have to accept a trade-off between economic development and environmental protection in decisions about public and corporate policy no longer makes sense; the two goals are consistent with each other. Buchholz urges readers to understand that this idea must sink into Western consciousness and become a part of ethical thinking for any kind of reasonable theories to be developed.

If we merge ethical standards in the analysis of the Amazon rainforest, it is my belief that we strengthen the arguments that favor the conservation of the rainforest. Sustainable development is only one of these ethical standards, perhaps the strongest principle. The United Nations World Commission on Environment and Development (UNCED) has recognized the importance of this principle and has defined sustainable development as "development that meets the needs of the present generation without compromising the ability of future generations to meet their own needs." Allocations that impoverish future generations in order to enrich current generations are, according to this criterion, clearly unfair. Therefore, it would seem unethical to destroy the Amazon rainforest since this would inevitably imply that future generations would be left worse off than present generations. Sustainability in other readings is often cited as the "grandchild effect." The idea is basically the same; the short-term economic gain of any action must be weighed against the long-term destruction of an ecosystem. We must base our decisions on whether our actions and behaviors will foreclose possibilities for our grandchildren.

But just as the concept of "sustainability" can be utilized to strengthen the notion that rainforests should be preserved, there are other concepts that should also be part of a contemporary discussion of environmental ethics. Specifically, the principle of "carrying capacity" advocated by environmental economists is an important one since it suggests that there are limits to what can be sustained in an eco-system. This notion suggests that there are boundaries to growth which, translated into the Amazon rainforest, suggests that no population within the rainforest can keep on growing indefinitely without causing irreversible damage. We must thus respect the limit dictated by the natural carrying capacity of the region before harmful effects take place.

Patricia D. Hartig (1997), author of the article "Sustainable Development: Principles Toward Environmental Ethics," argues that the practice of environmental law may well be the most critical area of the law for all humankind. Besides the principles of sustainable development and carrying capacity, Hartig lists anticipation and prevention; full-cost accounting; integration of economic, social and environmental factors; and efficiency, innovation, and continuous improvement as additional guiding principles that will help achieve a higher level of ethical behavior than that provided for in the rules of professional conduct.

5. Next Steps: Assessing Our Spaces of Freedom and Responsibility

Having discussed the ethical arguments in favor of conservation, it would seem appropriate to include certain recommendations for the future. As presented in the introductory paragraphs of this paper, there are primarily two forces driving the destruction of the Amazon rainforest: the first one being political and the second one dealing with economic interests. In practice, it would seem very difficult to expect that developing nations will completely reverse their political strategies and impede the migration of population into forestland. After all, the Rio Declaration on Environment and Development (1992) in its second principle grants countries a discretionary freedom of action by noting that

> States have, in accordance with the Charter of the United Nations and the principles of international law, the sovereign right to exploit their own resources pursuant to their own environmental and developmental policies, and the responsibility to ensure that activities within their jurisdiction or control do not cause damage to the environment of other States or of areas beyond the limits of national jurisdiction.

Nevertheless, the Rio Declaration is keen in recognizing the inherent interdependent nature of our eco-systems, and the concept of sustainable development is at the heart of its principles. In its third principle, for example, the Rio Declaration notes that the right to development must be equitable, respecting the needs of present and future generations. Therefore, as citizens of the world, it goes without saying that we must monitor the activities taking place in these sensitive regions to ensure that they are in accordance with the ethics of sustainability. To excuse ourselves of this duty by arguing that as individuals our spaces of freedom are too limited is not valid. We have an ethical obligation to use and increase our spaces of freedom. This can be achieved by building networks within and among all levels of society and government, industry and business, and non-governmental organizations.

The international community must also take its own ethical duties seriously. All nations share responsibilities for preserving rainforests. There should be active involvement to pursue policies that are in compliance with established multilateral agreements. The Rio Declaration (Principle 7) proclaims that "States shall cooperate in a spirit of global partnership to conserve, protect and restore the health and integrity of the Earth's ecosystem." Such cooperation should be made explicit by allocating financial funds to those nations having greater environmental endowments. These actions will answer the cries of many local government officials who are constrained by limited financial resources. As an example, the "Tropical Plywood Imports, Inc." case (Hosmer 1995) cited a Brazilian delegate to the ITTO (International Timber Trade Organization) who claimed "why is it that the tropical forest countries have to pay the price to do something about it? ... Environmentalists are always talking about our moral duty, but our people can't live on moral duty."

Finally, we should mention the role of multinational corporations and local businesses that have economic interests that adversely impact rainforest land. In his remarks made to the United Nations Correspondents Association, Stephen Viederman (1997) President of the Jessie Smith Noyes Foundation, argues that the incompatibility between multinational corporations and sustainable development arises because the "business of business is business, not sustainable development," and managers and shareholders direct greater attention to next quarter results rather than next century objectives. In brief, Viederman concludes that "multinational corporations and sustainable development are presently incompatible, and unless the UNCED and other international, national and local groups working on sustainable development recognize this fact, the only thing that will be sustained is the discussion, not the development." Timothy C. Weiskel (1997), Director of the Environmental Ethics and Public Policy Program of Harvard's Divinity School, also addresses this point when noting that "the environmental problems we face including everything from global warming to the relentless destruction of biodiversity stem from the fundamental mistake of enshrining metaphors of market valuation as the primary framework for formulating and legitimating public policy."

No one can argue that multinationals are more environmentally sensitive today than they were decades ago, but they still have a larger ethical and social obligation to protect the fragile Amazon rainforests. In this regard, we are reminded of the need for a more comprehensive and balanced concept of the firm—a concept that recognizes that the firm is a moral actor having economic, social and environmental responsibilities to be accounted for (see Enderle and Tavis 1998). This is not impossible to achieve, and companies like Monsanto, in the U.S., and Ciba-Geigy, now Novartis in Europe, have explicitly expressed their concern for the environment and have been able to secure a sound financial performance. Viederman (1997) argues that it is in the interest of businesses to become more environmentally sensitive since waste is synonymous with cost, and reduction of waste will contribute to profit. In a recent study cited by Viederman (1997), the financial benefits of improving the environmental performance of firms is said to have increased shareholder value by up to 5%. The key lies in the ability of managers and business to perceive the role of business ethics not merely as an instrument useful in examining business objectives or to increase profits, but rather as a value in itself that should permeate the entire corporate culture.

6. Conclusion

This paper has discussed the factual observations explaining the reasons for destruction and preservation of Amazon rainforests. Most importantly, however, the analysis has incorporated an ethical dimension that is necessary in the discussion of both economics and the environment. Unfortunately, the ethical dimension has been long ignored. According to the 1997 Seoul Declaration on Environmental Ethics, "the key lies in recognizing that human beings and the natural environment are interdependent and part of a larger entity, the Whole-Life-System."

Now more than ever we must understand that the role of environmental ethics is increasingly important. Just as the arguments of scandals, of economization, of good business, and of challenges (see Enderle 1993) help explain why business ethics is becoming so important, these same arguments can explain why environmental ethics is also momentous. Whenever we read about the unfortunate degradation that takes place in the Amazon rainforest, we should be motivated persistently to develop more proactive policies and not let business and environmental ethics lag behind. In a world where economic thinking and acting are penetrating and dominating more and more the domains of life, the argument of economization implies that ethical standards should be called upon to set boundary lines. Decision makers and the community at large should think about the strong ethical principles underlying the conservation of rainforest land because this perspective constitutes the best hope of solving future environmental crises. In this regard, the argument of challenges in business ethics is crucial since we will certainly face greater obstacles in the years ahead. Environmental ethics should understand these challenges and develop guidance to meet them.

References

Agenda 21. 1992. Programme of Action for Sustainable Development. Rio Declaration on Environment and Development: Statement of Forest Principles. 3-14 June.
Buchholz, R.A. 1993. *Principles of Environmental Management: The Greening of Business*. New Jersey: Prentice-Hall, Inc.

Callicott, J.B. 1992. "Environmental Ethics." In *Encyclopedia of Ethics,* ed. L.C. Becker and C.B. Becker, 311–15. New York, London: Garland Publishing.

Enderle, G. 1993. "What is Business Ethics?" In *Business Ethics: Japan and the Global Economy,* ed. T.W. Dunfee and Y. Nagayasu, 133–50. Dordrecht, Boston, London: Kluwer Academic Publishers.

Enderle, G. and Tavis, L. 1998. "A Balanced Concept of the Firm and The Measurement of its Long-Term Planning and Performance." *Journal of Business Ethics* 17: 1129–44.

Hartig. P. D. 1997. "Sustainable Development: Principles Toward Environmental Ethics." http://www.voyager.net/

Hosmer, L. T. 1995. "Case Study: Tropical Plywood Imports, Inc." In *Business Ethics. Readings and Cases in Corporate Morality*, ed. W. M. Hoffman and R. E. Frederick, 559–64. Third edition. New York: McGraw-Hill.

Hurst, P. 1991. *Rainforest Politics: Ecological Destruction in South-East Asia.* London: Zed Books LTD.

Myers, N. 1992. *The Primary Source: Tropical Forest and Our Future.* New York: W.W. Norton & Company.

Seoul Declaration on Environmental Ethics. 1997. *World Environment Day.* http://www.rona.unep.org.

The Rainforest Action Network (RAN). 1999. http://www.ran.org.

Viederman, S. 1997. Key Issues Underlying Earth Summit II, Agenda 21, Globalization and Sustainable Development. http://divweb.harvard.edu.

Weiskel, T. C. 1997. Selling Pigeons in the Temple: The Danger of Market Metaphors in an Ecosystem. http://divweb.harvard.edu.

PART TWO

Social Issues:
Compensation and Labor

"Same Job, Same Pay."
On Fairness in Compensation Packages for
Local and Expatriate Staff

Hannah Lu
George Cui
China Europe International
Business School (CEIBS)
Shanghai, China

1. Introduction

With more and more foreign investment coming into China, expatriate managers are sent to safeguard the money that has been put into a foreign country. These expatriates will be working side by side with their local counterparts and subordinates to achieve the common goal of their business organization. Their jobs are the same; their compensation packages are usually not. Very often it becomes an issue at the negotiation table, before a joint venture is established, and remains a topic among local staff afterwards.

It is not uncommon to hear the foreign part request a compensation package for its representative, usually the future general manager of the company, almost ten times more than what his Chinese counterpart, the vice general manager, can possibly receive. A most frequently quoted phrase by the Chinese side at such occasion is "same job, same pay." The obvious implication is that a company should compensate its employees fairly for the jobs they do, not for their ethnic origin. Although the foreign part may agree in principle to the notion, it usually has its own strong argument for the meaning of "same pay." The core value at stake is fairness.

This paper will discuss this issue based on a real life case, with our understanding both from the social-cultural perspective typically found in China and from the economic perspective representing western values (see Enderle and Tavis 1998). We also describe some negative effects of an unequal compensation structure upon a joint venture and provide our recommendation to deal with this problem.

2. The Case: Negotiations about Compensation Packages in a Joint Venture

When the joint venture negotiation between STU (Chinese company) and LMN (American company) approached the discussion of compensation package for the future top management, it was halted by a big gap in figure as well as in attitude. It was hard for the Chinese to accept it, as the Chinese factory director said, "Even my salary is only five times more than a workshop worker. Why should two people of the same level, the president and the vice president, be treated so differently?" The Chinese side asked for the same pay for its vice general manager as for the general manager. The request was difficult for the Americans to agree. Their argument was that the fairness of compensation should not be judged superficially by the figure, but rather by the standard of living that was associated with it. The American representative stressed that "An annual income of US$80,000 ~ 100,000 provides a decent standard of living for a company's president in America. The same amount in China, if we take into consideration the subsidized housing and other life necessities, would make the Chinese vice president a millionaire!" Although each side felt strongly about their own argument, in principle they agreed that employees should be treated fairly when their compensation package is decided.

But what happened later almost destroyed the already slight bit of common understanding. When the American representative finally said, "The board of directors of the joint venture will decide the compensation package for the vice general manager taking into account his level and the package of the American president," the Chinese side said, "The joint venture shall not pay the vice general manager directly, but pay the money to the Chinese parent company which will transfer the payment to the individual." It turned out later that the Chinese party did not intend to give the vice general manager the equivalent pay even if the American side agreed. The reason was simple. On the Chinese side, people would think it unfair for the vice general manager to receive a close-to-US-standard pay, knowing at the same time that the Chinese Chairman of the Board who remained on the payroll of the Chinese parent company received only one fifth of his subordinate (the Chinese vice president). The discussion over the fairness for employees soon became a fight for the fairness for investors. The American side pointed out that it would be absolutely unacceptable because they saw that portion of money kept by the Chinese parent company from the pay of the vice general manager as a "safety net." Safety net meant that the Chinese investor would be able to get some return even before the joint venture's bottom line figure was finally calculated. Even at a year of loss when the American investor would not get any dividend, the Chinese partner would still get several thousand US dollars deducted from the vice general manager's compensation. The Chinese party felt offended that their joint venture partner suspected them, a company with sales over RMB200 million (approximately US$25 million), using such a small amount of money as a safety net.

It took a couple of days for the American side to understand that "same job, same pay" in the joint venture was more of an issue of national dignity, while "same job, same pay" within the Chinese system was an issue of social justice and values of equality. In essence, both parties were still discussing fairness but under two drastically different social-cultural and economic perspectives.

3. Understanding from a Chinese Social-Cultural Perspective

"Same job, same pay" is stressed in front of foreign investors as a direct result of political pressure. Since the eighteenth century, China has been invaded by foreign countries and was forced into business with foreign countries after a series of failures. After years of struggling, China finally can stand up and face the foreign counterparts equally. As a result, the country and its people have become politically sensitive to any seemingly unfair deal in many aspects from business to personal compensation. When Chinese enterprises try to attract foreign investment and start formal discussion on bilateral economic co-operation, they will intuitively stress the principle of equality. It is usually a situation where the principle of equality is applied to the relation between two nations rather than between the individuals of the two sides of negotiation. Any inequality would directly hurt the national dignity of the Chinese people.

Looking from a cultural perspective, one will easily notice that the principle of fairness is widely accepted and admired in China. People naturally conclude that if both local and expatriate staff are of the same level at work in the same company with similar workload, they should receive the same pay. Any difference would be regarded as an unfair treatment. The foreign party may argue that the gap is due to different countries' living standards, but for Chinese people who live in a comparatively backward economy, their feelings are seriously hurt when they look at the tremendous difference in the absolute figures.

Collectivism is a characteristic of Chinese culture. People prefer to stay in harmony by sharing working space, a common attitude to certain affairs and an equally distributed benefit scheme. Take a look at the state-owned enterprises in the past; it is not surprising to see that the general manager's salary is only two or three times that of the labors. "Same job, same pay" is a guideline to ensure a harmonious family atmosphere. Now the pay scheme difference is larger, but it is not as large as that in other countries like the USA. This is only one of many illustrations of collective values in China. The historically evolved idea of equality lays more stress on superficial "sameness" than on the intrinsic value. As a result, the cultural values create an ethical dilemma for the Chinese party. How can it be possible to defend the national dignity and protect the social harmony at the same time by paying a consistent compensation package to the same individual? Balancing all these conflicts, we can understand why the Chinese party in the case above decides to claim the same pay for their manager as the US expatriate while only allocating a fraction of it to him. This is a "family issue" in which the foreign party should not intervene.

In reality, the Chinese party always compromises by reducing the Chinese top manager's pay. According to our past working experience, we know that such a compromising solution exists not only at the top management level, but also at the middle management level. Due to the global trend of "localization" (i.e., the replacement of expatriates by national managers) in joint ventures, more and more local employees are promoted to the position of middle or senior managers, their payment packages always ending up with this typical result of compromises, the consequences of which will be discussed later in this paper.

4. Understanding from an Economic Perspective

A compensation package is a reward that an employer gives to his or her employee in return for contribution to the growth of the company. Every employee is entitled to a certain specific package by virtue of employment contract. Besides a sign of appreciation and recognition of his performance, the basic purpose of the compensation package is to provide the employee with a decent or adequate standard of living. Therefore, the question of what constitutes a "decent" or "adequate" standard of living becomes a critical issue when such dispute over compensation packages for local and expatriate staff occurs. The answer to this question is, in part, subjective. But it largely depends on the economy in which the person in question originally lives. Different economies create different living environment for people in terms of accommodation, transportation, consumption habit and even expectation of life quality. A decent standard of living should be the one that is widely acceptable to the people of the same economic and cultural origin as the person in question, with the consideration of his job. Generally speaking, the change of working location should not cause any deterioration to the living standard of the person being transferred, in our case, to China. It is especially so when the job transfer is more of a requirement from the company than a choice by the individual. It is unfair to the individual to degrade his living standard for the sake of his company. On the other hand, it will be equally unfair to a local staff to request a package equivalent in figure to that of an expatriate but out of scale by local economic standard. He is not entitled to such request. Compensation package is first and foremost an economic term, although it can not be absolutely exempt from social or political influence.

In economic terms, it is not sensible to compare the values of the compensation packages on the basis of exchange rates. Rather, it is the purchasing power that defines their values. One dollar in America is not equal to one dollar in China in its purchasing power, which creates a difference in their power of creating living standard for the receivers. In our case, the Chinese side realized this and proposed that indirect payment process to discount the unfairness in the eyes of Chinese employees. Obviously, equality is not an adequate concept in this context to judge the fairness of compensation packages for local and expatriate staff. Equity is. It focuses more on the intrinsic value of the money as well as of the individual. Therefore, "same job, same pay" is in principle a good illustration of fairness, but it can be very misleading if it is only superficially interpreted by merely looking at the absolute figures instead of the value.

5. Consequences of Practical Compromise

In our case, as in many other similar situations, both parties reach an agreement with compromise. The company will pay the expatriate and local manager differently but with a substantial increase for Chinese manager. Such a compromise solves the problem at the negotiation phase. However, the gap remains, and unfortunately the gap usually brings negative effects upon the daily operation of a joint venture.

The unequal reward system causes disharmony between the local managers and their expatriate peers. Most Chinese cannot help feeling discriminated against, and such a feeling is hard to adjust. As a result, the co-operation between these managers is always poor. They do not communicate unless they have to, and the effect is not favorable in most cases. There is always a gap between the two functional areas which they manage. It gradually becomes bigger and bigger. In some extreme cases, an additional team or department has to be formed to meet the need of this vacuum area. Cost goes up for sure, and efficiency is hurt badly. Sooner or later, the company's financial performance will show this negative effect.

The co-operation between top expatriate manager and middle Chinese management is also poor. Many Chinese managers feel unfairly treated. When a tough situation requires close co-operation between them in order for the company to survive, they probably won't do their best to contribute their efforts. We know how dangerous it can be when inside management a conflict arises. In a factory that one of the authors worked for, she frequently observed that the local managers supported in words whatever the top manager instructed them, but as soon as the top manager left, they resumed their own way of working without implementing the instruction. When time came for report, many excuses were used to explain why the expected favorable result could not be realized. Since they were local employees, they could always say something that the top expatriate manager did not know, or was unable to prove. Further, the expatriate might be unable to make a confident judgement as to whether their local subordinate was telling a lie or a truth. When local middle managers were required to make suggestion in order to solve a practical problem, they usually talked a lot, but they did not really think it over and make efforts to find an effective solution. What they suggested always required further input, and it was never cost effective! If such problems happened again and again, the overall performance of the whole company could slip down very quickly.

Besides the group disharmony that unequal benefit program creates, there is a far worse possible result. Many local managers start to find their own way to cover the gap of compensation through kickbacks, negligence of job responsibility, and abuse of company property. Slowly, the culture of the company is contaminated in such a way that the subordinates follow the middle managers' examples. Relationship between supplier and customer becomes worse due to kickback requirements. Goods delivered by vendors may be of inferior quality as the suppliers regard them as a pay back of their kickback to local managers. Normal operation can be frequently interrupted, and loss in production becomes apparent.

6. Conclusion

The concept of fairness has been discussed all along in the history of ethics. People around the world have accepted it as one of the common core values of human society. Stemming from this core concept, a series of practical guidelines have evolved, which, unlike the core concept itself, are very culturally and economically specific. These guidelines are inevitably put under close examination when people of two completely different economies get together. "Same job, same pay" is such a case. It is usually difficult for people of the less developed economy to accept the gap, which is attributed mainly to the difference in the level of economic development. That explains why the Chinese side would take that gap as an insult to their national dignity. However, it should never be disregarded that compensation is an economic concept rather than a political one. Since compensation mostly takes the form of money, the purchasing power instead of the absolute figure should be the criterion to judge fairness because it is the purchasing power that will finally determine the receiver's living standard which should be adequate with respect to his job position and local economic conditions.

From an economic rather than political perspective, a compensation package is no more than the market rate for a person of certain professional skill level. It would only become an issue of national dignity if we were living in a world of planned economy where compensation level is a discretionary decision. A human decision can be discriminative, while a market rate is the result of the interaction between supply and demand. The core value base of such a market rate is the person's productivity. The best way to protect the national dignity is to improve the national productivity, which will improve its economy. Consequently, the compensation level of its general labor force will increase and certainly that of its managers will also. Artificially determined compensation level in defense of national feeling requires other ways to justify itself for its true value. Thus, "safety net" becomes an issue. In an effort to treat both local and foreign investors fairly, the government has suggested that the difference between the nominal and actual compensation figure of Chinese top managers be kept by the joint venture for its employees' welfare expenses. It again puts the principle of "same job, same pay" under serious question. Why should a group of people share the compensation paid for a few individuals for their job? Political compromises won't resolve a real conflict in economic concept.

"Same job, same pay," however, does bring up an issue that concerns the harmony of the working environment in a company. Any defect in the design of a fair compensation structure for local and expatriate staff can result in inefficiency and even act as a barrier to business co-operation. Copying compensation structures directly from Chinese parent companies will result in a double standard system, which is difficult to explain to local staff. When people start to feel unfairly treated, they will be unmotivated and, thus, hurt business. It would make more sense to both parties that a joint venture should have its own policy of compensation based on economically and ethically sound reasons. Even more important, these reasons must be effectively communicated to every one in the company to prevent disharmony within an organization.

Business ethics has considerable levels of universality which are brought forth by the basic nature of human beings. Commonality is also necessary to promote mutual interaction between countries as well as people. The issue of business ethics becomes complicated when people from different cultures, especially different economies, are involved. It is an issue that faces every one looking for international economic co-operation. In developing countries including China, eruptive economic transformation is under process, and they are typically composed of both market and non-market sectors. Thus, it is unrealistic to impose the western values upon other countries without expecting serious conflicts. At the same time, China and other developing countries should deepen substantive understanding of the ethical dimension of western cultures, making efforts to accept a degree of cultural diversity so as to enhance amicable economic partnerships and co-operation. It is important for every party to keep an open mind while holding its own ethical values in order to create an atmosphere of dialogue. Open dialogue between economies and cultures will lay a ground for developing a widely acceptable system of ethics and business principles.

References

Enderle, G. and Tavis, L. 1998. "A Balanced Concept of the Firm and The Measurement of its Long-Term Planning and Performance." *Journal of Business Ethics* 17, 1129–44.
Haas, R. 1994. "Ethics – A Global Business Challenge." In *Ethics in International Management*, ed. B. N. Kumar and H. Steinmann, 213–20. Berlin, New York: de Gruyter.

Adequate Salaries in Developing Countries

Victor Trujillo
Cheron's Latin American
Headquarters
Caracas, Venezuela

1. Introduction: What Salaries for Low-skilled and Highly-educated Employees?

For years, employees and employers have been fighting over salary increases. Although this is a common situation all around the globe, this fight becomes especially fierce in many developing countries where salaries are usually not enough to cover workers' most basic needs. In many cases, inflation worsens the problem as it creates a vicious circle in which a salary increase produces higher inflation (in higher proportion than the salary increase), which in turn results in employees demanding another salary increase and so forth. Employees end up watching their purchasing power diminishes over time.

From the employee point of view, this is an outrageous situation in which they only are affected. They cannot afford a decent standard of living while companies still make profits. In reality, this is a sensitive issue that affects not only employees, but also governments and corporations. Problems are perhaps more complex for multinational corporations with branches in developing countries as they face tougher criticism when employees compare what these companies pay to its developed countries' employees with their own decreased real salaries.

The situation worsens when such information is published in the developed countries where most multinational corporations are based. It is not unusual to observe public scandals over salaries paid by these companies in developing countries. The Nike Corporation sweatshop scandal is just one in thousands of possible examples of the ethical problem faced by these organizations. This company has sub-contracted facilities in China, Indonesia, and Vietnam which have been accused of human-rights violations, including child labor and "misery" salaries (lower than minimum needed for subsistence). The usual response is that such salaries are very competitive for that specific market and are consistent with productivity of those workers. Further, the existence of these companies' branches is usually tied to low labor costs: if wages are increased, these branches will not be competitive and therefore would not survive. Meanwhile, governments of developing countries usually argue in favor of bringing foreign investment in and stopping (or controlling) inflation by making a sacrifice that will pay off in the future.

If we analyze this problem from each party's point of view, each argument makes sense. Employees do have the right to demand a salary that allows them to cover their basic needs of housing, food, and health services, as well as some savings for personal growth. Corporations also have the right to earn a reasonable profit, and governments have not only the right but the obligation of improving their countries' well-being in the long run, which is usually measured by macroeconomic variables.

There is yet another question that many highly-educated workers from developing countries ask: Why do we get paid much lower salaries than our developed countries' counterparts, if we both are similarly trained and can add the same value to company's wealth? The multinational corporations' response again refers to productivity. The entire company's body of employees is not as productive as that of a developed country's branch. This results in a loss of motivation for these workers who are therefore likely to leave the country for better opportunities, thus starting another vicious circle as the developing countries' productivity decreases again and again when the most productive workers flee to developed countries.

Again, all parties involved in this problem have valid arguments. These kinds of workers usually have salaries which are very good for the economies they live in, but still they feel exploited, feeling they are paying for other people's short comings. Companies' arguments are again for competitiveness and survival while governments once more argue in favor of foreign investments and controlled macroeconomic variables.

These two problems seem to have no evident solution. If we choose to continue the status quo, workers will end up dissatisfied and in some cases living in distressful conditions. If we choose to increase salaries, corporations' survival in developed countries will be at stake and the state of these economies would be negatively affected as the previously mentioned vicious circles take place.

What to do? This is exactly what this paper intends to find out. I will analyze each argument in detail using the current situation in Venezuela as an example. Then I will try to derive helpful proposals for workers, corporations, and governments to follow in order to satisfy everyone's needs.

2. The Arguments

The standard to measure whether a proposition is the correct one to solve the problem has to be the common good, or how society is better as a whole. According to the Catholic Social Teaching, which is a very rich source on salary determination rightness, common good has to be taken into account when determining a just salary. In 1965, the Vatican Council II declared that "remuneration for labor is to be such that man may be furnished the means to cultivate worthily his own material, social, cultural, and spiritual life and that of his dependants, in view of the function and productiveness of each one, the conditions of the factory or workshop, and *the common good*" (Vatican Council II 1965). The same Vatican Council II defines common good as "the sum of those conditions of social life which allow social groups and their individual members relatively thorough and ready access to their own fulfillment" (Vatican Council II 1965). Hence, common good refers to a balance between collective and individual well-being. I believe this balance to be critical if society is to last in the long run. Preservation and development of society have to be the most important factors to take into consideration, not only in salary determination, but in every aspect of life. What hurts society hurts each of its components, so that if we make a decision that does not immediately affect us negatively but hurts another component of society, it will eventually hit us harder. Then it is in the best interest of every group in society to make decisions that do not harm any other group. Therefore, proposals included in this paper have to increase society's well-being in order to be acceptable.

3. From the Employee's Perspective

We will now analyze workers' arguments on both problems. Are their demands just? Do they have the rights they claim? In order to answer these questions, we will take a look at the current situation for Venezuelan workers, as it may help us in understanding the rightness of their claims.

During the 1970s and the early 1980s, Venezuela lived through its best era in economic terms. Oil prices had gone from less than $5 to more than $30 a barrel; therefore, the economy boomed, salaries were great and the government, which is by law the only owner of minerals in the country, subsidized food, transportation, housing and, in general, every citizen's basic needs. Workers could not have been happier.

In 1983 oil prices crashed. The country had to devalue the Bolivar (Venezuelan currency), and workers started to feel a decrease in their real income. In 1989, a new government implemented market economy measures that included freeing price controls. With an inflation level of almost 90% that year, workers' real income plummeted. Since then, different governments have implemented contradictory policies that have helped inflation to remain at high levels, therefore reducing workers' real income.

A good example of workers' real income deterioration can be seen in the retailers' industry situation during 1996. In this year, price levels rose more than 100% resulting in an nominal increase of retailers' sales of more than 90%. Workers' salaries for this industry increased by less than 40%. This means that the average worker for this industry can only purchase 70% of the goods he/she was able to buy one year before. Similar developments have been going on for more than a decade (OCEI 1998).

The current Venezuelan monthly minimum wage is around US$150. Even though it is true that the cost of living in Venezuela is lower than in the U.S., $150 is far below what is needed to cover basic needs like housing, food, and health services as many goods are either similarly or higher-priced than in the U.S. For example, the Mc Donald's famous Big Mac (often used as a real measure of exchange ratios) is priced at about $3. Eating a Big Mac would take 2% from a Venezuelan worker's salary, or eight times of what it takes from a US minimum-wage worker´s salary.

It is evident that a salary that helps cover basic needs is as much a right as the right to life. In the Nike scandal in Asia, many activists have accused this corporation of human rights violations, not only for allowing subcontractors to pay salaries below the legal minimum, but mainly because these salaries are far below the minimum needed for a dignified subsistence (Community Aid Abroad 1998).

Today, Venezuelan citizens have solved their needs by pooling resources. Entire families, including married children, live in the same place, share many expenses and so forth. However, as this situation continues, combined incomes are becoming insufficient to cover families' needs so that many workers are looking for alternative sources of income including crime. Therefore, it is correct to affirm that if workers do not get paid enough to cover a decent way of living, it will result in damage to society as a whole as crime and other social problems increase. This means that covering workers' basic needs is not only a just demand but also a necessity for society as a whole. Consequently, it is a non-negotiable issue in our search for a solution to the ethical problem faced by multinational corporations. Workers' basic needs must be covered by their salaries. In fact, Richard De George discusses that "American companies must pay at least subsistence wages and enough above that level to allow workers and their families to live decently" (De George 1993:51), in his proposed Ethical Guidelines for Multinationals Operating in Developing Countries. This is consistent with the Vatican Council II concept of fair salary mentioned earlier in this paper.

4. From the Corporations' Perspective

However, if corporations increase wages to the asked for level, their costs will soar, resulting in no profits (if prices remain constant). Instead, loss of money will drive companies out of business and workers will lose their jobs, resulting in an overall huge loss for society for the same reasons as stated above. Another possibility is that either governments or corporations themselves will decide to limit corporate profits in order to increase employees' wages, but this will result in corporations going to some other country in which they would be able to get a better, more adequate return for their investment. It will also hurt society as many workers lose their jobs and government loses income in the form of taxes.

If corporations decide to increase prices in order to cover increased wages, the inflationary vicious circle mentioned early in this paper will take place at a faster pace and, again, it will hurt the worker and hence society as whole. Therefore, workers' wages cannot be increased if everything else remains constant. It is evident that corporate profits are a necessity too. In fact, the Catholic Social Teaching has defended the concept of "fair profit," adding that it is not the only indicator of the situation of a company. There are "human and moral factors that are just as essential for the long-run survival of corporations" (John Paul II. 1991).

The situation described before applies only to developing countries. In contrast, most developed countries' workers do get paid more than enough to cover basic needs. Why such difference? Multinational corporations argue that such workers get paid more because they produce more. If a U.S. worker produces two items in the same period of time a Venezuelan produces one identical item, unit labor cost for the U.S. operation *is* half of that of the Venezuelan operation. If we take product's unit price around the world as constant, which is consistent with globalized *market* economies, the U.S. operation generates much more profit per unit than the Venezuelan, and such additional profits can be shared with workers in the form of increased salaries. Clearly, corporations take their profits before considering wages.

5. It Is Not Labor Productivity – It Is Corporate Profits

I have established that the argument of lower labor productivity is a perfectly valid reason for lower salaries in developing countries. However, we have to argue that the actual cause of lower salaries is lower profits (before taking into consideration labor costs), which in turn means higher costs. This means that every element that increases costs of operation for multinational corporations in developing countries compared to their operations in developed countries contributes to lower wages for the developing countries' workers. Labor productivity is just one factor affecting third world countries' salaries. In many cases it's the most important, while in other cases it is not so important.

In many cases other factors such as higher costs of raw material, technology, negotiations and risk do have an important effect on workers' salaries. Therefore, increasing labor productivity would help increasing developing countries' workers' salaries, but it will not solve the problem entirely.

Highly educated employees in developing countries can be as productive as their developed countries counterparts. Even though they have
similar qualifications, they earn very different salaries. For instance,
Procter & Gamble de Venezuela, C.A. (PGV), a subsidiary of the Procter
& Gamble Company based in Cincinnati, pays its entry-level, college-
graduate employees about US$800 per month. PGV is known in the
country as one of the best companies in terms of salaries paid to its
employees. In fact, only 1% of the people who apply to PGV gets a job
offer. Offering $800 per month to a college graduate in the U.S. would
be considered as an insult. Often the Venezuelan college graduate will
have similar qualifications as an American worker, having perhaps even
earned his degree from a U.S. institution. Of course, the cost of living in
Venezuela is lower than in the U.S., but it is still impossible to afford
a proper standard of living for a college graduate with only $800. Just
a small apartment's rent would take half the amount. PGV's employees,
who are lucky compared to the average Venezuelan employee, are sometimes dissatisfied and dream of going to Europe or the U.S. to improve
the quality of their lives. During my summer internship in PGV, many
employees expressed their desire to come to the U.S. when they found
out I was living here. When asked why, they answered that they were
sure they could get a good job that would allow them to rent a good
apartment, buy a good car, and save some money.

As we can see in the example above, if there is no difference in productivity between this kind of Venezuelan worker and their U.S. counterparts, then the difference in salaries must be the consequence of other
factors that make the Venezuelan operation of Procter & Gamble less
profitable (before labor costs) or more risky than their U.S. operation.

What drives higher costs in Venezuela is a complex matter. In addition to lower productivity, there is a lack of infrastructure for transportation, manufacturing, etc. There is also political, economical, and judicial instability that increase forecasting, legal, and "lobbying" costs as
well as risk carried by these companies. It is a very well known rule that
the higher the risk, the higher the return must be. Thus, when corporations take their profits first, they leave less money for their employees.

So far, we have determined the reasons behind lower salaries for developing countries' employees. Correcting this inequality between developed and developing countries is the solution for increasing employees' salaries and, thus, improving society's well-being. But who is going
to do it and how? Who is responsible for this action? Workers, corpora-

tions, or governments? Even though the problem is quite complex, I would like to offer some recommendations to solve it.

6. Recommendations

I stated that an increase in salary of workers to a level that covers their basic needs is the responsibility of society as a whole. Consequently, correcting the afore mentioned inequalities between developed and developing countries is everyone's responsibility.

Productivity can be increased with proper education, training, adequate technology, and a good infrastructure. It is employees' responsibility to get a proper education. For instance, if general knowledge training is provided in public schools, it is employees' duty to attend and acquire that knowledge. Government's responsibility is to provide the afore mentioned training in a appropriate way and to provide businesses with a good infrastructure to develop their businesses. Corporations' responsibility is to provide employees with specific job training and to maintain an updated technology to help increase employees' productivity.

However, the problem cannot be solved by each of the parties alone. Rather, they have to act together as they are all responsible for increasing productivity. "Establishing and maintaining the common good require the *cooperative efforts* of some, often many, people" (The Common Good 1998). Therefore, each party's responsibility is not limited to the actions mentioned before. In addition, they have to demand and insure that the other parties take their responsibilities. Employees have to demand their employers provide job specific training and implement adequate technology in their processes. They also have to demand the government provide general training. Similarly, corporations have to encourage employees to attend training sessions within and out the companies' programs, as well as pressuring governments to provide their citizens with adequate education and to implant a satisfactory infrastructure for businesses to develop. Finally, governments must require corporations to bring the latest technology to the country given that employees can now manage it, as well as encourage and stimulate employees to attend training programs.

Unfortunately, this is not happening. It is easier for multinational corporations just to take their profits and pay low salaries. They believe themselves to be behaving in an ethically correct manner since in most cases they pay salaries well above the legal minimum wage and are also providing employees with some training. Nike contractors' child labor use provides a good example. It is commendable that, in some cases, they pay higher than average salaries and that their employees are better off than the average Chinese, but by doing so they are helping to lower China's productivity. In the future, these teenage employees will not have an education good enough to handle the latest technology and processes because they were working at a time in which they should have been getting basic education. In the end, Nike is doing more harm than good to China's society.

Many multinational corporations are forgetting that they are still responsible for increasing productivity, that, in addition to provide training to their employees, they must require the other parties (especially governments) to do their parts. They are not applying the pressure needed for society's long-term development. Short-term mentality is responsible for this situation.

Although the current situation is harming employees only, it will eventually harm every component of society, including corporations. Multinational corporations must help in the development of third world countries because it is in their best long-term interest and because they have the moral obligation to do so. The Caux Roundtable's General Principle Two states that "Businesses established in foreign countries to develop, produce or sell should also contribute to the social advancement of those countries by creating productive employment and helping to raise the purchasing power of their citizens" (Principles for Business 1994). Multinationals' responsibility goes beyond the economic realm; they must also "engage selectively in cultural and *political* life" (Enderle and Tavis 1998:1133 f.).

Of course, corporations are not the only ones that lack responsibility. Governments are also responsible for the current situation. The huge levels of corruption in most developing countries suggests that government officials have little care for their society. These people put their personal wealth above society's goals, thus causing a huge damage to the less powerful people, the less-trained workers. Lack of infrastructure, education programs, and coherent economic policy has helped greatly to lower Venezuelan workers' real income.

Workers are also accountable for the current situation. They have evidently been unsuccessful in demanding their governments and employers do their part in the solution of our problem. In the Venezuelan case, highly educated individuals who are supposed to lead others have shown a serious apathy about the Venezuelan problems.

The above portrayal of the Venezuelan situation, which applies to many developing countries, seems hopeless. The proposal made above has been suggested before by many authors. It is clearly a way to increase productivity and lower other costs that keep developing countries' wages lower. However, execution of such proposal is quite difficult because none of the parties is really aware of their ethical responsibilities. They are particularly not conscious that their responsibility is extended to do whatever is in one's space of freedom that can push others to behave in an ethically correct manner. Everyone's space of freedom is certainly limited by a set of constraints (Enderle and Tavis 1998:1131f.). In many developing countries, these constraints have been overestimated by some, while others do not even realize they have such space of freedom.

It is logical that my last proposal be *ethics education*. This has also been proposed by the authorities of the Universidad Catolica Andres Bello (UCAB), my undergraduate institution, and it is the reason why I decided to study at the University of Notre Dame. According to Professor M. Cecilia Arruda, "Values [in Latin America] seem to have been forgotten. Materialism and selfishness have become strong rule, so that ethical behavior started to be seen with disdain in many cases" (Arruda 1997). This anti-ethics mentality has infiltrated most sectors in many developing countries and few people seem to realize the long-term negative implications of it. It is evident that a change is needed in the way many people look at ethics in these countries. Widespread ethics ignorance has to be eradicated so that everyone understands his responsibilities and the long-term benefits of being ethically correct.

Each component of developing countries societies needs to know it has a space of freedom, the limits of that space of freedom, and how to use that space so that it can make ethically correct decisions, which will eventually result in the common good. If we can make corporations, governments and employees aware of their responsibilities in preserving and developing the society they operate and live in, the first proposal would seem obvious to each of them. Areas of agreement would be easily reached, and specific proposals of easier execution would be made. Those really interested in society's long-term well-being must keep asking themselves: What else can we do to behave in an ethically correct manner?

References

Arruda, M. C. 1997. "Business Ethics in Latin America." *Journal of Business Ethics* 16:1597–1603. Also: *The Latin American Alliance*. http://www.latinsynergy.org

Community Aid Abroad. 1998. "Some Conditions Are Improving but Wages Remain So Low Workers Struggle to Subsist." *Religious and Social Investors Report on Nike and Reebok Factories in Indonesia, Vietnam and China*. http://www.caa.org/campaigns/nike.

De George, R. T. 1993. *Competing with Integrity in International Business*. New York: Oxford University Press.

Enderle, G., Tavis, L. A. 1998. "A Balanced Concept of the Firm and the Measurement of its Long-term Planning and Performance." *Journal of Business Ethics* 17:1129–44.

John Paul II. 1991. "Centesimus Annus." In *Ética y Negocios para América Latina*, ed. E. Schmidt. 1995. Lima: Universidad del Pacífico.

Principles for Business. 1994. The Hague, The Netherlands: Caux Roundtable Secretariat.

The Common Good. 1998. *Issues in Ethics*, Vol. 5, No. 1. http://www.scu.edu/ethics/publications/iie/v5n.

OCEI. 1998. Indicadores Económicos. Oficina Central de Información. http://www.ocei.gov.ve.

Vatican Council II. 1965. *Pastoral Constitution on the Church in the Modern World Gaudium et Spes*. http://www.stjosef.at.

Life in the Fields:
An Exploration of Migrant Labor
in America's Agricultural Industries

Kevin Kreutner
University of Notre Dame
South Bend, Indiana, USA

We suffer in Mexico because there is no work.
Then we suffer in America because there is...
Rigoberto Cortez (1997)

1. Rigoberto Cortez: A Case from Life

When Rigoberto Cortez was nineteen years old, he faced a difficult dilemma. He had a newborn baby girl, a two-year-old son, a wife, and no job. He lived in a small village near Tecoripa, Mexico. With no way to provide for his family, Rigoberto left Mexico and illegally entered the United States. He had many friends who had made the quest to America in the past, and he was fairly confident that once he found his way to Santa Ana, California, he'd be able to find some familiar faces.

Rigoberto made it to Santa Ana without too much trouble and soon found himself working in the strawberry fields of Orange County. He lived in a small apartment with seven other strawberry pickers and sent the majority of his earnings back to Mexico to feed his family. Eventually, Rigoberto made a friend who worked for a restaurant and soon managed to get a job as a busboy. Years later, an amnesty law gave Rigoberto a legal right to work in the United States. Today, he is a cook in Southern California, and his family still lives in Mexico since they can not enter the United States legally. Afraid of the dangers associated with crossing the border illegally, Rigoberto visits them one month a year and hopes that someday he can bring them to America.

2. Migrant Labor in US Agricultural Industries

In a mass consumer society like that which exists in the United States, people rarely give much thought to how the products they buy make their way into department stores, shopping malls, and supermarkets. Currently, there is more attention being placed on how domestic companies operate in developing nations (Grow 1996). There is, however, an equally important issue to be examined within our borders. This issue involves the use of foreign, often illegal, migrant workers in our agricultural industries. These are the people who pick the strawberries American children snack on, harvest the lettuce served in fine dining establishments, and collect the grapes to turn them into premium Napa Valley cabernets.

Each year, approximately two million migrant workers, ninety percent of whom come from Mexico, harvest agricultural products in the United States (The Economist 1993b). An estimated twenty thousand people pick strawberries in California each year (Bacon 1997:20). Exact figures are difficult to derive due to the nature of the migration. Industry experts appearing before Congress in 1992 claimed that between 30% and 70% of all foreign agricultural workers nationwide held doctored immigration documents (The Economist 1993b). This migration, both legal and illegal, accounts for over twenty percent of all new labor growth in the United States (Kossoudji 1996:902). Once in the United States, migrants find a crowded job market that allows employers to pay low wages which in turn results in many living in extreme poverty. For the workers, poor economic opportunity in their home country forces them to do whatever is necessary to feed their families and survive.

This immigration brings to the table a plethora of contemporary issues including illegal immigration, NAFTA (North American Free Trade Agreement), health care, education, crime, and more. In this paper, the ethical considerations surrounding migrant agricultural labor will be examined. In doing so, the case of Rigoberto Cortez will be utilized to aid in an understanding of the realities which these migrants face.

3. What Is the Ethical Issue?

The further one researches the use of migrant labor in the United States, the more difficult it becomes to narrow down the true ethical issue involved. There are issues involving wages, housing, health care, and employer sanctions, to name just a few. In order to create a specific examination while also incorporating all relevant areas, this discussion will focus on one specific moral dimension of this issue. For the purpose of this paper, the ethical imperative involves looking into pros and cons associated with migrant labor work conditions. In other words, is it morally correct for agricultural industries knowingly to utilize migrant workers in the manner in which it is currently operating? Rigoberto Cortez's introductory statement above exemplifies the ethical dimension under examination. Before it is possible to explore both sides of this debate, it is essential to define exactly what life is like for migrant workers.

4. The Life of a Migrant Agricultural Worker

Just as no two lives are the same, it is impossible to try to typify exactly what a migrant worker experiences. The "average" life is defined from the examples that have been made public. Generally, one would have to imagine that there are more cases of injustice than those reported. On the other hand, if the researchable examples are only of rare extremities, it is possible to base a judgement on a inaccurate poor estimation of the problem. Starting with this objective orientation, the conditions of migrant workers will be examined by looking at what appears to be the three main areas in ethical question: wages, housing, and health concerns.

4.1. Wages

Because of the nature of how workers are compensated, it is a challenge to measure an accurate wage. There are a variety of estimates available. Between 1982 and 1994, it appears that the nominal field labor wage in California rose little if any, in many areas remaining below the legal minimum wage (Bacon 1997:18). One study estimated that real wages in California have declined at least twenty percent over the past two decades. For instance, the same report pointed out significant wage drops in the strawberry and broccoli industries (Estrada 1997). A 1995 federal study suggested that the actual average wage for migrant workers was only $5,000 per year (Beall 1996).

Field laborers are generally paid according to how much they produce. For example, it is common practice for strawberry pickers to be paid by the basket. Sometimes the payment per basket picked is a function of how many workers show up each morning. "On days when there were a lot of people (who wanted to work), they would pay us way less than when there were only a few 'Vatos'" (Cortez 1997). One strawberry picker described that on his first day, he thought he made $20 for eight hours according to the piece rate system, but he couldn't be sure until the foreman paid him at the end of the week (Bacon 1997:19). PCUN, a union originally started by cucumber pickers, claims that only workers in their prime can work fast enough to earn $5 per hour (Klinkenberg 1997).

Attempts to determine an accurate wage are also affected by involuntary deductions paid by the workers to farmers. In one worst case scenario, workers were actually forced to live on the farm and were permitted to buy grocery and hygiene items from the farmers only. Workers were paying a reported $5 for a pack of cigarettes and $2 for a can of chicken noodle soup. Many who were new to the United States had signed a "contract" to work a three week harvest. At the end of the three weeks, some were forced to stay even longer because their purchases exceeded earnings, and they were threatened with deportation (Copp 1996:38). Rigoberto Cortez remembers being forced to pay for water while working under the California sun: "They charged us $1 and we knew that it had just come out of the garden hose" (Cortez 1997). One farm owner consistently required employees to do calisthenics before work and to pack berries at the end of the day, all without pay. The United Farm Workers (UFW) estimated that the practice cost workers, whose average salary is $8,500 a season, 5 percent of their pay (Bacon 1997:18).

It is no surprise that workers are treated in this manner. Federal law exempts farm workers from union protection, overtime rights, job security, and number of hour guarantees. The law was originally drafted to protect the farm owners from being overly responsible because of the perishable nature of their crops (Klinkenberg 1997). Undocumented workers are often signaled out from those who possess legitimate documentation. One study found that "the hypothesis that unauthorized immigrants are chosen into low-paying, low-skill farm jobs and that their earnings are lower compared with legal workers is validated" (Taylor 1992:890).

In short, it is obvious that the wages paid to agricultural workers, regardless of legal status, are far from what most would agree is the standard in American society. Unfortunately, the exploitation of migrant farm workers expands far beyond the realm of wages.

4.2. Housing

Most migrant laborers move around from crop to crop depending upon where work is easily available. They also rarely have enough money to place a standardized deposit, have no credit history, and often lack verifiable identification and past residences. Thus, it is nearly impossible for them to find long-term housing. Generally, they find housing in one of two ways. The first involves housing that is mandated, offered, or otherwise initiated by the farm owner or employer. The second involves people who charge exorbitant amounts for squalid housing, taking advantage of the desperate situation of the workers. Whichever case it may be, the housing conditions faced by migrants and their families are in demand of closer scrutiny.

There is no shortage of cases of migrant workers living in deplorable locations. One example involved people who were living in a one-room wooden shack that had exposed wiring and an only occasionally functioning refrigerator and stove. The bathroom shared between many such shacks was a small dirty outhouse with public showers generally devoid of hot water (Copp 1996:40). In Hillsborough County, Florida, code inspectors had to evacuate a migrant labor camp because the residents were in imminent danger from a potential fire or gas explosion. The trailers in the camp had been equipped by farm owners with gas stoves and heating utilizing tanks typically used for backyard barbecues. In some instances, copper tubing was used to transport the gas through holes in the trailers' walls – creating a serious explosive danger. At least one of the trailers used a garden hose for indoor plumbing (Jimenez 1997).

Because the migrant workers have such a difficult time finding any housing, they are often charged far more than normal. One woman describes a decrepit one-bedroom house being rented for $950 per month in an area where larger, nicer houses rent for much lower. This home was shared by seven adults and seven children, most of whose fathers were working the crop picking circuit. The house, along with many others like it owned by the same couple, had broken heaters, damaged ceilings, no trash service, and exposed wiring. Thirteen year old Rosa Cyphers told the Los Angeles Slum Housing Task Force, "there are big fat cockroaches everywhere; it's like there are millions of them." Her mother, Sandra Cyphers, added that their house had been without water for months (Williams 1996). Another couple described funding their $800 per month rent by renting out space on their front lawn and building makeshift "shacks." Thousand Oaks, California code enforcement officers discovered that a total of fifty legal and illegal immigrants were living in twelve such structures on the property (Jimenez 1997).

Although these are only a few examples that do not represent all migrant workers, it seems clear that migrant laborers do not have equitable access to proper housing. The lack of sanitation, along with other conditions, can often have a serious effect on the health and safety of migrant labor.

4.3. Health and Safety

Agriculture is considered one of the most hazardous occupations in the United States. There are a wide array of dangers associated with the migrant workers' lifestyle including those directly associated with the work as well as those which are indirectly caused. During the Helsinki Commission's hearings on Farm Worker Health and Safety, health experts went into detail to describe the dangers of working in the fields, living in squalid housing, and traveling to work in unsafe, overcrowded vans and trucks (Gaston 1993:31).

Workers also face greater risk of disease. The Centers for Disease Control found that farm workers are six times more likely to develop tuberculosis than the general population and have a diabetes rate three times higher. They are also significantly more prone to parasitic and infectious diseases, maternal and newborn health problems, hypertension, and alcoholism (Gaston 1993:32). An American Journal of Public Health finding linked many problems to poor water quality at many migrant labor camps. It indicated that migrant workers generally have higher rates of intestinal problems, especially those transmitted by water. It concluded, "drinking water supplies in migrant worker camps are often contaminated with bacteria" (Ciesielski et al. 1991:63).

Actual work in the fields exposes workers to a variety of dangers. For instance, picking strawberries requires that one stand hunched over in order to remain agile and reach the fruit. Kneeling causes one to be slow and thus earn less due to the compensation system. Over the length of a harvest, day after day, eight hours a day, this can cause serious chiropractic and other problems. Some of the workers, especially the elderly, have a difficult time standing upright after work each night (Cortez 1997). Agricultural workers also face serious risks from the use of pesticides in the fields. On one reported instance, a woman was almost killed when a pilot slightly missed his target while dropping a poisonous insecticide (Copp 1996:39). Despite extensive worker appeals, the California State Assembly voted in 1996 to delay the prohibition of methyl bromide, a toxic pesticide used on almost every strawberry field to kill parasites (Bacon 1997:19). Rigoberto Cortez reveals, "nobody likes to work after they spray, you can smell all of the stuff and it gets kind of hard to breathe. Every once and a while some 'Vato' will get too dizzy from it and pass out" (Cortez 1997).

It is important to note the dangers that some of the health issues can have on the general populace as well. In one instance, nearly 9,000 Los Angeles students and teachers were exposed to hepatitis stemming from a strawberry picker (Navarrette 1997). Proponents of the controversial California Proposition 187 that bans access to medical attention for illegal immigrants point out the potential danger to the food supply associated with the bill. Although not abundantly significant for this paper, it would be foolish not at least to consider the general health effects for the general population in looking at the ethics of the migrant labor system.

5. The Ethical Debate

It is clear that there are a variety of undeniably poor aspects in the current system. Obviously, it is impossible to argue that one would choose to live the life of the migrant worker. Some of the instances mentioned cited specific cases while others involved general conditions inherent with the occupation.

It would be quite easy to dismiss immediately the ethical argument in favor of the use of migrant labor. After all, it is difficult to condone or justify the circumstances described earlier. At this point, however, it is important to realize that the responsibility for the areas discussed above falls upon many shoulders, not just the farmer or landlord. One of these is our representative government and, thus, the public as a whole. If nothing else, as will soon be explored, the farmers and landlords are merely acting out of personal, capitalist self-interest.

5.1. The Argument in Favor of Using Migrant Labor

There are many different reasons to defend the use of migrant labor in agriculture. Recognizing that all the laborers are on the fields by choice is the first place to begin. There is no indentured servitude involved. Nobody forces the workers to show up for the harvest year after year. This fact opens up many different defenses for the current, market-driven system.

There is no doubt that the workers involved are better off dealing with those conditions than returning to Mexico. If the opposite were the case, they'd return to their homelands. One worker explains, "[in Mexico] you work all day and they pay you 80,000 pesos [approximately $30 at the time] per week. That's why one comes to the United States" (Cantu 1995:401). Despite the fact that often families are separated by the harvest season, they still find it to be lucrative and worthwhile. Without this availability of income, albeit in less-than-ideal conditions, many families would be even worse off. One Agriculture Ministry Agent explains that despite attempts being made to dissuade migration and despite the risks, people will keep traveling to the United States because it still beats starvation (Dillon 1996).

Another defense of migrant labor use involves necessity on the part of American farmers, who have been facing economic problems of their own. Years of drought in California, for instance, caused some farmers to lose their lands in the 1980s. Using migrant workers allows farming operations to reduce production costs and have a flexible labor supply; it also allows higher organizational flexibility (Cantu 1995:413). Growers have a basic dependence on this abundant migrant labor supply. In 1985 a cold freeze that threatened many strawberry crops hit San Francisco. When the media publicized the farmers' plight, 400 workers quickly descended on the fields and saved the crop. One Florida farmer admitted that without foreign workers, his crops would rot in the fields (Vanpelt 1996).

The seasonality of the harvest for almost every individual farm makes it impossible for the farmers to provide amenities like health insurance, stable wages, and long-term housing. Many farmers explain that they do not like some of the conditions, but they are unable to do much more. Most economic studies point to the fact that low wages are not due to racial/ethnic discrimination but rather due to the enormous oversupply of labor (Estrada 1997:13). Farmers also point out the fact the Americans are extremely price conscious and would ultimately have to pay much more for products if conditions were to be improved. A National Consultation on Migrant Farmworker Ministry emphasized that farmworkers play a crucial role in keeping our supermarkets filled with "an Eden-like abundance of inexpensive fruits and vegetables" (Copp 1996:38). Another study found that as long as consumers are accustomed to low prices, while at the same time growers are losing control of their water supply due to deregulation, the pressures on farmers to keep costs down will continue (The Economist 1993a).

Migrant labor is often looked upon as a stepping stone to better jobs. People can enter the United States with nothing and survive working the fields. By following the harvest, they come in contact with many people and areas, and eventually a better opportunity should arise. Many workers, once they learn some English, eventually find restaurant careers that offer a much better standard of living. In short, the fields can offer one a chance at the American dream. Without it, the people will have no opportunity or means by which to survive upon initially entering the country. "I came to the United States with $30. Three days later I had money daily and a place to sleep. As bad as it was sometimes, I don't know what I would have done without the strawberries" (Cortez 1997).

In short, migrant labor can be viewed as a necessary evil in the development of American agriculture and the lives of the workers. To some extent, this is an "ends justify the means" viewpoint. Although deplorable in some ways, a system has been created that allows farmers to earn a profit and offers poverty-stricken immigrants a means for survival.

5.2. The Argument Against the Current Migrant Labor System

There are infinite ways to dispute the use of migrant labor. The strongest case against the current system does not focus on the practice of using migrants in the fields but rather on the manner in which they are treated. For the purposes of this debate, the argument against the current system will be structured directly to combat the major points made in the argument for, as well as to add a few more.

The hallmark reasoning of the laborer's choice to enter the United States and work in the fields is viewed as weak to shallow at best. It is true that workers come here by choice, but it is really a function of the fact that they have no other choice available. People will do just about anything to avoid starvation. Just because life on the fields is better than death does not justify what these people are forced to experience. The workers are often powerless to fight the conditions to which they are subjected. Many of the workers do not have green cards and so are afraid to complain (Williams 1996).

In the past, workers did attempt to improve their situations with limited success. Starting in the 1960s, the United Farm Workers under the leadership of Cesar Chavez used strikes, civil disobedience, and boycotts to press for better wages and conditions. At its peak, the UFW had over 100,000 members in California alone (The Economist 1993a). Today, that number is as low as 25,000 nationwide (Bacon 1997:19). Further, a number of tactics have been used to limit the power of the workers to bargain collectively. In one instance, a farmer plowed under a field where workers had begun to organize a strong union, threatening to continue to do so until it stopped. Another woman described being fired after she started to organize a union group and was even shot seven times in the arm by a foreman after her union contemplated a strike (Bacon 1997:21). The UFW has even tried to move past the farmers by lobbying some of their major customers for change. This has been done with quite limited success. For instance, despite making a pledge to listen to the UFW, the E&J Gallo winery later refused to open talks with the union (Snyder 1996).

Those against the current system are quick to admit that improving conditions would ultimately result in higher prices at the supermarket. However, they claim, this is placing prices where they should be to begin with. They argue that the lower prices are really only a function of the torture that the workers endure. The UFW, combined with AFL-CIO, organized a national campaign called "Five cents for fairness" which stated that if everyone paid an extra five cents per basket of strawberries, workers could be provided with improved wages, medical insurance, and overall housing conditions (Bacon 1997:22).

The issue of upward mobility is also controversial. There is much evidence to prove that there is little such opportunity, especially for those who lack legal documentation. One study concluded that finding better work was dependant on gaining skills and education that the migrants simply cannot afford, causing "the distinction between free and unfree labor to begin to erode." The same finding found that the likelihood that growing numbers of migrant farmworker families will experience intergenerational poverty is great and increasing (Estrada 1997:13). Another study suggests that neither education received in Mexico nor additional education gained in the United States (excluding learning English) is helpful in advancing in the U.S. labor market (Kossoudji 1996:901).

Farmers often claim that they use migrant labor because there is no domestic labor force willing to do the work. Opponents of the labor do not disagree with this fact. Yet, they explain that the farmers are taking advantage of the laborers because of the desperate situations they face in their home countries. One workers' advocate explains, "why would you expect a U.S. worker to say 'sign me up'? Nobody raises their children to be migrant workers" (Beall 1996).

The basis for the argument against the current system is simple to see. It is quite clear that the field workers would not be treated so poorly if they had any power to change conditions. The farmers are truly exploiting them because of their misfortunes. Employers often discriminate directly against the workers because the workers are unlikely to force their employers to comply with U.S. labor laws. Such an action would often only open them up for deportation (Kossoudji 1996:911). This intentional discrimination proves the fact that this current system is not based on any sound ethical foundations. If the arguments in favor of migrant labor were correct, then farmers would be able to allow workers to bargain collectively without intimidation and to give them the opportunity to have some control over their own lives without threatening them with violence and deprivation.

5.3. The Ethics: A Personal View

Without question, the practices associated with migrant labor are unfair, unjust, and unethical. The public is quick to close its eyes to questions of basic humanity because of the often illegal status of the workers and the risk of higher fruit and vegetable prices. My discussions with Rigoberto Cortez provided great insight into exactly how the workers feel. His description mainly presented migrant life as being one of desperation and humility. He continually wished to point out that the workers know they are being taken advantage of but have little recourse (Cortez 1997). The National Consultation on Migrant Farmworker Ministry found that despite the fact that Mexicans are generally very religious people, the quality of life is so poor that deeply religious Mexican farmworkers are often cut off from their own spirituality and become unable to take solace in their faith (Copp 1996:40). With all this in mind, I believe that actions must be taken to ensure some minimum level of decency in our agricultural fields. The United States is the richest nation in the world, and it is deplorable to think that we knowingly allow these conditions to exist, continue, and even escalate.

6. Recommendations: What Should Be Done

There are several ways to go about forcing a change in the current system. For the most part, they are based on two different premises. The first is that government takes a hand in improving migrant life, and the second involves creating an environment where farmers will be forced to improve conditions because of a lack of labor supply.

There is no doubt that the government essentially has been ignoring the problems currently embedded in migrant life. In the early years of the century, the Bracero program allowed migrants to harvest for the season and then return to Mexico. The workers lived in government sponsored camps that provided hot showers, indoor restrooms, medical care, and community recreational activities (Cannon 1996:15).

Although currently there are some calls for a new Bracero-type program, most current legislation on the books does little to help the workers. In fact, most of the current effort would do quite the contrary. One California bill under debate would grant some aliens the right temporarily to work the harvest, but would allow employers to withhold one quarter of their salaries until they returned to Mexico (The Fresno Bee 1996). In Washington state, Governor Locke recently vetoed a bill that would lower housing regulations for migrant worker camps, stating that it "fails to address the basic conditions of the workers and the children who would reside in the structures" (Navarrette 1997). In California, Governor Pete Wilson created the "Targeted Industries Partnership Program" to check on labor contractors with bad reputations. The program is, however, only a fact-finding endeavor with no legal authority. Another California bill was struck down that would make growers personally liable for any breaches of labor regulations which occur on their property (The Economist 1993a).

Despite the fact that there are calls for government to get involved with this issue, it does not appear as though anything is soon to be accomplished legislatively. This certainly should change. Our government has an obligation to ensure that these types of exploitation do not continue, especially when they are so apparent. At the very minium, our government must do two things. First, migrant workers should be granted the same union privileges as exist in other industries to give them an opportunity to fight for themselves. Second, housing regulations should be enforced to prevent landlords form abusing tenants. In short, the government needs to stop turning a blind eye to what it knows is going on. There are already wage restrictions, housing regulations, and OSHA codes in place; but somebody needs to enforce them.

The second plausible "solution" to the problem takes government essentially out of the equation. If farmers were not able to get a sufficient supply of migrant labor because of the harsh living and working conditions, they would be forced to improve wages, housing, etc. Common consensus is that this will only occur through sustained economic growth in Mexico. Jorge Castaneda, a Mexican writer and professor suggests, "Mexican stability is the only true deterrent to migrant labor" (Vanpelt 1996). It is hoped that the development of a significant Mexican middle class, through the help of NAFTA (programs), will work to limit the hordes of workers turning to the US for survival. If this plan does work, however, it will most certainly take decades.

In conclusion, the most important recommendation is probably the hardest to implement. The American public needs to have greater humanitarian concern for the manner in which it buys all of its goods and services. People need to look at what they buy and how it gets to the stores. As long as there is no public outcry, little will be done to change the system. It is very easy for us all to ignore the problem by claiming that it is government's responsibility to look into these things. Unfortunately, we all know that our representative government will only act if the public calls for it to do so. If people boycotted strawberries one season to make a point, there is little doubt that field conditions would change. There needs to be an understanding that by purchasing the fruits of this labor one is essentially supporting and promoting migrant labor practices. Without such an understanding, the suffering and exploitation will continue.

References

Bacon, D. 1997. "The U.F.W. Picks Strawberries." *The Nation* 14 April: 18–22.

Beall, P. 1996. "Growers Ask for Easier Immigration." *The Wall Street Journal* 28 February.

Cannon, B. 1996. "Life and Social Interaction in a New Deal Farm Labor Camp." *Agricultural History* 1 January: 1–32.

Cantu, L. 1995. "Keep On A-Goin': Life and Social Interaction in a New Deal Farm Labor Camp." *Sociological Perspectives* Fall 38: 399–415.

Centers for Disease Control and Prevention. 1997. "Pregnancy-related Behaviors Among Migrant Farm Workers." *The Journal of the American Medical Association* May: 1512–16.

Ciesielski, S., Handzel, T. and Sobsey, M. 1991. "The Microbiologic Quality of Drinking Water in North Carolina Migrant Labor Camps." *The American Journal of Public Health* 6 June: 762–5.

Copp, J. 1996. "Fruit of Justice Stills Eludes Farmworkers." *Migration World Magazine* May–June: 38–41.

Cortez, R. 1997. Personal Interview (12 October).

Dillon, S. 1996. "INS Beams Message to Migrants to State Home." *The Ft. Worth Star-Telegram* 12 January.

Estrada, R. 1997. "Declining Wages of Migrant Farmworkers Result of Labor Oversupply and Not Racism." *Chicago Tribune* 8 April.

Gaston, M. 1993. "Health Needs of Migrant and Seasonal Farmworkers." *Migration World Magazine* January-February: 31-32.

Grow, D. 1996. "Prayers for Economic Justice are Answered." *Minneapolis-St. Paul Star-Tribune* 11 September.

Jimenez, T. 1997. "Officials Order Shack Dwellers Out of Converted Properties." *The Los Angeles Daily News* 19 April.

Klinkenberg, J. 1997. "Bittersweet Reclamation." *St. Petersburg Times* 23 September.

Kossoudji, S. and Cobb-Clark, D. 1996. "Finding Good Opportunities within Unauthorized Markets: U.S. Occupational Mobility for Male Latino Workers." *International Migration Review* Winter, 901–24.

Navarrette, R. 1997. "Conflicting Legacies of Cesar Chavez." *The Sacramento Bee* 13 April.

Snyder, G. 1996. "UFW March Focuses on Sonoma County." *The San Francisco Chronicle* 4 May.

Sylvain, P. 1993. "Migrants Chase an Elusive Dream." *Bangor Daily News* 21 August.

Taylor, J. 1992. "Earnings and Mobility of Legal and Illegal Immigrant Workers in Agriculture." *American Journal of Agricultural Economics* November: 889–97.

The Economist. 1993a. "Strawberries and Circuit Boards: Migrant Labor." 27 March.

The Economist. 1993b. "A Giant Sucking Sound: Immigration." 5 June.

The Fresno Bee. 1996. "An Open Door for Illegal Aliens in Congress is Sure to Exacerbate the Already Huge Problem of Illegal Immigration." 14 March.

Vanpelt, D. 1996. "Unwelcome Mat is Out: Job Fears and Business Needs Collide as Congress Debates the Immigration Bill." *The Tampa Tribune* 15 April.

Williams, F. 1996. "Couple Are Accused as Slumlords." *The Los Angeles Times* 16 August.

Child Labor
in the Orange Juice Industry in Brazil

Michelle Amestoy
Melissa Crosbie
University of Notre Dame
South Bend, Indiana, USA

1. Problem

Brazil is the world's leading orange juice supplier. According to a study conducted by the U.S. Department of Labor, 15 percent of the 70,000 fruit pickers in the state of Sao Paulo are estimated to be younger than fourteen. In 1996 the Brazilian exporters of citrus products signed an agreement to end child labor but have not cooperated to extinguish this practice (The Bradenton Herald 1998). Now the U.S. has stepped in to help eliminate child labor in Brazil through several organizations like the International Brotherhood of Teamsters Union, the International Labor Rights Fund, and the U.S. Customs Service. This paper examines the issue by first providing a background of the orange juice industry in Brazil. We then review the economic conditions in Brazil, followed by the underlying factors contributing to the child labor problem. Brazilian laws are then discussed, as is the responsibility for enforcing these laws. A brief discussion on ethical imperialism is presented. The paper then concludes with our recommendations on eradicating the child labor problem.

2. Background of the Orange Juice Industry in Brazil

The orange juice industry did not exist in Brazil thirty years ago. It began with an influx of new technology into the country as opposed to simple expansion and addition of factories. Today, orange juice is one of Brazil's leading agricultural export commodities. In 1996 orange juice was Brazil's fifth largest exported product, totaling 1.4 billion U.S. dollars (Brazil Embassy). A large percentage of orange juice traded on the world markets comes from Brazil. Most people think that Florida produces a majority of the orange juice sold; however, most of the Florida orange juice produced meets the U.S. demand and very little is exported. In fact, the U.S. actually has to import orange juice from Brazil to meet all U.S. demand. The growth in the orange juice industry is currently coming from European demand and is being met by Brazilian markets.

The overall business climate in Brazil has been favorable to multinational investors. Brazil has a sound legislative system that has enacted statutes providing the strictest intellectual property rules in Latin America and also has a tremendous natural resource base (Inside Brazil 1997). More specific to the orange juice industry, Brazil also has an advantage over its U.S. competitors in that it pays very low taxes for access to American markets. Brazil often sets the world price for oranges, since its production level is almost twice that of Florida's and its production costs are lower. The main cause of the lower production costs is that Brazilian companies are not subject to the same strict labor and environmental standards as U.S. producers (Brazil's Orange Juice Industry).

There are four major players in the Brazilian orange juice industry: Cutrale, Citrosuco, Cargill and Louis Dreyfus Citrus. In addition, U.S. companies also purchase products from Brazil. One example is Minute Maid, who may purchase anywhere from 20% to 40% of its orange juice supply from Brazil (Deogun 1998). It is projected that the Asian and Eastern European demand for orange juice will rise five to six percent in Europe and ten to fifteen in Asia. How will Brazil meet this rise in demand? Brazilian companies will meet it through expansion and with the use of child labor. One company has chosen to expand beyond Brazil. Sucocitrico Cutrale, Brazil's largest juice exporter, purchased two Minute Maid processing plants in Florida which will help them manoeuver around the high tariffs that have limited their access to U.S. markets in the past (Moffett 1998).

3. Economic Conditions

Approximately 25% of the Brazilian population live below the UN absolute poverty line. 14.3% of the children in Brazil between the ages of ten and thirteen are working. Of the 70,000 fruit pickers in the Tabatinga region of Sao Paulo, approximately 15% are children who earn about $3.00 per day for working fourteen hours (Teamster). Brazil is the fifth largest country in the world and has a population of more than 162 million people. About one-third of the population are children fourteen and under. Brazil is primarily an agriculture country with coffee, sugar and soybeans as it's main exports (Athers).

The FY 1996/97 orange juice production in Sao Paulo was projected to be approximately 16% above the previous year's output. This was attributed to a larger harvest and more oranges being processed (FAS Online). The forecast for FY 1998/99 does not appear as positive. The orange juice industry has predicted slower growth due to environmental conditions that have already forced companies to begin increasing the price on oranges sold in the U.S. According to Philip Lesser, director of economic and market research at the Florida Department of Citrus, long-run prices of orange juice stock are likely to rise, and the Sao Paulo region will see a decreased output during the FY 1998/99 (Dow Jones News Service 1998).

The economic environment will impact the orange juice industry and may increase the use of child labor due to the lower wages these children demand. Companies are currently experiencing poor production of oranges and will need to reduce their operating costs, thereby using child labor to reduce their wage expense.

4. Political Environment

Brazil's president, Fernando Henrique Cardoso was re-elected in October 1998. Under the Cardoso regime, interest rates have risen and sales have fallen in his attempts to bring Brazil's inflation under control. Cardoso's policies to fight inflation worked. Inflation fell from more than 1,000% to less than 5%, but at the expense of large consumer debt and worker layoffs. Throughout his term, the Brazilian government continued to operate in a deficit situation and failed to enact spending cuts and to raise governmental revenues to sufficiently cover expenditures. As of October 1998, Brazil's deficit was $32 billion including interest payments, or 7.3 % of GDP (Goering 1998).

During Cardoso's next term, the government is expected to negotiate a bailout with the International Monetary Fund, to stabilize the real (Brazil's currency unit), and to slash both the budget and the retirement systems. In the private sector, companies are already attempting to cut their operating costs through actions such as cutting outside maintenance services and reducing utility usage (Goering 1998).

Because Brazil is currently in a large deficit situation, money will not be readily available to fund child labor reform efforts. This will negatively impact the strength of future reform efforts such as educational voucher programs (subsequently described), whose past impact has been positive.

5. Existing Brazilian Laws

Brazilian law provides free and compulsory education for children between the ages of seven and fourteen. In 1988 Brazil instituted child labor laws that established fourteen as the basic minimum age for work in Brazil. However, there are two exceptions to this rule: (1) A child learning a profession or a trade can begin at twelve and (2) children required by a judge to work can do so at an earlier age (Athers). This is the only child labor law that exists in Brazil to date.

6. Who Is Responsible for Enforcement of Child Labor Laws?

In Brazil, the Ministry of Labor assumes child labor law enforcement. Since there is a shortage of both inspectors and inspections, enforcement is often minimal (U.S. DOL Study 1994). Another difficulty with enforcement is that the problem varies significantly from one part of Brazil to another. In some areas the inspectors are very lethargic, and scholarship programs don't exist which makes it harder for families to survive without the child's income. In other areas, many of the orange growers contract with co-ops for labor and don't know exactly who is working for them (Moffett 1998). Are the growers responsible for enforcement of the labor laws, or is someone else responsible?

The Teamsters are investigating the orange juice industry in Brazil to determine if child labor practices are apparent. If child labor exists, the Teamsters plan to file a complaint with the U.S. Customs office to ban the import of Brazilian orange juice (Schneider 1998).

In reality, no single entity can assume full responsibility for the eradication of child labor as the problem is too widespread. All people involved in the orange juice industry have spaces of freedom in which they can work to change the child labor practices evident here. Local grove-owners can ensure that children are not present in their fields through frequent inspections of workers. Since local grove-owners often use co-op companies to provide labor, these co-ops also bear some responsibility in determining that all hired workers meet the minimum age requirements of employment. If the co-op companies provide transportation services for grove workers, the transportation providers can assume oversight responsibility by reporting to the transportation owners the numbers of children traveling to the groves. If the numbers are significantly high, the transportation company owners can decide whether or not to renew their contracts with the co-op companies. Any of these individuals can also report such practices to local, state, or governmental authorities.

7. International Labor Organizations Addressing the Child Labor Issue

One of the most widely known international organizations and one that has published extensively on the child labor issue is the International Labor Organization (ILO). Founded in 1919, the ILO was based on the principle that social justice is a viable component of durable peace. The ILO has officially been recognized as a leading organization in the human rights field, earning the Nobel Peace Prize in 1969. As far back as 1973, the ILO recognized that child labor was becoming a serious issue, especially in developing countries. They developed and ratified a Minimum Age Convention stating that the minimum age for admission to employment should not be less than the age of completion of compulsory schooling. This has been a large problem in Brazil. The 1994 edition of UNICEF's *State of the World's Children* reported that Brazil had one of the lowest primary school completion rates in the world. Why are the children not in school? One plausible reason is because they are out working in the groves and on other agricultural venues to help support their families. One interesting fact about this convention is that it was ratified by so few members (sixty-two). Governments of the non-ratifying countries justify their position on technicalities. In response, the ILO planned to discuss new standards to suppress extreme forms of child labor in 1998 and to adopt and ratify new conventions sometime during 1999 (ILO).

In 1996, the ILO first produced an entire document exploring the problem of child labor. The document provided two main reasons that child labor is still of great concern: the large number of children affected, and, more importantly, the negative repercussions on the personal development of children caused by beginning a life of permanent employment at too young an age. As can be expected, child labor participation rates rise in rural areas. However, the report also stated that the total volume is increasing due to the rapid urbanization evident in most developing countries. The type of work performed, as well as the industry environment, has different effects on its participants. The agriculture sector is considered particularly dangerous for health and safety reasons, since workers are exposed to harsh climate conditions that cause quick fatigue, dangers from insects and other animals, sharp and primitive tools and long working hours. Toxic chemicals and insecticides also contribute to an unsafe work environment (Child Labor).

8. Past Actions and Attempts to Solve the Problem

The International Programme for the Elimination of Child Labor (IPEC), an extension of the ILO, began to implement an action plan in 1992 with the approval of the Brazilian government. The program's purpose is to research, publicize, and mobilize different sectors in communities to address the issue of child labor. Additional duties of the IPEC include training union representatives to collect and disseminate information on the plight of child workers and providing financial support for these children. The IPEC program currently operates in thirteen Latin American countries.

In cooperating with the ILO and IPEC, the government of Brazil sent a strong message about its intent to eliminate child labor now. In contrast, until 1993, the Ministry of Labor did not formally recognize that problems with forced labor existed. Further, since that time, government efforts to solve these problems have been weak. In 1994, a campaign was launched with the intent of raising public awareness of the risks involved in child labor, pressuring the government to take a more active role in solving the problem, helping unions and employers monitor child labor usage, and eliminating the problem entirely. The program was started and supported by the ILO, UNICEF, and Herbert de Souza (Betinho), a Brazilian social activist (U.S. DOL Study 1994).

Various non-governmental organizations (NGOs) concerned about child labor are also active in Brazil. In 1990, an NGO coalition was created to assist in passing legislation on this issue. The coalition is the DCA Forum in Defense of the Rights of Children and Adolescents and is still in existence today (U.S. DOL Study 1994).

In 1996 the Brazilian Association of Citrus Exporters signed an agreement banning the use of child labor. Also in 1996, the Sao Paulo Chamber for the Sugar and Alcohol Sector signed an agreement with the Sao Paulo government pledging to eradicate child labor. Although these actions can be construed as positive, the problem again lies with enforcement.

In 1997, senior officials from twenty Latin-American countries met in Cartagena, Columbia to reaffirm political commitments to stop the most intolerable forms of child labor. The meeting was an attempt to unite international experts, government officials, and union and trade employees. Statistics presented by the ILO at the meeting showed that in the Latin American region, 20–25% of all children between the ages of six and fourteen are currently working to help support their families. To restate this statistic, one out of every five Latin American children are employed. The percentages are highest in the labor sector, composing almost 60% of the child labor force. Restating again that children who work often do not attend school or drop out of school at an early age, the ILO called for increased educational reforms as a priority in the fight against child labor (ILO Press Release). UNICEF has provided support of reforms to strengthen Brazil's education system (U.S. DOL Study 1994). According to an IBGE study, Brazil will enter the 21st century with an estimated 16 percent of adults and children who cannot read or write, in spite of the 1998 Constitution determination to reduce illiteracy and standardize the education process (IBGE).

9. Current Actions

Poverty is the greatest single force that contributes to the addition of children into the workforce (Child Labor). Many families in Brazil depend on their children's income to support the family. Without this income, many families would not be able to live in adequate conditions. The government is trying to reduce the reliance of families on their children's income by providing them with vouchers. The voucher program provides every family with R$50 to enroll their children in school. The child must attend 75% of his/her classes each month to receive this voucher (New Steps). The ILO also believes that policies limiting or gradually decreasing the average family size can also have the positive benefits of reducing child labor and improving school attendance.

It is often believed that children are more likely to become employed than adults given certain circumstances, including the following: when child labor is less expensive or less troublesome than that of adults, when labor is scarce, or when child skills such as dexterity are highly valued. In reality, however, any labor cost-savings obtained through the use of child workers is small. These findings cast doubt that child labor is a necessary ingredient in a competitive-edge company mix (Child Labor).

A group of diverse activists in the central Brazilian communities is striving to eradicate child labor in the orange groves. They are using police and labor inspectors to stop buses, vans, and trucks headed for the fields and inspect who is on board. This effort has reduced the number of children being transported to the groves. For example, in July 1998, one of these raids found that of the 2,200 workers who passed through the checkpoint only 4 were children (Moffett 1998).

Citrovita Agro Industrial Ltd., a large juice producer, has confronted the child labor issues by funding an educational center for underprivileged youth. The local educational authorities are also providing financial aid to families so the children won't be forced into labor to provide for their families (Moffett 1998). The national government has also made child labor a campaign issue. President Cardoso's re-election campaign includes a "nationwide scholarship program aimed at keeping children out of the workplace" (Moffett 1998).

Another organization that is involved in attempting to eradicate child labor in the Brazilian community is the Abrinq Foundation. This organization was established in the late 1980s as a result of a series of episodes of violence against children. The main goal of the foundation is to ensure the rights of the child according to both national and international standards. The Foundation utilizes four areas of strategic intervention: political actions, communication, fund-raising, and exemplary operation of projects to educate people about the child labor problems in Brazil. In 1995, Abrinq created the "Child-Friendly Corporation Program". To apply a child friendly seal, companies must meet the following criteria:

• Take on a formal commitment not to hire children under the age of fourteen.

- Disseminate this commitment throughout their network of customers and suppliers.
- Develop or support a social program for children or a professional training program for adolescents.

During the first year of the program, 264 companies were authorized to use the seal. As of November 1996, twenty-three new companies had joined the program (Salazar).

The problem with this program is the lack of monitoring after the seals are distributed. The Abrinq Foundation believes that enforcement responsibilities fall on unions, government, and the press. Other companies have taken more drastic approaches to curbing the use of child labor by cutting ties with growers that violate the child-labor laws in Brazil (Moffett 1998).

Other countries are also becoming involved in this Brazilian issue. For example, the orange-growing industry in Australia is threatened by cheap Brazilian imports, blaming child labor for the low prices of the foreign products. Although the Australian Food Council assured native farmers that any shipments from known users of child labor would be boycotted, the head of Brazil's own trade union movement contends that this is not being done. Kjeld Jakobsen, the international head of the Centrale Unica dos Trabalhadores, has publicly stated his belief that there is no practical way to avoid using child workers in Brazil and that juice importers were being deceived into thinking their products were child friendly. "Without the necessary inspections and with no way of enforcing the laws in Brazil, [suppliers] could not be certain of what they are importing."

10. Ethical Implications

There are three basic ethical frameworks that can be used to assess the behaviors of other countries. The first is Universalism, a widespread and objective sets of guidelines about ethics that are common across all cultures. According to this framework, all countries should outlaw child labor since employing under-aged children violates their basic human rights. International codes of conduct are based on this principle.

The second framework is Ethical Relativism, which follows the belief that ethical behavior in any one country is determined by its own unique culture. Under this framework, child labor can be viewed as a necessary practice due to a country's poor economic environment, and thus it should be an accepted form of labor. On the brink of financial crisis, Brazilians might argue that the latter statement best describes their current situation.

The third framework is Ethical Imperialism, which states that cultural beliefs and standards of one particular culture should be imposed on other cultures. Many countries believe the U.S. is attempting to force its own ethical standards, which denounce the use of child labor, upon Brazil. A vivid example of this can be seen in the recent efforts of the United States Congress which passed a law that bans foreign products made with child labor. This law has loopholes that make enforcement difficult. As written, the ban "applies to products made by a child laborer confined against his or her will." The controversy inherent in this law results from defining "confined against his or her will." For example, customs officials define working "against your will" as requiring proof of coercion by the employer. On the other hand, child advocates believe that any underage worker is by definition working against his/her will. The confusion will only be expanded as economic and political conditions change and as various foreign cultures are introduced to this law.

Since the economic, political, and socio-cultural systems of Brazil and the U.S. differ, we believe that the U.S. should not impose its own child labor standards on workers in Brazil. However, some efforts should be made to educate people on the harmful effects of child labor ultimately on a country's population.

11. Our Recommendations

In order to eradicate the problem of child labor in Brazil, one must first consider the economic conditions that exist. Much of the population is poor and cannot survive without the income their children earn. How can this be changed? One way to alter Brazil's economic condition is to raise worker wages. The government also needs to take a more active role in strengthening Brazil's floundering economy by reducing expenditures and/or increasing revenues.

The government can also help to alleviate the child labor problem through increased educational reform, specifically by investing more into programs that provide families with money for their children, contingent upon the children attending school and meeting certain educational levels. These levels could include basic math, reading, and spelling skills. These types of programs could work to slow the use of child labor, since they provide an incentive for parents to keep their children in school. As part of this program, parents also need to be educated as to the importance of an education for their children. This would allow the children to move from working in the fields to working in more technically advanced jobs, so the parents ultimately would receive more income from their children. The programs should be instituted throughout the country. Possible funding sources include NGOs, international organizations, and private investment sources.

The media can also play an active role in helping to eliminate child labor by exposing companies who practice this type of behavior. Child-friendly and watchdog organizations can use media coverage to publicize and call for boycotts of companies who use child labor to produce their products.

Techniques that can be employed at a corporate level include anonymous hotlines, executive surprise visits, and corporate pressure on companies that use child labor. By instituting anonymous hotlines, individuals exposed to child labor practices can report such incidences without fear of personal repercussion. Executive surprise visits can serve as a means of enforcing company policies that prohibit the use of child labor. Companies can choose not to purchase or import products originating from known child laborers.

Another technique to eliminate child labor is to strengthen the current enforcement of child labor laws. The government should heavily penalize companies that choose to use child labor in their businesses. The government could enlist child labor organizations, local governments, and nationally recognized background institutions to help enforce these laws. These organizations could offer rewards to individuals or other organizations that report and/or capture child labor practices. The press could signal the government's intolerance of the use of child labor to the Brazilian population.

To conclude, all of the recommendations described above require funding without which the results achieved by these techniques would be limited. We believe there are institutions in place to help combat the child labor issue in Brazil, but all individuals must expand their efforts and take additional action to eradicate the problem.

References

Athers, L. "Children in Brazil: Child Labor." http://www.tulane.edu.

Brazil Embassy. http://www.brasil.emb.nw.dc.us.

Brazil's Orange Juice Industry: Fast Track to Profit. http://observer.soc.american.edu/112braz.htm.

Child Labor: What's to Be Done? http://www.ilo.org.

Dow Jones News Service. 1998. Commodities Review. 30 October.

Deogun, N. 1998. "Florida Orange Shortage Takes Its Toll as Tropicana Is Raising Juice Prices 10%." *The Wallstreet Journal,* 29 October.

FAS Online. http://www.fas.usda/gov.

Goering, L. 1998. "Brazilians Facing Tough Decisions." *Chicago Tribune,* 4 October.

IBGE. http://www.ibge.org.

ILO. http://www.ilo.org.

ILO Press Release. "At Least 15 Million Children Work in Latin America." http://www.ilo.org.

Inside Brazil. 1997. "From Oil to Orange Juice, Investors and Brazil Discover Mutual Benefits." 5 February.

Moffett, M. 1998. "Citrus Squeeze: U.S. Child-Labor Law Sparks a Trade Debate over Brazilian Oranges." *The Wall Street Journal,* 9 September.

New Steps Towards the Eradication of Child Labor in Brazil. http://www.brasil.emb.nw.dc.us.

Salazar, M.Ch. "Mobilizing Corporations Around Actions to Eradicate Child Labor in Brazil." Preliminary Version.

Schneider, M. 1998. "Teamsters Eye Child Labor in Brazil." *Associated Press,* 18 March.

The Bradenton Herald, FL. 1998. "Unions Target Minute Maid in Dispute over Child Labor." 14 January.

Teamster. http://www.teamster.org.

U.S. DOL Study. 1994. Use of Child Labor in American Imports.

PART THREE

Ethical Issues in the Health Care

The Commercialisation of Gene Therapy

Elizabeth D. Klein
Imperial College
University of London
London, England (U.K.)

1. Introduction

Gene therapy involves the use of the body's information-carrying genetic material, deoxyribonucleic acid (DNA), which controls heredity, to combat and control disease. This can be done by either adding DNA to the body or by altering the body's own DNA, and generally involves the use of human DNA on human diseases. However laudable combating disease is, by using human DNA on human subjects, we open a number of ethical and moral "cans of worms." For instance, will we just alter human DNA with respect to disease? Or will we also use this as a means to select for "fashionable" characteristics such as height and hair colour? As our understanding grows, will individuals with a genetic disease become a focus for prejudice and discrimination? In my opinion, we must address and debate these issues now, before the use of gene therapy becomes a common occurrence, and this whilst we still have the opportunity to influence the debate.

To further the debate, this paper will cover a number of topics in relation to ethics and gene therapy. An initial explanation of genetics and how gene therapy works will be given, followed by an overview of some ethical theories that will be useful in this debate. The paper will then continue with an analysis of some ethical issues with respect to research, therapy itself and commercialisation.

2. What Is Gene Therapy?

2.1. What Are Genes?

DNA is a long complex molecule that is packed and folded into chromosomes so that it can fit into cells. Each section of DNA forms a gene that is a unit of heredity that determines the structure of a protein in the body. Proteins are complex and make up all the essential constituents of the body, from red blood cells to muscles to the brain. A mutation or a change in the genetic code (DNA) can cause disease. Examples may be found in sickle cell anaemia (the red blood cells are sickle shaped because of one mistake in the gene that "codes" for red blood cells) or cystic fibrosis (thick mucus is produced which blocks the lungs, again caused by a simple mistake in the code). Other changes, such as a change in chromosome number (as with the extra chromosome seen in Down's Syndrome), can also cause disease. The techniques used in gene therapy to combat these diseases will be different for the different types of change present.

2.2. How Is Gene Therapy Done?

Gene therapy involves the use of genetic engineering techniques in order to alter or replace defective genes in the human genome. In other words, the treatment attempts to cure genetically-based diseases by introducing normal genes in a patient to overcome defective genes. The techniques can either be performed on somatic cells (the cells that do not pass on genetic information to offspring, that is all cells in the body except for sperm and eggs) or on germ-line cells (sperm and eggs). The most radical techniques would involve the alteration of the defective gene in germ-line cells, which would mean that future generations would never get the disease.

2.3. Historical Trends

Gene therapy is not the first attempt to alter the genetic makeup of the human gene pool (variety of genes present in different humans). Eugenics developed the idea that continuous selection for breeding of the fit (i.e. those most well-adapted to the environment) and concomitant removal of unfit genes would be advantageous (Carter & Williams 1970; Penrose 1971; Sinsheimer 1987). However, this would need the co-operation and consent of the majority of the population. Eugenics has in the last fifty years come into disrepute because of its association with the Nazi era. The new eugenics, which would involve alteration of the germ-line cells, is quicker and more powerful.

3. Definitions of Ethical Frameworks

Ethics in relation to medical and genetic matters could be considered to have started with the ancient Greek Hippocratic Oath, which required physicians to "do no harm." Medical ethics then developed through the centuries, with the 1864 code of ethics by the American Medical Association and the Nuremberg Code of research ethics on human subjects, which was developed after World War II (McGee 1998). A number of theories have developed over the years that can be used as a basis for looking at ethical issues of gene therapy. These are discussed below.

3.1. Teleological Theory

In this theory "morally right actions are determined by their non-moral values" (Beauchamp & Childress 1983:19), with non-moral values being such things as pleasure, knowledge and friendship. In other words, the ethical action revolves around "the greatest good for the greatest number," a sort of global cost-benefit analysis (Moon 1995).

3.2. Deontological Theory

This theory is the opposite of the teleological theory above and was first unambiguously formulated by Kant. In this theory, duty is independent of the concept of good and "moral worth of an action is independent of consequences" (Beauchamp & Childress 1983; Moon 1995). Kant's categorical imperative has much to offer a discussion on gene therapy. It is:
1. act only in ways that you would want all others to act;
2. always treat other people with dignity and respect (Moon 1995).

3.3. Human Rights

A discussion of gene therapy is also a discussion of the important issue of human rights. A right is defined in terms of claims, with moral rights being defined in terms of moral principles and rules (Beauchamp & Childress 1983). One of the more relevant human rights with respect to gene therapy is the right to life and safety to which each individual is entitled.

3.4. Beauchamp & Childress' Four Principles

Beauchamp & Childress developed four principles with respect to biomedical ethics in 1983. These four principles are:

- AUTONOMY – to undertake moral and ethical action a person must be autonomous. Since the individual can determine his or her course of action, the individual's autonomy and so their right to choose must be taken into account.
- NONMALEFICENCE – this principle involves the belief that one should not do harm to an individual.
- BENEFICENCE – this involves the requirement that one must contribute to the welfare of the individual. Positive steps are required to fulfil this principle.
- JUSTICE – justice is comparative in that each individual has an equal claim to fairness and human rights. One must also act justly towards an individual, allowing them what is owed (Beauchamp & Childress 1983; Moon 1995).

3.5. UNESCO Framework

UNESCO set up a working committee as part of the International Bioethics Committee in 1995 (Edgar & Tursz 1995) to look at Human Gene Therapy and came up with the following minimum ethical framework when considering a gene therapy programme on humans:
1. the respect for human dignity and worth;
2. the right to equality before the law;
3. the protection of rights of vulnerable individuals;
4. the right not to be subjected without free consent to medical or scientific experimentation;

5. the right to the highest attainable standard of physical and mental health and associated rights to health care;
6. the right to protection against arbitrary interference with privacy or with the family;
7. the right to enjoy the benefits of scientific progress and its application; and,
8. the right to freedom for scientific research.

4. Ethical Issues with Respect To Research And Therapy

The first human trial of genetic therapy techniques to combat disease took place in 1990 when a child with ADA deficiency (bubble babies) was treated with some success. By 1998, over 300 gene therapy clinical trials involving 2,000 patients were under way (SCRIP 1998), although no one product had yet been approved for sale. It was initially thought that single-gene inherited diseases would be the easiest and first to be treated, but gene therapy applications to cancer, degenerative neurological diseases and HIV have proved popular. Approximately 57% of these clinical trials involved treatments for cancer with only 10% looking at inherited genetic disorders (Loss & Phillip 1998). The first approved gene therapy-derived cure is likely to be approved in 2000 in the U.S. and is a novel therapy to treat AIDS-associated blindness (CMV retinitis) developed by the pharmaceutical company Novartis (Loss & Phillip 1998).

4.1. Human Guinea Pigs

To be approved and sold to combat disease gene therapy must be tested on humans. The question of whether or not it is right to test on humans has been asked many times before in relation to therapeutic drugs and techniques and currently, all therapies need to undergo clinical trials to prove efficacy and safety prior to approval. However, the question is now more difficult because we are dealing with gene therapy that can alter human DNA. Any testing performed by physicians must not contradict the Hippocratic Oath, particularly in terms of not doing any harm. Platt (1970) holds that experimentation is only valid when it is considered that the risks are small, the benefits large and that any experimentation is for the patient's sake. But this begs the further question of whether experimentation to further research is ethically correct.

Much current work on gene therapy is necessarily experimental with no guarantee of success for the individuals on whom the experiments are being conducted, but with the prospect of success in the long term. Platt (1970) answers this question by suggesting that the researchers and clinicians must have a willing collaborator in the "guinea pig." The guinea pig must be fully informed of the experiment and not coerced in any way into becoming a test subject; he or she must also be made to understand that the experiment may not improve the quality of their life. Many people may view this as their last chance and they will therefore not necessarily act rationally (Cooper 1995).

While adult guinea pigs can exercise their right to choose, what about the rights of child guinea pigs, as well as the rights of the future generations brought into the world by the test subjects? The latter question will be dealt with below in the section on germ-line cells. The former question, however, poses a difficult dilemma: as children cannot necessarily articulate or even understand the problems associated with gene therapy, how can they make a choice? If they cannot make a choice, do their parents have a right to make the choice for them?

Many of these children may be suffering from dreadful genetic diseases that would give them a life span of only a few years, for example, Tay-Sachs, with no hope of alleviating their symptoms or delaying an untimely, and in some cases painful, death. Looking at it in this light presents an alternate view, that is, can parents deny their children the chance that experimental gene therapy may present? (French Anderson 1987). The ultimate responsibility lies with the parents (Carter & Williams 1970; Kieffer 1979).

4.2. Somatic Cells

The large majority of gene therapy techniques that are currently being used and developed are for somatic cell therapy (cells that do not pass genetic information on to offspring) because:
1. current understanding and discovery have only extended as far as somatic cell therapy;
2. as this therapy does not involve passing genetic material onto future generations, it is the choice of the individual.

Many people do believe that it is ethical to insert DNA into a human in order to alleviate suffering from a disease as long as it follows the strict guidelines used for clinical trials and approval of therapeutic drugs

(French Anderson 1987). Above all, human gene therapy must be safe, it must confer advantages to the sufferer and must ensure that there is not a transfer of DNA to germ-line cells by mistake (Berger 1995). Current thinking points to a public lack of knowledge over gene therapy, but a general acceptance of somatic cell therapy for the treatment of disease (Walters 1991).

4.3. Germ-line Cells

Germ-line gene therapy is now becoming theoretically possible to accomplish, although in a rough way, with researchers managing to clone a sheep (the famous Dolly) and producing numerous animal models for disease with technologies that could be applied to humans. This kind of gene therapy has not yet been conducted due to the technical and moral difficulties associated with it. However, it is important to discuss this issue now, because of it will possibly be used in the future and we have a responsibility to future generations. Will the inserted gene adversely affect any offspring or future generations?

It is impossible to predict with accuracy the effect of naturally occurring mutations (which may be benign) on genetically engineered DNA, and so the question arises as to whether is it ever ethical to pursue this type of therapy at all. (French Anderson 1987). Germ-line gene therapy would have greater societal impact than somatic cell therapy and therefore demands the consent of society as a whole (Harris 1992).

Kieffer (1979) summarises some of the issues that should be considered in connection with genetic responsibility:

- it is the right of every child to be born with a sound mind and body; determining what is genetically normal or acceptable is fraught with hazards;
- it is morally irresponsible to knowingly bear defective children; rather than considering the genetically handicapped as public health hazards, it is preferable to consider them a positive sign of genetic diversity;
- the determination of who is acceptable based on genetic categories can be too easily extended to other categories of social usefulness;
- individuals have a responsibility to the human gene pool.

French Anderson (1987) propounds three conditions that should be met before germ-line gene therapy is undertaken:

1. there should be considerable previous experience with somatic cell gene therapy;

2. there should be adequate animal studies that establish the reproduc-
ibility, reliability and safety of germ-line gene therapy;
3. there should be public awareness and approval of the procedure.

4.4. Prohibition of Research?

Even if there was a desire to prohibit or at least police this kind of
research, it would not be possible to do so. The only way to monitor it
would be to make it as open and as answerable to public opinion as
possible. Researchers themselves are not unethical. However, they sometimes do not consider the ethical issues involved in a piece of research
because they are too involved in it. In fact, by delaying research because
of concerns over misuse, further suffering could ensue for individuals
who have a genetic disease, which would in itself be unethical.

4.5. Gene Therapy for Enhancement

Developing somatic cell genetic therapies to treat life-threatening diseases seems to be becoming ethically acceptable. However, if researchers are able to treat diseases in this way they may also, theoretically, be
able to manipulate such characteristics as height, pattern baldness and
skin colour. Along with ethical and philosophical conundrums over enhancement issues, there is unlikely to be any consensus over the appeal
of each enhancement and the risk profile will be greater for cosmetic
gene therapy than for disease prevention and treatment (Wivel 1999).

5. Ethical Issues with Respect to Commercialisation

5.1. Should It Be Possible to Profit from Humans with Disease? Who Should Gain from Commercialisation?

Answers to the questions above can be arrived at by viewing current
practices in the pharmaceutical industry. As in the pharmaceutical industry developing drug therapies, there are high costs associated with
developing gene therapy, a long time frame and huge risks (Scott-Ram
1992). No company will be willing to invest the time and effort needed
without some guarantee of a pay-back. This relates to the current concentration on cancer and HIV therapies, where there are much larger
groups of people who are more willing to pay for treatment than those
with single-gene defects.

This pay-back also allows further research to continue through increased investment in the company. Other expenses are also incurred, including insurance, setting up clinical trials and pursuing patents. However, this still does not answer the first question of profiting from human suffering. This is not necessarily ethical as it does not follow the principle of justice as proposed by Beauchamp & Childress (see above). The sufferers must be treated justly and fairly and this can be more difficult if the pursuit of money gets in the way. Managers are therefore in an ethical quandary: who do they have more of an ethical responsibility to – the shareholders, for whom they must make a profit, or the consumers? (Strudler 1994). The answer depends on the viewpoint of the reader. In a sense, all the shareholders are consumers and therefore the managers have more of a responsibility to the consumers, but the shareholders are making an initial investment and therefore will demand their return first.

5.2. Patents

One of the ways that companies can retain the profits from their investments in gene therapy is through the use of patents. The world's main patent offices have all agreed that DNA and other living material is patentable (Scott-Ram 1992) but a number of arguments have been put forward against this. One of the more persuasive arguments is that products involving human DNA and proteins are a "discovery" and not an "invention", and are therefore unpatentable (Coghlan 1995). Alternatives to patents are being proposed, with some arguing that human DNA and proteins should be commonly owned by the public and in no way patented, and others suggesting using copyright (Coghlan 1995; Scott-Ram 1992). A further complication is relating the commercialisation of germ-line gene therapy to patents: what is a gene therapy and "artificial" in the first generation then becomes part of the gene pool may subsequently become "natural" in future generations. Can the patents relate to future generations?

5.3. Genetic Testing

An issue that is allied to gene therapy is that of genetic testing. This is a more developed field than gene therapy with a number of tests already available to either identify an individual as a carrier (i.e. they have a defective gene but do not develop the disease) or as a sufferer, for example tests for Tay-Sachs and Hodgkinson's. A pertinent ethical dilemma in this area is: is it right to test for a disease that cannot at this moment be cured? Genetic testing could lead to discrimination against the individual or family in a number of areas.

5.4. Job Refusal

If testing becomes commonplace, individuals with a genetic disease or a predisposition to a disease could be refused jobs. One argument for this is that blood or cells taken for genetic testing does not violate any rights, although others would argue that it violates the rights to privacy and the principles of nonmaleficence and justice. Some would argue that it is ethically incorrect to refuse a job on the grounds of genetic disease and it is the responsibility of the company with this knowledge to safeguard the health of the individual by making the work environment "safe" such as preventing those people with a predisposition to asthma from working in an non-conducive environment. Managers, though, may argue that they have a responsibility to their shareholders not to put an additional burden on their investment by employing someone who may require a lot of time off and sick pay, and in the U.S., insurance payments (Strudler 1994).

One of the major difficulties with the setting of company policy with respect to genetic testing is that managers may attach excessive importance to results from genetic testing. Another issue is that research is proceeding at such a pace that those people who are ill now may not be ill in the future with new gene therapies and pharmaceuticals. Another question arises from this issue: is this discrimination at all? By refusing to allow a blind person to be a taxi driver, we are not discriminating against him or her, we are in fact protecting their best interests. Is this not the same by protecting those with a predisposition for a genetic disease from working in an area that might aggravate their symptoms? (Strudler 1994).

5.5. Insurance Refusal

In the U.K., insurance has been refused to those found to have a predisposition to Hodgkinson's Disease. However, this is more of an issue in the US where employers pay for health insurance of their employees. The Disabilities Act of 1990 holds that genetic discrimination is illegal, but it does not cover insurance companies and so they can refuse insurance to those with a genetic disease (Kiernan 1995; Strudler 1994).

5.6. Social Prejudice

By discriminating against those with a genetic disease, stereotypes are being reinforced and disability is seen in an even worse light than currently. An underclass of "gene poor" people could develop (Taylor 1998). As Kieffer (1979) summarises: "the determination of who is acceptable based on genetic categories can be too easily extended to other categories of social usefulness."

This could exert ever-increasing pressure to abort foetuses found to have a genetic disease, or to genetically engineer or even to sterilise those with the genetic disease to stop them passing their genes to the rest of the gene pool. This ignores the important issue that diversity in the gene pool allows quick adaptation to changing surroundings, and the presence of eccentrics and geniuses. Without Van Gogh's mental problems would he have been able to produce the art that he did. Do we really want to live in a society where everyone is the same? It also ignores the principles of nonmaleficence and justice and basic human rights.

6. Conclusion

In this paper a number of issues have been discussed including the ethics of research, therapy and commercialisation of gene therapy using some ethical theories defined above. For instance, using the teleological theory the eradication of disease through gene therapy benefits the "greatest number" by reducing the monetary and social burden on society of those suffering from a genetic illness. Through discussion, scientists, politicians, health workers and other interested parties can work to find a solution.

However, in all of this discussion it must be remembered that: "Broad scientific, metaphysical, or religious beliefs often underlie our interpretation of a situation in which we must act" and so a universally acceptable code of ethics will be difficult to attain (Beauchamp & Childress 1983). The International Bioethics Committee (Edgar & Tursz 1995) has tried to develop a framework based on international standards. However, the extent of global ethical and cultural diversity means that a framework based on one set of scientific, metaphysical, and religious beliefs may be too restrictive.

Given that this is a global issue connected with collective "ownership" of the gene pool, an effort must be made to develop a global framework. With this revolutionary and powerful new technique to improve life, we must also link social responsibility, individual freedom and an ethical conscience. In fact, the pursuit of improvement of the conditions of life is one of the mainstays of the search for an ethical code (Curtin 1994).

Public opinion is also changing rapidly, and so what is unethical now may be ethical in the future and vice versa (Cooper 1995; Platt 1970). When in-vitro fertilisation (IVF) gave the first test-tube baby in 1978 there was much debate over the ethical implications of such a technique. It is now considered commonplace, although some ethical debate still surrounds assisted conception. Gene therapy is a complicated issue and further discussion should take place, for example, using a consensus committee to involve the public. This occurred with plant biotechnology (U.K. National Consensus on Plant Biotechnology).

References

Beale, G. 1971. "Social Effects of Research in Human Genetics." *The Social Impact of Modern Biology*, ed. W. Fuller. London: Routledge & Kegan Paul.

Beauchamp, T. L. & Childress, J. F. 1983. *Principles of Biomedical Ethics*. New York: Oxford University Press (2nd ed.).

Berger, A. 1995. "Safety Ruling Opens Gene Therapy to Women with CF." *New Scientist* 3 (June).

Carter, C. O. & Williams, B. 1970. "Genetics and Moral Responsibility." In *The British Broadcasting Corporation and the Contributors. Morals and Medicine*. London: Baylis & Sons Ltd.

Coghlan, A. 1995. "Licensed to Sell the Stuff of Life." *New Scientist* 11 February:12–3.

Coghlan. A. 1995. "Jumping Genes Pave the Way to Safer Therapy." *New Scientist* 18 March.

Coghlan, A. "Tumours Yield to Direct Approach". *New Scientist*.

Cooper, K. 1995. "Happy Anniversary, Strictly Speaking." *Journal of the American Society of CLU and CHFC* 49 (January):31–2.

Curtin, L. 1994. "Human Problems, Human Beings." *Nursing Management* 25 (May):35–9.

Edgar, H. & Tursz, T. 1995. "Report on Human Gene Therapy." UNESCO International Bioethics Committee Annual Report, chap. 3.

French Anderson, W. 1987. "Human Gene Therapy: Scientific and Ethical Considerations." In *Ethics, Reproduction and Genetic Control*, ed. R.F. Chadwick. London: Routledge.

Harris, J. 1992. *Wonderwoman and Superman: the Ethics of Human Biotechnology*. Oxford: University Press.

Harris, J. 1997. "Cloning and Bioethical Thinking". *Nature* 389.

Kieffer, G. H. 1979. *Bioethics: A Textbook of Issues*. Massachusetts: Addison-Wesley Publishing Company.

Kiernan, V. 1995. "U.S. Bans Gene Prejudice at Work." *New Scientist* 13 (May).

Loss, I. & Phillip, M. 1998. "Genetic Therapy." *HSBC Securities* 17 April.

McGee, G. 1998. "Bioethics: an Introduction." http://www.med.upenn.edu/~bioethics/outreach/bioforbegin/beginners.html.

Mestel, R. 1995. "High Hopes for Gene Therapy in Newborns." *New Scientist* 20 May.

Moon, C. 1995. *Lecture Notes on Business Ethics Full-time MBA*, London: Imperial College, University of London.

Orkin, S. H. & Motulsky, A. G. 1995. Report and Recommendation of the Panel to Assess the NIH Investment in Research on Gene Therapy, 7 December.

Penrose, L.S. 1971. "Ethics and Eugenics." In *The Social Impact of Modern Biology*, ed. W. Fuller. London: Routledge & Kegan Paul.

Platt, Rt. Hon. 1970. "The Lord. Human Guinea Pigs." In *The British Broadcasting Corporation and the Contributors. Morals and Medicine*. London: Baylis & Sons Ltd.

SCRIP. 1998. "Complete Guide to Gene Therapy." *SCRIP* (July).

Scott-Ram, N. 1992. "Biotechnology Patents – Issues, Problems and Perspectives." *SCRIP Magazine* (July/August):6–10.

Sinsheimer, R. L. 1987. "The Prospect of Designed Genetic Changes." In *Ethics, Reproduction and Genetic Control*, ed. R.F. Chadwick. London: Routledge.

Stock G. & Campbell, J. Summary Report: Engineering the Human Germline Symposium. UCLA Program on Science, Technology and Society.

Strudler, A. 1994. "The Social Construction of Genetic Abnormality: Ethical Implications for Managerial Decisions in the Workplace." *Journal of Business Ethics* 13 (November):839–48.

Taylor, R. 1998. "Superhumans." *New Scientist* 3 October.

U.K. National Consensus Conference on Plant Biotechnology. 1994. Final Report 2–4 November.

Walters, L. 1991. "Human Gene Therapy: Ethics and Public Policy." *Human Gene Therapy* 2:115–22.

Wilson. J. M. 1998. The Human Genome Project: Science, Law and Social Change in the 21st Century. The Institute for Human Gene Therapy. http://www.med.upenn.edu/ihgt/info/prospcts.html.

Wivel, N. 1999. Gene Transfer for Enhancement. http://www.med.upenn.edu/ihgt/info/topic1.html.

Health Food Products in China:
Are They Really Healthy?

Yan Guo
China Europe International
Business School (CEIBS)
Shanghai, China

1. The Emergence of the Health Food Market

Health food is a very popular word all over the world. According to the official definition, the term *health food* refers to a category of food products that not only bears the common food characteristics but also can regulate human physiological functionality, so that it can be applied to certain population group, although it does not aim for curing diseases (State Technical Inspection Bureau 1997).

This definition was, however, not made until 1997. The market had responded much earlier. The health food industry emerged from almost nothing to a remarkable industry in just a couple of years. In 1987 there were merely 100 manufacturers making a turnover of less than RMB1 billion. In 1994 this figure rose to over 3,000 manufacturers with a total sales of RMB30 billion (US$3.5 billion). The largest manufacturer alone topped RMB1 billion in sales that year (Lin Zhaojun 1998).

However, along with the quick growth, there were a lot of problems which in turn hampered the sound growth of the industry. In 1995, sales quickly dropped down to less than RMB25 billion. In the following years, coupled with an unfavorable economic situation, the market continued to shrink, although this year (1999) it is anticipated to bounce back a bit.

The emergence of the health food industry can in part be explained by economic growth. People are indeed much better off in recent years. For the first time they can afford something besides their basic needs. And the first thing they want to take care of is themselves. Aging is another important factor. Life expectancy is getting longer which means there are more elderly people who need to pay more attention to their health. However, there are many other things that contribute to the success of the health food industry.

The *herbal medicine concept*. Unlike in many other countries, traditional herbal medicine still plays an important role in China. The herbal medicine theory has one assertion that the food and the medicine are of the same origin. This means that some foods have therapeutic functions and can be used as drugs. Many people mistakenly generalize the idea and believe that all herbal medicines can be taken as food. Older people have more faith in herbal medicine than the young generation. I must say that herbal medicine is a precious heritage from our forefathers. Yet, it needs prudent scientific study. Some of the therapeutic functions are hard to explain from the modern medical viewpoint. Other functions are hard to evaluate. There are still others whose functions have been misused. Health food inherited this concept as well as many of the herbal medicines. And since these medicines are said to have been treated by modern technology, they are even more appealing to a worried public.

The *natural concept* is another influential factor in the health food industry. Some natural health food active ingredients are often called 'Neutraceutical' to indicate a rather harmless substance with special therapeutic effect. The new version of U.S. Pharmacopoeia even enlists some species. (The 9th Supplement of USP23/NF18 enlists Betadex, Cellacefate, Feverfew, Chamomile, Gingko, Oriental Ginseng, St. John's Wort, etc.) However, in the US, the ingredients are often simpler and more easily identified. The popular ones seem to be those recently published from medical research finding. They are nothing more than a simple or compound form of active ingredients, such as gingko biloba, spiranula, etc., whose functionality has been approved by research. In China, the word natural is also associated with "healthy," "clean," and "free from side effect." And since all herbal medicines are naturally grown, it is logical to market the products under this concept. The ingredients, however, are more complicated because they include both those introduced from the West and many others handed down as health enhancing food, although the functions are often untested.

Versatile functionalities is another alluring factor. Unlike modern synthetic medicine, in which each drug targets a single symptom or disease, traditional Chinese herbal medicine is believed to cure the patient through a holistic approach. One herbal medicine or a compound of different herbal medicines can have multiple effects that not only cure the disease but also strengthen the body. It is certainly a good deal to buy one product and cure all diseases and still build up the health. Many health foods have been promoted to be even more versatile than ever. The product brochures often include many functions that are appealing to even very healthy people.

2. Food or Drug?

Realizing the need to have some first-hand information on the health food market, I did my first investigation in a randomly selected store, in a supermarket in Minhang (near Shanghai) where I checked the health food counter. There were over 200 different kinds of health food on sales at this five-meter-long counter. Many of them are packed in the typical medicine package, small boxes that contain small jars, capsules or pills. And since the over-the-counter drugs were also on sale at the same counter, it was almost impossible for people to distinguish the health food from the medicine. There were quite a few leaflets scattered on the counters for promotional purposes. I picked up the one on the very top. It was a leaflet for a product in two variations. One was called *Heaven Spring*, which is an oral liquid. The other was called *Heaven Liquid*, which is actually a dilution of the same in liquor. Except for this difference, the claimed quality and functions are very similar. I must say that picking this leaflet was entirely out of convenience. Yet this leaflet is very typical in its claims among the industry. In order to illustrate many of the problems, I would like to use the descriptions on this leaflet as an example later.

Because of particular claimed curing functionalities, health food products should be classified as medicine and be put under supervision of the State Drug Administration (SDA). But in practice the majority of these products are marketed under the food category. The reason is simple: it is much more difficult to register a new drug than a new food. Although not so rigorous as in developed countries such as the United

States, in China, in order for a new drug to be introduced into the market, the marketer will have to supply numerous data on the drug's therapeutic effect, toxicology, etc. from a long period of clinical trials. The manufacturer also has to be approved by SDA, and the production procedure has to comply with good manufacturing practice (GMP). The product can only be sold through certain distribution channels. Advertising is also constrained. On the other hand, as a food product, the marketer only needs to obtain a production license and a hygienic license, which are much easier to obtain. There is virtually no special requirement on the distribution and promotion of a food product. Although new laws and regulations have gradually be introduced, the problem has never been fully solved.

3. Ethical Issues

There were reported complaints from the earliest growth of the health food industry. The earlier complaints focused on quality, such as low concentration, or on overly exaggerated advertisement. Most recently, questions were also raised on the functionality and on the possible long-term implications to human health. The consumption rush has finally calmed down during the past two years, although many brands still enjoy handsome sales. And with the shift in public interest, the media has gradually reduced the focus on these topics. However, many of the problems still exist today.

The first issue of ethical concern is the proclaimed *mysterious active substance*. In the U.S., most products contain one or more of the active ingredients whose functionality is known through scientific research. In China, however, the marketers specifically try to promote their products as containing something mysterious which works better than any known substance. They either claim to be a compound of Chinese traditional herbal medicines processed with modern technology, or they claim their products are extracted from such traditionally healthy foods as turtle, snake, pearl, etc. A few others have been taken from western medicine, such as taurine, cysteine, and docosahexenoic acid (DHA), etc. In this case, many marketers print out the ingredient name in a short form, like DHA, so that no one can really understand what it actually is. One particular Shanghai brand claimed to contain some miraculous bacteria that would "eat up body trash." For *Heaven Spring* and *Heaven Liquid*, the leaflet claimed that their main active substance is one precious herbal medicine that can not be found except in the plateau above 4,000 meters of the Qinghai-Tibetan region. Such herbal medicine, therefore, experiences both extreme cold and extreme heat in the same day. "The extreme weather molded its unique function," as claimed by the leaflet. That is not all. "The products are a combination of over forty different precious herbal medicines, extracted by using modern technology." The Heaven Liquid even has sort of a "Brandy taste." These mysterious substances enable the marketers to demand extra profit because of their rarity. Many consumers also like to pay for it because of their superstition. The problem is, since the active ingredients are not known, there is no way to verify the effectiveness in a scientific method.

With the different ingredients came the second problem of *their functions*. Before 1995, the marketing was so heavy that these health foods seemed to be more functional than any kind of drugs on earth. In 1995, however, the legislative authorities took some action, and now the ads have to be more modest. The new Food Hygiene Law prohibits any food products from claiming therapeutic functions. Even then, the functions as promoted by the marketers are dubious. The Heaven Spring and Heaven Liquid leaflet listed a total of thirteen "auxiliary" therapeutic functions, which would treat problems, including heart abnormality, hypertension, immune dysfunction, and cancer. Besides, there are "eleven nutritious therapeutic function."

A third problem is the *small size of dosage and its low active substance content*. Calcium pills are a good example. Due to the dietary structure in China, where people eat more vegetables and less meat and dairy products, the whole population lack calcium. An average adult would need about 400 milligrams calcium besides their food each day. Considering the absorption rate, he would need to take about 1.5 grams of calcium each day. But calcium pills contains so low calcium that he would have to take from 32 to 130 different calcium pills each day to meet that demand (Anonymous 1997)! The birds' nests is another case. Last time my mother-in-law came to see my wife and me, she bought as a gift one big pack of one brand of "Birds' Nest." Later we found out in a report that this brand contains so little birds' nest that it is hardly detectable during the quality inspection (Jia Lie et al. 1995). The birds' nest case is especially interesting in that it is estimated that the total available natural birds' nests in China is a mere dozens of kilos. Yet, the total proclaimed content in all the birds' nest health food added up to dozens of tons, a figure over one thousand times the actual amount!

That is, on average, one is enjoying 0.1 percent of the labeled amount that one has paid for. Clearly this is serious fraudulent behavior. However, before the *Administration Measures of Health Food Act* was enacted in 1996, no law required the content of the active ingredients to be labeled. Even if the labeling is correct, in the case of the calcium pills, the consumer still needs to have some knowledge as to the level of dosage to take the pills correctly. In the case of the bird's nest, no one has any knowledge of how much is the correct level.

The fourth problem is the *high price*. At present the prices for each package of ten gram oral liquid ranged between RMB5.98 to 209 (US$0.7–25). Very few brands are sold cheaper than RMB30, but plenty are over RMB100. And this price range is substantially lowered as compared with the peak year of 1994. The sheer prices makes it affordable to a substantial part of ordinary citizens. Yet considering the income level, this is by no means cheap. Furthermore, such a package is often only for a one-two weeks period, which means, on a per month basis, the expenses have to be at least double. One manufacturer priced his product at RMB200 per package, giving the vendor RMB90 per package discount. The cost of fish oil is less than RMB10 per bottle, the manufacturer sells at RMB15. But in the market the price averaged at RMB170–260 per bottle, a price more than 10 time the cost (Fei Zhiping 1999)! No wonder an executive from a fairly "honorable" manufacturer exclaimed: "the profits are just so attractive!" I do not mean high profit is bad. But the fact that people are willing to pay is certainly due to their belief in the nearly miraculous function of health food products. The customer is not interested in how much the marketer earns, but rather how much benefit one receives from the product. The marketer knows this very well and is thus able to shape the customer's beliefs by excess advertising. The question here is not high profitability per se, but rather the marketer's misleading information sent to the customer.

The last problem I want to discuss is the *potential threat to human health*. This problem is particularly acute to children. Given the absence of responsible clinical trials for a long enough period, the long-term effects of these products on human beings are unclear. One particularly popular brand that targets children is believed to contain steroids from such animals as the snake and the chicken. What long-terms effects this would have on children is not at all mentioned. And the general public has never put forward this question due to lack of proper medical knowledge. Such a problem is threatening because the effect will not show up until many years later. Who would take responsibility by then? What responsibility can be taken?

Effectiveness is the central part of all these problems. Is the mysterious ingredient effective, does it function as described, what is the proper dosage and level of concentration, is the effectiveness worth its cost, or does this effectiveness has any side effects? A more prudent and responsible approach would begin by conducting extensive research and taking clinical trials over a long period of time. The active ingredients have to be identified and tested. The problem, however, is that many of the manufacturers are too eager to make quick profits at the cost of the their customers.

4. Wide Concern

The issues concerning the health food raised wide publicity in China during the past few years because of the vast number of consumers who were directly affected. There are three interest groups concerned in this matter: the marketers who market the health food so heavily; the general public who consumes the products in the belief that they will enhance health; and the regulative authorities who should protect the interest of the people.

The general public who consumes the health food should be the beneficiaries of this industry. They are not and should not be experts in the products. They deserve the right to know the exact content, the detailed effects and the possible temporary and long-term side effects of the products. It is the marketers' responsibility to provide such information. However, the consumers do need to have basic knowledge on nutrition and health, so as to protect themselves from misleading information. They should also stay away from the superstition that there is some kind of elixir that can keep them healthy. For many exercise is the best medicine.

The administrative authorities have tried to regulate the market at the beginning of the industry. In 1987 the *Administration Measures on Health Drugs* was first endorsed. This was intended to include only some herbal medicine that has health functionality, but since the administration was delegated to authorities on the local level, the product range was soon out of control. It was not until recently, when the problem went out of control, that new legislation was introduced. In 1995, the first *Food Hygiene Law* was enacted. Based on this law, the Ministry of Health published the *Administration Measures of Health Food* in 1996. And in 1997, the *General Standards on Health (Function) Foods* was published. It stipulated the definition, basic principles, classification, technical prerequisites, testing methods, and labeling requirements, etc. The *Standards* also stipulated that the function food should also label the minimum (and in some case maximum) content of the active ingredients. Moreover, the labels "shall not introduce, describe or imply that the product has *curing* functions" (State Technical Inspection Bureau 1997). In January 1999, the state finally decided to abrogate the *Administration Measures on Health Drugs* (Peng Dan 1999).

The focus is still largely on *the marketers*. They have the legal and moral responsibility to ensure the quality and the function that their products claim to have. In those days when lacking regulatory standards, they were to make sure that careful study and clinical tests be performed to ensure safety and functionality. Even after the *General Standards on Health (Function) Foods* was published, many of these issues still exist. Though the compliance level is much higher today, some problems can never be solved simply by means of legislation. Some of the doubtful ingredients are still in use. The prices are still very high. Some imported brands or ingredients have the same problem.

5. Conclusion

The new laws require existing health food products to undergo a new registration procedure. Up to the beginning of 1999, there were some 1,400 products approved for sale. These were mainly the second generation health foods, whose safety have been recognized through time and medical research. However in this particular industry, the legal framework proved to be inadequate in many ways. Laws and regulations which are too rigid might destroy the vitality of the industry and might eliminate many potential products that might otherwise be very good to the human health. The solution to these problems is largely in the hands of the marketers. They should keep in mind their responsibilities for the public and provide those products that are developed under responsible evaluation of the functions and effects.

The consumers, in the meantime, should educate themselves to have a basic understanding of the advancement and limitations of modern life science. They will therefore be less likely to be persuaded by false claims of irresponsible marketers. Another point in the Chinese context is that the debilitated consumers should seek damages through possible legal actions. This not only can relieve their damage, but also set precedents for other consumers and perfect the laws.

The last thing I need to point out is people's view on health. Traditionally the Chinese people have not learned the fact that exercise is the key factor in keeping healthy. As a result, the majority of the population does not have enough exercise. So when people's health start to deteriorate, they do not realize that they would need more sport, but try to compensate by taking some kind of tonics. And health food is the latest version of tonic. If only people can have enough exercise, with the help of the health food, they would be much healthier.

References

Anonymous. 1997. "Calcium Supply Should Be Noted by the Public." *China Health & Nutrition* 3.

Anonymous. 1998. "Health Food Consumption: Follows the Ad." *Natural Health Products* 10.

Fei Zhi-ping. 1999. "Deep Sea Fish Oil: Sham as Genuine." *Jiefang Daily* 2 February.

Ji Mei. 1999. "China Health Products Market, Hard Now but Prospecting." *China Health & Nutrition* 1.

Jia Lie et al. 1995. "A Study on the Analysis of Bird's Nest Drinks." *China Food Hygiene* 9 April.

Jiang Pei-zhen et al. 1998. "An Analysis on the Demand for Health Food in Shanghai Urban Residents." *China Food Hygiene* 10.

Li Lian-da et al. 1998. "To Develop Function food with Chinese Characteristics." *Natural Health Products* 1.

Li Xiao-yu. 1998. "The Situation of Health Food Development and Administration." *China Food Hygiene* 10 June.

Lin Zhao-jun. 1998. "'Apollo' Ten Year's Gains and Losses." *Natural Health Products* 10.

Liu Jian-wen. 1998. "The Actuality and Prospect of Health Products Market." *China Health & Nutrition* 12.

Long Fu. 1998. "The Diet Food Market to Be Slimmed." *Natural Health Products* 8.

Peng Dan. 1999. "China Will Abrogate 'Health' Drugs." *China Chemical News* 4 February.

State Technical Inspection Bureau. 1997. "General Standard on Health (Function) Food." *China Health & Nutrition* 7.

USP23-NF18. Ninth Supplement 4490.

Ye Xing-qian. 1998. "Trends in US Health Food Development." *Natural Health Products* 3.

Ethical Dilemmas of Addictive Products' Promotion in America and in Poland

Bożena Kochman
University of Warsaw,
Warsaw, Poland

1. Business Ethics and Social Responsibility

In the last two or three decades business ethics has become an independent discipline spreading like a vine in the West, especially in the United States. In Poland as well efforts are being made to give this discipline academic status and to increase its role in the conduct of economic transactions. The intensive development and rapid institutionalization of business ethics may be easily explained by the fact that not only theoretical but also practical goals are placed before this discipline (Lewicka-Strzałecka 1996).

These practical objectives consist in "the relationship between the efficiency of human actions, their effectiveness in business and economic life, and the impact on the field of social action known as ethics" (Ryan 1996). Because of the diversity and complexity of various economic aspects it is difficult to define the real and precise nature of the last principle. According to Henry Hiż's definition "ethics is a property of social activity that must be judged by its results" (Ryan 1996).

The increasing call for more ethics and social responsibility created this new discipline and secured its strong position in the field of business. Wojciech W. Gasparski states that:

Business ethics task is to point out that among people the society is composed of those who not only believe in amoral business, but also many of those – business people included – who acknowledge the necessity of considering ethical frames of business activities … Business ethics does not destroy business, as some business people fear, it improves in the similar manner that engineering improves cars, not destroying them, but installing catalysts. This is the way to civilize technology and to civilize the economy (Gasparski 1996).

Such a philosophical approach towards business and ethics creates the need for defining the codes of conduct which state the norms people of business should follow. Every firm, institution or enterprise that wants to succeed has to adopt such a code. Especially public institutions like mass media must care about ethical behavior. Serving audiences is their task so they are constantly exposed to their judgment. When the matter is particularly disputable like, for instance, advertising of addictive products the mass media should definitely act according to their ethical criteria.

2. Advertising Ethics

In modern advertising the two operating ethical systems are (1) an external system based on mandated, institutional codes, guidelines, formal regulations, and organizational procedures and (2) a personal system that commonly relies on human judgement of what is right and wrong." The first system constitutes formal bodies such as governmental and industry regulatory guidelines, media advertising policies, and agency clearing practices. The second system is composed of individual decisions, which are made on the bases of the ethical assessment of the immediate and long-run effects of individual actions (Dunn et al. 1990:76).

Advertising practitioners nowadays are mostly conscious of ethical issues and have institutional standards and procedures in place to handle unethical practices. Business success is build on long-term considerations, and most individual advertising practitioners and their agencies operate in an ethical manner, knowing that actions taken in the short-run for personal and organizational gain might cost them more down the road – perhaps their job and their business. Thus, they strive to maintain high ethical standards and socially responsible advertising practices. Once a free-swinging, unchecked business activity, advertising is today a closely inspected and heavily regulated profession. Advertising's alleged past excesses and shortcomings have created layer of laws, regulations, and regulatory bodies. Consumer groups, governments, special interest groups, and even other advertisers now review, check, control, and change advertising.

3. General Government Advertising Regulations in America and in Poland

Both Polish and American governments have long struggled with the very controversial nature of this kind of advertising. They have tried to reach a consensus on whether to allow the companies to advertise alcohol and cigarettes in the mass media. A long lasting debate over its ethical dimensions is undertaken by various consumers groups, special interest parties and individuals. Opponents and defenders stick to their arguments which taken separately are in a way justifiable and right. Nonetheless, nobody can question the consequences of smoking and drinking alcohol and no one ought to ignore the frightening numbers of diseases and deaths these addictions cause. Thus, through the history lots of restrictions have been put into life in order to limit the advertisements of these harmful products.

In the U.S. different states have different regulations governing what can and what cannot be advertised and what can be depicted in ads. Some states forbid advertising for certain types of wine and liquor, and most states restrict the use of federal and state flags in advertising. But generally in America there is a ban on advertising hard liquors and its derivative products on TV and in the radio. The advertising industry is supervised by the advertisers themselves through transacting agreements and mutual controlling their own moves.

Twenty-five years ago the spirit producers and the mass media signed a voluntary agreement about not putting the hard alcohol ads on television which was later expanded to the radio. The advertisements of beer and wine are permissible on TV provided that good manners and caution are maintained and also that they are consistent with federal and state laws. However, in these ads, the advertisers should avoid presenting the act of drinking in front of video camera. It is forbidden to give the strength of the advertised drink, suggesting that it will make somebody stronger. As for the radio the advertisements of wine and beer are allowed under the condition that they are discreet and in the good taste.

Since 1971 advertising nicotine has been prohibited on TV and in the radio. In the press all the ads of tobacco products need to have a warning note with information about the bad influence on people's health.

In Poland, for the first time in its history, the law about education in sobriety and alcohol prevention creates integrated and complementary organizational system of activities in the sphere of prophylactic and solution of alcohol problems. The basic document in which the aims, strategies, methods and main tasks of government administration are stated is the National Program of Prophylactic and Solving Alcohol Problems. It was accepted by the government in August 1996.

On 29 September 1996 the new government regulation called Alcohol Prevention Law came into life in Poland according to which: "It if forbidden to carry out advertising of alcoholic drinks." That means displaying and showing alcoholic products. But the core issue is the definition of exactly what constitutes advertising, and that point remains ill-defined in the new law. The advertising of any beverage with more than 1.5% alcohol content has been illegal since 1992 in Poland. But advertisers, faced with minor infractions, defied the law often tacking amounts for fines onto bills for service.

Thus, outlawing alcohol ads is nothing new, but under the new law enacted in September alcohol advertising becomes a criminal act and carries a penalty ranking from zl.10,000 to zl. 500,000 ($3,571 to $178,571). Criminal status also means media offenders could lose their jobs and media organizations would be closed down. The sharpened guidelines address alcohol advertising as part of an overall regulation on alcohol in Poland.

The ban on cigarette advertising in Poland is restricted to radio and television, and cigarette companies now have to put larger health warnings in the press and on posters and billboards. According to the new "Anti-nicotine" amendment of Ministry of Health to the ruling from 5 December 1996 (enacted on 14 August 1996), the warning notes have to be twice as large as they were before and they have to cover the area of 20% of the ad. There is also change in the sentence which should say: "smoking cigarettes causes cancer and heart diseases." What is more it must be placed black on white or white on black in capital letters at the top of the advertisement.

4. Recent American Ethical Cases in Addictive Products Advertising and Promotion

The cases that I examine support the idea that any philosophy or course of action that does not take the public interest into consideration is vulnerable in today's business environment. Compared to earlier decades, today's firms face more critical public and governmental scrutiny and an environment in which regulatory and litigious actions are a constant possibility. The more enlightened business climate creates the need for a trusting relationship between a firm and its various publics. As a consequence of this new look at the world of economy today new discipline of business has emerged. It is called "business ethics"– "and is supposed to analyze moral rules in the economic world". This fresh discipline has encouraged people of business to seek higher moral standards and made them aware of various dilemmas and temptations. Unfortunately there is often not complete agreement as to what constitutes ethical behavior. At the extremes like for instance advertising of alcohol and tobacco there is not much dispute. With the increasing public consciousness and constant drive towards healthy lifestyle more and more people consider this issue as unethical and unacceptable. Things get even worse when the companies evidently target their products to already endangered communities like minority groups.

Let's take the example of two recent cases where targeting the ghetto with products that some saw as undesirable brought a crescendo of criticism. These were PowerMaster strong beer and Uptown cigarettes which have been subjected to community and ministerial protests charging that business firms were foisting unhealthy and unsafe products on susceptible and easily influenced ghetto youth. In the case of PowerMaster the sin was targeting malt liquor to ghetto youth via promotion by rock stars, billboard advertising, and a name that critics maintained was highly suggestive in the most negative sense. So PowerMaster and Uptown's aggressive advertising campaign met not only with the violent protests but also with the government support against these alleged perpetrators of abusive practices. Yet more sober observers raised the question of why black consumers could be allowed the same right to make their own buying decisions as whites.

As for morality and ethics of advertising and selling strong beer the comparison with other alcoholic alternatives is necessary. Gin, vodka, whisky, or even wine have far more alcoholic content than strong beer. However, in the example of PowerMaster where malt liquor is stronger than regular beer the difference is not so significant. The morality lies in the fact that this alcohol was advertised and sold in the endangered area, in the ghetto neighborhoods where the urban youth is highly responsive to the powerful promotion and becomes victims of unscrupulous marketers. What is also worth mentioning is that teenagers below the legal drinking age are exposed to the advertisements as well and they are tempted by young drinkers in the nice surroundings. Thus, when it comes to underage drinking the critics condemn advertising of beer and wish it would be banned from TV and the radio.

It is generally accepted that minority groups are more easily swayed and far more vulnerable to aggressive promotional blandishments. But defenders of beer and liquor marketing disapprove of the ill defined paternalism and they favor people's free choice of the products. According to them no one ought to tell them what they should and what they should not consume.

Another aspect of defense is that since 1935 it has been illegal for beers to advertise their alcoholic strength in commercials or on containers so full disclosure of alcohol content is impossible and thus the public cannot be well informed. This is one of the reasons for the questioning ethics behind advertising beer because the public cannot weigh the possible dangers against the pleasures.

Related to this round of denunciations was another event that received even wider attention: Joe Camel, the cartoon character in the promotion of Camel cigarettes, which somehow and without reasonable expectations found an almost unprecedented appeal-to children. The potential for such a beloved cartoon character to influence children to smoke was appalling and unacceptable to large sectors of American society, including the American Medical Association.

The next move of the American cigarette industry which was also met with public negative opinion was turning its promotional efforts overseas. As the Western Europe proved to be inefficient market the U.S. tobacco industry focused its attention and aggressive promotional efforts on more hospitable grounds of Eastern Europe, the Far East, and developing countries. Considering their vulnerable market and susceptibility towards American influence some Western cigarettes like Marlboro for instance are better recognized there than in the U.S. The image of a cowboy on the Western environment creates the special and exotic atmosphere which adds additional value to the Philip Morris brand.

Analyzing the overseas push by U.S. tobacco firms we should point out that it is widely accepted that every company has the right to improve its financial conditions and strengthen position on the market. When the firm is prosperous enough it is free to enlarge its market to other countries no matter what kind of products or services it offers. Nevertheless, we can question the ethics of promoting the use of tobacco in foreign countries when the industry is under a health cloud in the United States where most mass media promotion is banned. The other issue is that although cigarette smoking is generally considered dangerous to health even life threatening no one is entitled to judge the tobacco makers, growers, advertisers and retailers negatively if the tobacco users smoke consciously with their own responsibility. The same argument of what is ethical speaks for targeting foreign markets and minority segments by tobacco industry. After all the individuals are free to decide about themselves.

Pertaining to these criticized promotional strategies is the sponsorship of such athletic events as the Virginia Slims Tennis Tournament, geared to healthy young women athletes but supported by a product deemed anathema to good health by medical experts and a substantial part of society. This is the sphere where social and ethical dilemmas prevail. On one side there is an unhealthy product, agreed upon by all specialists except tobacco industry, and on the other side there is sponsorship of athletic events for women which probably wouldn't be held without such financial help. So let's try to answer the following questions objectively: Do we refuse to accept this sponsorship? Do we ban all cigarette promotion that appear to have some tie-in with health and fitness? Does the evil outweigh the good?

Although there are so many ethical controversial issues in the U.S. no one can argue that American mass media are the world's most diverse, rich and free. But their dazzling resources, variety and influence cannot be rated by the envy they arouse in other countries. Their failures are commonly excused on the grounds that they give people what they want. A world of new communication technology requires a coherent national policy, respectful to the American tradition of free expression and subject to constant public scrutiny and debate.

No tenet of American democracy is more fundamental or more jealously guarded than freedom of expression in the media, enshrined in the First Amendment. This is the argument that advertisers of addictive products such as alcohol and cigarettes often remind of. They say that restrictions that deprive the consumer of information are considered unconstitutional.

5. Polish Ethical Controversies in Alcohol
and Cigarette Advertising and Promotion

Considering the case of Łańcut Distillery, I can say that this company and generally all Polish liquor producers do not use such aggressive promotional strategies as companies from the Western countries. It is true that they use other possible ways to inform the public about their products but their strategies do not take drastic forms like targeting towards minorities, youth or foreign markets. Maybe it is connected with still developing advertising field of business in Poland or maybe with the whole concentration on the American leader companies and their advertising tactics.

The marketing executives of Łańcut Distillery state that the new regulation from 9 December 1996 highly restricted advertising industry and it 'tied hands' of domestic spirit producers especially. It discriminates Polish liquor makers and leaves free market to foreign products which are still advertised in foreign TV stations through satellite television. The adds of alcohol can also be found in air flights where the ban on alcohol doesn't reach and it again makes foreign industry in a favorable position.

The executives admit that the new law will limit the sales of Łańcut Distillery and other domestic products in some way and foreign liquor makers will benefit from it significantly. Everybody is familiar with the saying that 'Advertising is the base of trade' so nobody should expect the increase of sales in this situation. But as it is already visible on the Polish market the spirit companies try hard to find other ways to circumvent the ban and successfully advertise their products in the radio and on the billboards, especially, under the cover of non-alcoholic drinks. It is particularly popular with the beer industry. The public is flooded with the ads of non-alcoholic beer and other ways of reminding customers of the beer brands. It is enough to turn on the radio and in a minute you will hear spots like "EB sound", "TYSKIE playing" or "BROK'n'Roll". Therefore, this is the sphere where the relationship between ethical conduct and the law is confusing and raises lots of rhetoric questions.

Liquor makers, faced with so much fuss about the ethics and morality behind advertising, often emphasize that even if alcohol and cigarettes were not advertised the consumption of them would not fall anyway. They are positive that without the ads many people would still be addicted if they are not able to control their indulgences. The whole matter consist in the fight for the culture of responsible drinking particularly of high percent alcoholic beverages. And this liability falls within the liquor producers' cognizance and also others like institutions and authorities dealing with education and dissemination of cultural alcohol using. What can be added is the fact that nobody forces customers to buy and use the specific brand in the excessive amounts.

Taking the legislation into consideration the spirit makers think that advertising alcohol and other addictive products IS ethical because it leaves to the potential client or the receiver of the ad the possibility of choice. The pure information does not equal with the force to purchase a product.

6. Conclusion

All the examples that I have presented consider the ethical aspects of the business which are most often debated nowadays. Since "Business Ethics" strengthened its position on the economic market these cases will long remain hot and touchy. However, when a company wants to succeed or remain in business it must learn from its own mistakes or from other firms. It must be wary and take care to avoid situations and actions that clearly violate the socially accepted norms of behavior and thus might harm its trusting relationship with the general public.

References

Dunn, W., Barban, A. M., Krugman, D. M., Reid, L. N. 1990. *Advertising. Its Role in Modern Marketing*. The Driden Press.
Gasparski, W. W. 1996.
Lewicka-Strzałecka, A. 1996. "Moral Reasoning in Business Ethics." In *Human Action in Business*, eds. Wojciech W. Gasparski and Leo V. Ryan. New Brunswick: Transaction Publishers.
Ryan, L. V. 1996. "Introduction." In *Human Action in Business*, eds. Wojciech W. Gasparski and Leo V. Ryan. New Brunswick: Transaction Publishers.

PART FOUR

Corporate Case Studies

Values Behind Strategic Management: the Alima-Gerber Case

Agnieszka Szumska
American Studies Center
Warsaw University
Warsaw, Poland

1. Introduction

As the business environment becomes increasingly competitive and dynamic, strategic thinking becomes more critical. It cannot be forgotten that formulation, implementation and control of the organization's strategy depend on human input into the company's operations. Thus, interpersonal relationships and values shared are important factors in the organization's performance.

This paper is an attempt to prove that *human involvement in strategic management is a key factor for successful Alima-Gerber operations.* The company has been chosen by no accident. Alima-Gerber represents one of the first examples of privatized capital in Poland. Due to American capital investments and continuous efforts to improve the firm's competitive position Alima-Gerber has been in the forefront of the best developing companies in the south-east region of Poland and is a national leader in the baby food industry.

Chapter Two of this paper explores the concept of strategy, strategic management, and their importance for the company's performance. Chapter Three discusses the first stage of the strategic management process, that is determining the mission and goals of an organization. They are used as a yardstick against which the company's success is measured. Prior to selecting a strategy, top managers evaluate the company's competitive situation by matching its strengths and weaknesses with the environment's opportunities and threats. This is the subject matter of Chapter Four. Only then can an organization decide about the strategy it wants to adopt. Chapter Five considers formulation of the corporate-level, business-level, an functional-level strategies. Strategy implementation, discussed in Chapter Six, is the work of the entire organization. The company's structure and culture are the two tools for implementing the strategy. Lastly, Chapter Seven explores strategic control, that is monitoring the organization's progress in attaining its goals.

2. Strategic Management – the Concept

The greatest challenge for a successful organization is change and uncertainty accompanying it. Therefore, a company develops its strategy which provides a way to deal with change. A strategy gives direction to diverse activities, even though the conditions under which those activities are carried out are rapidly changing.

Alfred Chandler states that strategy "is the determination of the basic long-term goals and objectives of an enterprise, and the adoption of courses of action and the allocation of resources necessary for carrying out these goals" (in Cole 1994).

Strategic management can be viewed as a series of steps in which top management ought to accomplish the following tasks:

1. Establish the organization's mission and develop its goals.
2. Conduct competitive analysis (analyze the opportunities and threats that exist in the external environment, and examine the organization's internal strengths and weaknesses).
3. Develop strategies (corporate strategies, business unit strategies, and functional strategies) in the context of external environment's opportunities and threats, and the organization's strengths and weaknesses, and matching the organization's mission and goals.
4. Implement the strategies.
5. Get involved in strategic control and modify either the strategy or its implementation to ensure that the desired outcomes are attained (Bartol & Martin 1991).

Although the chief executive officer is ultimately responsible for the organization's strategic management, he or she relies on other individuals, including members of the board of directors and other top managers.

There is a strong positive relationship between strategic management and good performance of a company. A primary benefit is that it provides an organization with consistency of action. Additionally, strategic management process forces managers to be more proactive and conscious of their environments. Lastly, the process involves different levels of management which encourages commitment on the part of participating managers and reduces resistance to proposed change.

In the face of fundamental changes in the environment or the internal situation, it may be necessary to modify or change the strategy itself. The strategic management process must be in place to ensure continuous reevaluation of these key elements and determine whether changes are needed.

3. Organizational Direction

Organizations are founded for a purpose. It is vital that stakeholders understand the reason for the company's existence, that is, the company's mission. It "sets a business apart from other firms of its type and indentifies the scope of its operations in product and market terms" (Rue & Holland 1989). It is also the first stage of formulating the company's culture (Zbiegień-Maciąg 1996:35).

The mission statement of an organization, at the corporate level, is stated in fairly broad terms. Gerber Products Company corporate mission is as follows:

> The people and resources of Gerber Products Company and its affiliated companies are dedicated to providing quality products and services at reasonable prices, and to meeting the needs of our customers in a responsible and responsive manner as we have for more than three generations (Rue & Holland 1989).

In establishing goals and objectives a clear sense of the company's purpose is necessary, because it is difficult to know where one is going if one does not first know who one is. Goals represent the desired general ends toward which all efforts are directed. Objectives are specific, and often quantified, versions of goals. They permit the assessment of organizational performace.

The values and needs of those who set goals will greatly influence the goals that are finally established. Since any group consists of nu-

merous individuals and every individual's values and actions constitute the group performance, as Ludvig von Mises claims, it is of vital
importance to coordinate the human force in order to avoid disintegra-
tion (von Mises 1949). Because of the diversity of these interests, top
management and board of directors face the difficult task of attempting to reconcile and satisfy each of the stakeholder groups, while pursuing their own sets of goals. By the successful balancing of various,
and often conflicting goals, management proves its unique value to
the organization.

In case of Gerber Products Company, the result is as follows:

> Corporate Management will provide strategic planning and direction to:
> - maintain our position of leadership in the marketplace
> - maintain our recognition as an authority in the field of infant health, nutrition, and care
> - grow through aggressive consumer marketing and sound diversification and acquisitions
> - protect and increase the value of our shareholders' investments (see Rue & Holland 1989).

Businesses are expected to operate in a manner consistent with society's interests. Social responsibility can be defined as "the moral and
ethical content of managerial and corporate decisions over and above
the programmatic requirements imposed by legal principle and the market economy" (see Rue & Holland 1989).

In the Gerber Products Company mission statement we read:

> We strive to meet our social responsibilities and to improve the quality of life
> for our customers, our communities, our shareholders, and our employees.
> Our reputation, established on honesty and quality, is a heritage we treasure
> and must continue to earn every day. We commit ourselves and pledge our
> resources to the continued quest for excellence so that future generations may
> also recognize and rely upon the integrity of Gerber Products Company (see
> Rue & Holland 1989).

Ethics of individual managers are closely related to issues of corporate social responsibility. Ethics is concerned with what is right and what
is wrong. It is normative and prescriptive, not neutral. It addresses
a question of what ought to be.

Because businesses exercise such a pervasive influence upon the economic, political, and social life, the general public has the right to expect
high standards of moral conduct from business executives as individuals
and from the corporation as a whole. Therefore, effectiveness and effi-

ciency, which as praxiological dimensions characterize human action, must be supplemented with the third dimension – ethics (von Mises 1949).

4. Organization's Competitive Situation

Before managers can devise an effective strategy, they need to analyze the organization's competitive situation. Such an assessment can be made with SWOT analysis. It is a method of analyzing the organization's competitive situation that involves assessing organizational strengths and weaknesses as well as environmental opportunities and threats. The company's macroenvironment is formed by political-legal, economic, technological, and social systems and trends which affect all firms.

As an example of the impact of political-legal sector on Alima-Gerber's operations, consider the Polish tax law that provided tax relief to firms with foreign capital. The condition was to purchase shares for at least ECU 2 million (about $ 2.6 million) in companies operating in areas threatened by unemployment. Thanks to it Alima-Gerber was exempted from the income tax amounting to $ 11 million (Świderek 1992).

Economic forces, such as gross national product, interest rates, and inflation, also have a significant impact on business operations. The effects of technological changes are expressed in new products or services, alternate processing methods and changes in complementary products or services.

As regards social forces, population trends can dramatically affect business opportunities. Since bottoming out in 1975 at 3.2 million, the birth rate in the United States was continuously rising throughout the 1980s. It definitely was a positive phenomenon for Gerber Products Company. In recent years, however, Gerber overestimated the U.S. birth rates, and as a result, it overproduced. Gerber had to look for other markets, like the Polish market where it could sell its products.

Managers recognize the various opportunities or threats arising from macroenvironmental changes through environmental scanning – the gathering and analysis of information about relevant environmental trends. Companies that produce competing goods or services operate in a more specific environment – an industry environment. From the praxiological point of view competition is not looked at as fighting for market share, and strategy has a solely metaphorical meaning. The role of the competition consists in assigning every member of the social system the job which they are best at so as they would be better able to serve the whole community and all its members (von Mises 1949).

Porter argues that there are five forces which work together to determine the type and direction of pressures on profitability that will be found in a given industry. They include: rivalry among existing competitors, threat of new entrants, threat of substitute products, bargaining power of buyers, and bargaining power of suppliers (Porter 1979:84–8; Porter 1980).

Intensity of rivalry manifests itself in the form of price cutting, advertising battles, new-product introductions or modifications, and better consumer service. In the United States, about 85% of the baby food market is controlled by only three national brands: Gerber, Heinz, and Beech-Nut. In 1984 Gerber's market share was 70.9%, while Beech-Nut's was 15.8%, and Heinz's only 13.2% (Rue & Holland 1989).

On the Polish market, Alima-Gerber has an 85% share of juice market with the certificate of the Institute of Mother and Child. On the baby food market Alima-Gerber is a winner having 60% market share (Unsigned 1996c). It is extremely difficult for new entrants to compete against Gerber's long established quality image and economies of scale it has achieved in baby food production. Substitute products are alternative products that satisfy similar consumer needs but differ in specific characteristics. Heinz instant baby food is a major threat confronting Gerber. Nevertheless, both companies are vulnerable to the use of home processed baby food.

The more buyers are able to dictate the terms under which they will make their purchases, the more powerful they are. If suppliers are in position to dictate the terms on which supplies will be obtained, they are said to be powerful. The baby food firms generally have the upper hand with regard to ease of change in suppliers, due to the large number of suppliers available to them.

In conducting a competitive analysis, the company's management also needs to give considerable attention to how organizational factors affect the competitive situation of the company. The firm's organizational factors include: organizational, human, and physical resouces. In an optimal setting, all three types work together to give the firm a sustained competitive advantage.

Organizational resources include functional areas like finance, marketing, production, research and development, and other. Financial analysis shows much about the financial resources of the firm and how well they have been utilized.

Analysis of the marketing function requires inclusion of the product-market issues, and much of that is external to the company. Today, Gerber's main thrust in promotion is in direct mail advertising and sampling. Through its marketing research division, Gerber purchases various lists from hospitals of families with new infants. The mail sent to the parents includes information on company products and booklets on infant care. The company reaches 90% of parents with babies through hospital kits or mailings (Rue & Holland 1989).

A firm's production department communicates and interacts very closely with the research and development group. Alima-Gerber specialists put much attention to maintaining high quality of their products. The Alima-Gerber's advantage lies in the fact that it knows how to process baby foods without destroying their nutritive value (Rudolf 1995). All Alima-Gerber products are prepared under the supervision of and recommended by the Mother and Child Institute.

Even the most superb organizational and physical resources are useless without a talented work force of managers and employees. Each firm's human resources (HR) are unique. This uniqueness stems not only from the fact that every organization employs a different set of human beings, but also from the specific synergies that are the effect of combining each company's HR with its particular organizational and physical resources. In this context, the organization's personnel and their knowledge, abilities, commitment, and performance reflect the firm's HR programs. Al Piergallini, Gerber's chief executive officer, believes that Alima-Gerber's most valuable assets are the company's management and employee qualifications (Choroszy 1992).

Physical resources are one of the key elements for successful company operations. Within two years from Alima-Gerber acquisition (till 1994), Gerber invested $11 million in machines, equipment ans other fixed assets of the company (Nowiny 1994).

5. Strategy Development

Having made the macroenvironmental and industry analysis, and the assessment of the organization's strengths and weaknesses, the managers must consider strategic alternatives. Many organizations develop strategies at three different levels: corporate level, business level, and functional level (Bartol & Martin 1991:192–4).

Corporate-level strategy addresses the overall strategy that an organization will follow. Corporate strategy development involves selecting by the company's managers a grand strategy and using portfolio analysis to determine the various businesses that make up the organization.

A grand strategy provides the basic strategic direction at the corporate level. Strategic alternatives at this level can be placed into one of the four basic categories: growth startegies, stability strategies, defensive strategies, and combination of the previous three.

Growth strategies are selected by firms to increase their profits, sales, or market share. They are used by U.S. businesses more often than all the other strategies altogether. Growth strategies have been adopted by Gerber Products Company. The key growth strategies are: concentration, vertical integration, diversification.

A concentration strategy focuses on a single product or service, or on a small number of closely related products. There are three approaches to pursuing a concentration strategy: market development, product development, horizontal integration. One of the examples of market development is as follows: In the 1960s, Gerber Products Company expanded into many foreign countries. Today, Gerber foods are available in 160 countries around the world (Rue & Holland 1989). Horizontal integration occurs when a company adds one or more businesses that produce similar products or operate at the same stage in the product-market chain. This happened when Gerber bought 60% of Alima's stock in 1992. Now, Gerber owns over 99% of Alima-Gerber shares (Unsigned 1996c).

Vertical integration occurs when a business moves into areas that serve either as suppliers to or customers for the company's products. When a business grows by becoming its own supplier, the process is known as backward integration. If a business integrates by moving into an area that serves as a customer of its products, the process is referred to as forward integration.

Diversification takes place when an organization moves into areas that are clearly distinct from its current businesses. There are two types of diversification strategies: concentric diversification, and conglomerate diversification. Baby foods are the product for which Gerber is best known. But in 1960, Gerber extended its product line to nonfood products. A vinyl baby pants and bibs manufacturer was acquired. Gerber also has a furniture division which offers chests, cribs, car seats, mattresses, and humidifiers, and operates an insurance business (Nowa Europa 1994).

All the previously discussed growth strategies can be implemented either through: internal growth, acquisition, merger, or joint venture. Stability strategy is adopted when an organization is satisfied with its current situation and wants to maintain its size and current lines of business. Defensive strategies are used when the firm's performance is disappointing or, at the extreme, its survival is at stake. They may take the form of: turnaround, divestment, or liquidation. Combination strategies are used when a company simultaneously employs different strategies for different organizational units. In fact, most multi-business organizations use some sort of combination strategies.

Many firms operate multiple business units in different environments and various situations. The most frequently used portfolio analysis is the Boston Consulting Group (BCG) growth-share matrix. It uses relative market share and market growth rate to compare the businesses in a corporate portfolio.

The *star* is a fast-growth, high-share business. It requires considerable investment to finance its growth. The *cash cow* is low-growth, high-share business, like the Gerber's baby foods group. This established and successful SBU needs less investment to hold its market share. Thus, it produces a lot of cash that the company uses to pay its bills and to support other SBUs that need investment. The *question mark* is a low-share SBU in high-growth market. The *dog* is a low-growth, low-share business, like the Gerber's children's apparel, furniture, and insurance groups. They may generate enough cash to maintain itself, but do not promise to be large sources of cash.

The strategic question at the corporate level was: In what industries or businesses should the organization operate? The appropriate question at the business unit level is: How should a company compete in the chosen industry or business? Michael Porter has outlined three generic *business-level strategies* that can be followed to gain competitive advantage over firms operating in the same industry. These are: cost leadership, differentiation, and focus strategies (Porter 1980). "Generic" means that they can be widely applicable to a variety of situations.

Cost leadership strategy emphasizes organizational efficiency so that the costs of providing products and services are lower than those of competition. One of the main threats to Gerber is the fact that Heinz sells its baby food products to the grocer at a lower price than Gerber. While Heinz has a cost advantage over Gerber, the latter emphasizes excellent quality control standards in the production process (see Rue & Holland 1989).

Differentiation strategy, adopted by Gerber, involves developing products and services that are perceived as unique in the industry. Gerber has established a reputation of being trustworthy since it was the first company to enter into the baby food market. For over 50 years, Gerber has dedicated all its efforts to providing quality products. The Gerber baby is a symbol for quality and is recognized and trusted by more parents than any other trademark in baby products. The slogan "Babies Are Our Business" became one of the best known mottos in many countries, and is still prevalent in advertising and in consumers' minds (see Rue & Holland 1989).

When following a focus strategy, the business specializes by establishing a position of overall cost leadership, differentiation, or both, but only within a particular market segment; not industrywide.

The appropriate generic strategy would depend, at least to some extent, upon the particular stage of its industry's life cycle. In theory, an industry progresses through certain stages during the course of its life cycle: embryonic, growth, shakeout, maturity, decline. The U.S. baby food industry is in the maturity stage. It is reached when the market demand for the industry's outputs is completely saturated. Almost all purchases are limited to replacement demand, and industry growth is either low or nonexistent. In some cases it might be even negative.

The business's competitive status and the external forces in its industry life cycle stage determine which generic strategy is appropriate for a given business unit. Gerber has adopted a differentiation strategy with the baby food industry in the maturity stage. At this stage the industry approaches zero or even negative growth, there is an emphasis on cutting costs and/or differentiating products to maintain sales levels. Without market expansion, competing successfully with high prices becomes increasingly difficult. Smaller businesses are likely to adopt either the focus:low-cost or focus:differentiation strategy, whereas larger businesses would follow the low-cost or differentiation strategy. Gerber is following the differentiation strategy.

After developing corporate-level and business unit strategies, management must turn its attention to formulating *functional strategies* for each business unit's functional areas. All organizations, regardless of their size, must perform certain functions: purchasing and materials management, production/operations management, finance, research and development, human resources, marketing. The role of functional strategies is spelling out the specific ways that functional areas can be used to support and strengthen the business-level strategy.

Purchasing and materials management functional area holds responsibility for the procurement of materials that are later processed by the production department into finished products for the marketing function to sell. Organizations that use the differentiation strategies, like Gerber, stress the procurement of high-quality inputs, even if they cost more than alternative offerings.

Production/operations management (POM) involves the process of transforming inputs (raw materials and parts) into outputs. Businesses following the differentiation strategy stress POM strategies that yield superior quality, which is true of Gerber Products Company. Gerber's corporate mission states that: "The people and resources of Gerber Products Company and its affiliated companies are dedicated to providing quality products and services" (see Rue & Holland 1989). This is achieved by employing the total quality management system. The company looks to appropriate choice of raw materials, packaging, and technological processes as well as to assuring good sanitary conditions on production lines, storage rooms, and transportation (Sznajdrowska).

The finance function includes not only cash management, but also the use of credit and decisions regarding capital investments. Business units that adopt the differentiation generic strategies, Gerber among them, employ financial strategies that fund quality improvements. They place the highest strategic priority on quality rather than on financial considerations.

Research and development (R&D) area has two basic components: product/service R&D and process R&D. Gerber, which competes with differentiation strategy within its baby food business, engages in product/service R&D. Gerber First Foods fruits and vegetables introduced in October 1986, captured 9% of the baby food market by the end of fiscal year 1987. New products introduced by Gerber between 1980 and 1989 account for 15.8% of the total Gerber food line (see Rue & Holland 1989).

All functional areas depend on the availability of human resources (HR) to implement the strategy. HR management aims to build a work force that enables the organization to achieve its goals. It involves planning for future HR needs, recruiting personnel, placing people in jobs, compensating them, evaluating their performance, developing them into more effective employees, and enhancing their work environment. All the Alima-Gerber workers have the opportunity to learn English. The company spares no expense on specialist courses and training (Barlik 1996). Business units that adopt the focus:differentiation or differentiation strategy should form reward systems that encourage output improvements and innovations. In Alima-Gerber, the Commission of Posts Evaluation developed a job evaluation and employee ranking system. The most important criterion in this system is the expertise, and in it: innovativeness, creativity, professional education, and experience (Unsigned 1995).

Marketing consists of four strategic Ps: product/service, pricing, place (distribution), and promotion. How these various marketing strategies are planned and executed depends on the particular generic strategy adopted by the business unit.

In the 1950s, Gerber was the first baby food company to use television advertising. Today, the firm reaches 90% of its customers (parents with babies) mainly through direct mail advertising and sampling (see Rue & Holland 1989).

It is essential that the business unit's functional areas be tightly integrated. A company that is able to mesh its functional strategies smoothly is more likely to attain a competitive advantage based on superior product design, superior customer service, and superior speed.

6. Strategy Implementation

Strategies not only must be well formulated to match environmental opportunities and threats, but also must be carried out effectively to assure an organization's success. Strategic implementation requires managers to consider two aspects: organizational structure and corporate culture.

Achieving a fit between strategy and structure is a complex process involving decisions about how activities will be grouped and how groups will be coordinated.

The company can grow in two directions: vertical and horizontal. Vertical growth is the increase in the number of levels in the company's hierarchy. The number of employees accountable to each manager represents that manager's span of control. The organization which is comprised of many hierarchical levels and narrow spans of control is called a tall organization. Alima-Gerber represents this organizational type. Because of a narrow span of control, managers have a relatively high degree of control over their subordinates. Additionally, jobs of both managers and employees in tall organizations tend to be narrowly specialized. As a result, authority in this type of a company is usually centralized at the top of the hierarchy. A flat organization, unlike the tall organization, has a few levels in its hierarchy and a wide span of control.

Horizontal growth is the increase in the breadth of the organization's structure. This is done through segmentaion of the organization into departments and divisions to accomodate the development of more specialized functions. A company may adopt one of a number of different structural types to implement its strategy, such as: entrepreneurial structure, functional structure, divisional structure, matrix structure (Rue & Holland 1989:210). Entrepreneurial type is used by small businesses, which consist of an owner-manager and a few employees. At this stage, no formal assignment of responsibilities is necessary.

As the company grows, the President, once involved in all functions of the enterprise, finds that his or her role is becoming less operational and more managerial. Each of the new employees is assigned to perform a specialized function. The functional structure is a combination of similar activities and the separation of dissimilar activities on the basis of function. Alima-Gerber has adopted this structural type. Alima-Gerber's functional areas have been characterized in detail in Chapter Four.

The supreme authority in the company is the Board of Directors whose task is to coordinate the work of functional departments. The board monitors results of executive leadership, approves mission and strategies proposed by top management, determines executive compensation and holds responsibility for governance. At Alima-Gerber the authority is granted to its: Board of Directors, Supervising Board, Shareholders Meeting (Statute of Alima-Gerber).

The Board of Directors at Alima-Gerber consists of three to seven people, whose term lasts for three consecutive years. The board members as well as the company's chief executive officer (CEO) are appointed and suspended by the Supervising Board. Alima-Gerber's Supervising Board continuously monitors the firm's performance and presents a report on the company's operations at the Shareholders Meeting. It approves the Board of Directors' statute and suspends its members in case of serious misconduct. The Shareholders Meeting enables

Alima-Gerber's shareholders to participate in the decision making process. The Shareholders Meeting examines and approves the report on Alima-Gerber's operations, decides about the way profits are shared or losses covered (Statute of Alima-Gerber).

Divisional type is usually found in organizations facing diversity in markets, products, and technologies. Matrix type is a combination of the functional and the product/project structures. Successful strategy implementation requires a culture that is appropriate to, and supportive of the firm's strategy. Corporate culture refers to the dominant values and patterns of behavior that are accepted and practiced by the members of a particular organization.

The linkage between corporate culture and strategy is crucial. Strategy proceeds from guiding beliefs which are the roots and principles upon which the company is built. They are the philosophical foundation of the corporation. As a rule, they are included in the company's mission statement. Some of the Gerber's guiding beliefs are:

- to meet our social responsibilities and to improve the quality of life for our customers, our communities, our shareholders, and our employees;
- to strive in all things and with all people, to do the best they can and make our best better;
- to observe and maintain the confidence of those who buy and use our products and services (see Rue & Holland 1989).

While guiding beliefs are precepts upon which strategies get formulated, daily beliefs affect whether strategies get implemented. Daily beliefs are rules and feelings about everyday behavior. They are situational and change to meet different circumstances.

Though Alima-Gerber had little to impress Gerber with at the beginning, it was working hard to catch up with its parent company. Maria Potocka-Bielecka, who was Alima-Gerber's Director General in 1992, realized that in order to equal Gerber, Alima-Gerber had to work on its work organization, productivity, new technologies, and improving product quality (Warzewska 1992).

There is an emphasis on continuous improvement of Alima-Gerber employees' professional competence. Company sponsored training is closely connected with career planning, that is preparing young people for positions which they may move to in a few years. Alima-Gerber provides its employees with the opportunity to acquire at least the basic knowledge of English or computers (Kortlan 1995).

Some other ways of strengthening the company's culture include:
- recruiting people (especially managers) who will fit into the firm's way of looking at things;
- emphasizing key aspects of culture (e.g. quality, customer care, pride in the job, safety-consciousness, etc.) by means of company newsletters and notices;
- ensuring that managers and supervisors emphasize cultural norms in the course of everyday tasks.

Alima-Gerber's newsletter *Aktualności* claims that the attitude: "Personally I hate you, but I will try to cooperate with you for the good of our company." is definitely positive and worth promoting if the firm's success is to be attained (Unsigned 1996a).

Culture, like strategy, is a top-down phenomenon. If the chief executive officer (CEO) ignores culture, he or she will be formulating a strategy without grounding it in what the company stands for. On the other hand, if he or she works with the culture to strengthen the corporation's strategies, he or she makes a step towards the organization's success.

First of all, a leader serves as a deliberate role model, teacher, or coach. His or her visible behavior communicates assumptions and values to subordinates. Alima-Gerber's chief executive officer, Ryszard Wojtkowski, is an authority in the company. He is open to people, quick in decision making, and a good organizer. The way top management allocate rewards and status is still another factor that has considerable impact on the corporate culture. Leaders can communicate their priorities by linking pay raises, promotions, and formal recognition of accomplishments to particular behaviors. At Gerber, pay raises are tied to innovativeness and creativity. For example, on 1 January 1996 salaries at Alima-Gerber increased by 15% on average. But employees who had good results at work received pay raises which went well over the 15% mark (Szeliga & Twardowski 1996).

7. Strategic Control

After establishing the organization's mission and goals, and developing its corporate-level, business unit, and functional strategies in the context of external and organizational factors, the company puts the strategy into motion. However, it is of vital importance that progress be continuously monitored through strategic control.

Strategic control involves determining the extent to which the organizational strategic plans are successful in attaining the company's goals and objectives. Assessing whether the organization has done the right things (effectiveness) is just as important as doing things right (efficiency), and all of this must be analyzed in the context of the company's ethics.

The strategic control process has several major steps (Bartol & Martin 1991:600):

- determination of environmental and organizational elements that need to be monitored;
- establishing standards with which the actual performance of the company can be compared;
- performance measurement (takes form of both quantitative and qualitative evaluations);
- comparison of the company's performance to the previously established standards;
- if performance meets the standards or exceeds them, no corrective action is necessary;
- if standards are not met, remedial action must be taken.

It is expensive and virtually impossible to control every aspect of the organization's activities. Therefore, top management selects, on the basis of the company's mission, goals and objectives, what elements of the environment and organization need to be controlled. Since uncertainty is already enclosed in the notion of human action, the problem of probability is essential for praxiology (von Mises 1949).

Macroenvironmental forces must be continuously monitored because changes or shifts in the macroenvironment have strategic consequences for the company. The company, through strategic control, modifies its operations to defend itself better against external threats and to capitalize on opportunities that may arise. For example, Gerber's operations in the U.S. were threatened by a birthrate slowdown, which until 1990 was expected to increase only 1% annually. Consequently, Gerber's top management had to extend markets for their baby products outside the country. Since the company's corporate objective is to develop through acquisitions (see Rue & Holland 1989), Gerber's remedial action, in the face of the shrinking home market, was the acquisition of Alima in 1992 (Unsigned 1996c), and thus finding additional buyers for their baby foods.

Monitoring the industry environment is another part of strategic control activities. The task is, again, to modify the organization's operations so that it can better capitalize on opportunities and better defend itself against threats that arise in the industry. Gerber, Heinz and Beech-Nut control as much as 85% of the baby food market in the U.S. In 1984, Gerber's baby food market share was 70.9%, while Beech-Nut's – 15.8%, and Heinz's – 13.2%. However, the situation changed in the late 1984 and early 1986 when glass was reportedly found in Gerber products. This caused Gerber's market share to drop by 16%, some of which was gained back due to continuous efforts directed toward aggressive consumer marketing and establishing the company's quality image (Kotler & Armstrong 1991:625–6).

Internal operations constitute the last area to be monitored in the strategic control process. Here, the strategy formulation and implementation are evaluated.

The Alima-Gerber's overall sales in 1995, planned for $ 23 million, ultimately exceeded $ 37 million. Operational profit, which was supposed to be negative ($ 2.334 million), eventually was positive, which speaks for the improving economic condition of the company (Unsigned 1996d).

Evaluating the organization's performance can be accomplished in a number of ways. However, management must also take into account external variables. Thus, the company's performance is compared with operations of its competitors. This is done through competitive benchmarking. The term refers to the process of measuring the company's performance against that of the top performers in the industry.

Benchmarking standards can be based on published information that is widely available. For example, *Fortune* annually publishes the most and least admired U.S. corporations with annual sales of at least $ 500 million (Wright et al. 1994:248). "List 500" published in *Gazeta Bankowa* is the Polish counterpart. Alima-Gerber was at 226 on the "List 500" published in May 1996, with sales of PZL 105.4 million and gross profit of PZL 1.9 million (Unsigned 1996b).

Another competitive benchmark that is used is the company's relative product/service market quality. There is a positive relationship between the quality of products that companies produce and the profitability of those firms.

Eventually, the company's relative market share can be used as an alternative competitive benchmark. Managers at all levels in the organization are partially evaluated on their contributions to the company's gains in relative market share.

Generally, an effective communication system helps provide assurance that strategies are implemented as intended, that employees cooperate in carrying out the company's plans, and that these plans are carried out with reasonable efficiency.

8. Conclusions

In times of increasingly competitive and dynamic business environment strategic management is critical for ensuring the organization's success. However, it is human involvement in strategic issues that is the key factor for successful company operations. As it has been argued, this is also true of the Alima-Gerber company.

First, determining the firm's mission and goals requires top executives to take into account not only their personal values and wants, but also needs and values of other stakeholders, like customers, employees, general public, suppliers and creditors. An explicit mission guides a variety of decisions which insiders, as well as outsiders, make regarding their association with the organization. It is important, therefore, that the mission be explicitly communicated to avoid misunderstanding of the fundamental purpose of the organization.

Second, Alima-Gerber and Gerber strategic planners must understand the current state of the macroenvironment and their industry if the strategy to be devised is to be successful. The strategic management process forces the company's managers to be more proactive and conscious of their environments. It gets them into the habit of thinking in terms of the future.

Having made the macroenvironmental and industry analysis, and the assessment of the organization's strengths and weaknesses, the Alima-Gerber and Gerber managers must consider strategic alternatives. The company's success depends, in great part, on the proper choice of suitable for the business corporate-, business- and functional-level strategies. Since the process involves different levels of management, it encourages commitment on the part of participating managers and reduces resistance to proposed change. Lastly, coordinating strategies across the three levels is critical in maximizing strategic impact.

Strategies not only must be well formulated, but also must be carried out effectively to assure organization's success. Implementing Alima-Gerber's strategies is the work of the entire organization. A spirit of togetherness, teamwork, and cooperation prevailing in the organization helps achieve better results and leads to success. Strategically appropriate culture certainly facilitates the firm's strategic actions.

Finally, strategic management requires that the managers continuously reevaluate and, if necessary, adjust the strategic plan based on changes in the external and actual organizational performance. An effective communication system helps provide assurance that strategies are implemented as intended, that employees cooperate in carrying out the company's plans, and that these plans are carried out with reasonable efficiency. Only then is the organization capable of surviving in the continuously changing business environment.

Clearly, but for the people constituting the organiztion's human resources engaged actively in the strategic management process, no company would be able to compete effectively on the market.

References

Barlik, E. 1996. "Alima-Gerber. Polish Staff. American Strategies." *Rzeczpospolita* 19 January. In Polish.

Bartol, K. & Martin, D. 1991. *Management*. New York: McGraw Hill Inc.

Choroszy, R. 1992. "The Difficult Way to Privatisation. Alima in the Gerber Family." *Polska Zbrojna* 4 March. In Polish.

Cole, G. A. 1994. *Strategic Management*. London: DP Publications.

Kortlan, D. 1995. Paper delivered at a seminar "Personnel Management – Strategies and Methods", October 1995, Warsaw.

Kotler, P. & Armstrong, G. 1991. *Principles of Marketing*. Englewood Cliffs: Prentice Hall.

Mises, von, L. 1949. "Human Action: A Treatise on Economics." *Praxiology* No 3–4 1996.

Nowa Europa. 1994. 6 July. "The Swiss in America." Signed: TOM. In Polish.

Nowiny. 1994. 8 August. "Swindle or No Swindle?" Signed: (raw). In Polish.

Porter, M. E. 1979. "How Competitive Forces Shape Strategy." *Harvard Business Review* (March–April).

Porter, M. E. 1980. *Competitive Strategy: Techniques for Analyzing Industries and Competitors*. New York: Free Press.

Rudolf, W. 1995. "New Challenges." *Nowiny* 25 May. In Polish.

Rue L. W. & Holland G. P. 1989. *Strategic Management. Concepts and Experiences*. New York: McGraw-Hill.

Świderek, T. 1992. "Alima Exempted from Tax." *Gazeta Wyborcza* 22 May. In Polish.

Szeliga, K. & Twardowski, J. 1996. "Alima-Gerber's Move." *Nowiny (Biznes Nowiny)* 29 February. In Polish.

Sznajdrowska, W. "Quality as a Priority in Baby Food Processing (Alima-Gerber S.A., Rzeszów)." Internal Alima-Gerber Report. In Polish.

Unsigned. 1995. "Posts Evaluation." *Aktualności* Alima-Gerber's newsletter (October). In Polish.

Unsigned. 1996a. "Corporate Culture – the Basis for Organizational Success or Failure." *Aktualności* Alima-Gerber's newsletter (January). In Polish.

Unsigned. 1996b. "Going up the List 500." *Aktualności* Alima-Gerber's newsletter (June–July). In Polish.

Unsigned. 1996c. "About Alima-Gerber S.A." *Welcome to Małopolska*. In Polish.

Unsigned. 1996d. "Alima-Gerber S.A. – Positioned for Continued Success." *Connections* a business newsletter linking all Gerber associates (June). In Polish.

Warzewska, B. 1992. "Processed Food." *Rzeczpospolita* 27–28 June. In Polish.

Wright, P., Pringle, C. D. & Kroll, M. J. 1994. *Strategic Management. Text and Cases.* Boston: Allyn & Bacon.

Zbiegień-Maciąg, L. 1996. *Ethics in Management.* Warszawa: Centrum Informacji Menedżera. In Polish.

The Liberian Ship Registry:
An Ethical Evaluation

Keven Kelleher
Kerry Ward
University of Notre Dame
South Bend, Indiana, USA

1. A Brief History of Liberia

Liberia is a nation whose roots stem from two sources, the tribes of western Africa and the Government of the United States. In 1816 the first group of American settlers reached the shores of what would be come Liberia. The settlers consisted of freed slaves from America, African Americans who had been born free and several missionaries from the Baptist, Presbyterian, and Methodist faiths. The earliest settlers had the support of the president of the United States at the time, James Monroe, and several other key figures in the U.S. Government. The goal of the earliest settlers was "the black resettlement of the African western coast" (Kramer 1995). Settlers continued to stream into the country, and, even though nearly half ended up victims of the harsh climate and new diseases, in 1847 Liberia was established as an independent country.

Liberia's ties to the United States were unmistakable. Its constitution was modeled after the Declaration of Independence, and its capital was named after James Monroe. It has also benefited from numerous aid packages and timely military presence from the United States. Through the years it has endured numerous overthrow attempts, but the country has survived, although with less land than in the original establishment. Both France and England forced Liberia to cede parcels of land to the Ivory Coast and Sierra Leone. Its main industries have been rubber, which was of such high quality that Firestone established a plant in the country, and steel, which attracted Republic Steel. In the mid-twentieth century Liberia began what has become one of its leading industries, shipping registration.

Although the history of Liberia has been riddled with conflict, it took a severe turn for the worse in 1980. In April 1980, Samuel Doe recruited primarily members of his own tribe for membership in the Army, and he then led this army in a coup in which the government was overthrown. He murdered the incumbent and nearly all of his staff and declared himself leader of the country at age twenty-eight. In 1985 he won elections which were speculated to be rigged, and between 1985 and 1989, he "viciously put down alleged coups" from several of his former allies (Conciliation Resources 1). His methods included murder, torture and ethnic cleansing of the countryside in favor of his own tribe, the Krahn.

In 1989, after several more years of brutal repression from the unpopular government, aid was cutoff to the government. Doe became extremely unpopular, and an American-educated member of the National Patriotic Front of Liberia (NPFL), Charles Taylor, led a rebellion into northern Liberia. The goal of the invasion was to overthrow Doe, and it sparked a civil war. The only thing that stopped them from quickly capturing Monrovia was intervention by the Economic Community of West African States cease-fire Monitoring Group (ECOMOG) (Conciliation Resources 2). ECOMOG established a cease-fire in the early parts of 1990, but the fighting grew more intense, and Doe was eventually kidnapped, tortured and killed in September 1990. Since there was no leader of Liberia, ECOMOG established control over Monrovia and began to institute a cease-fire. There were several factions vying for leadership of the country, including the NPFL led by Taylor.

The search for a leader of Liberia continued, as did the fighting. A transitional government was established by ECOMOG, and several peace accords were written and then broken between the years of 1991–95. Civilians, children and even five American nuns were among the casualties during these years. After years of bloody fighting that left over 150,000 people dead and nearly $2/3$ of 2.3 million people living in Liberia displaced, elections were finally held in 1997. Charles Taylor, the man who many believe was integral to initiating the civil war, was elected president.

The costs of the civil war were extensive and not over to this day, as fighting continues to break out periodically. The civil war killed an estimated 10% of the population and displaced another 80% (West-Africa.Com). In addition, an estimated 10% of all the fighters were children under the age of fifteen (Conciliation Resources 3). Large scale massacres and cannibalism were widespread, pregnant women were disemboweled and an estimated 25,000 women were raped during the war (One World News Service). In 1994 the World Health Organization reported that 77% of the high school age students had seen someone raped or killed. The casualties resulted from indirect actions as well, as it is now estimated that 56% of all of the country's children suffer from some form of malnutrition (Africa News Service 1).

The ten years of ongoing civil strife has had a substantial economic impact as well. This impact can be seen in three ways. The first of these is that a majority of the economic infrastructure has been destroyed, including once profitable diamond mines, rubber processing plants, and a thriving timber industry. The second way in which the conflict has contributed to the deterioration of the economy is by driving so many people from the country. Among the hundreds of thousands of refugees were a majority of the nation's "business people with their expertise and capital" (The World Fact Book 1998). The most devastating impact of the departure of such individuals is that most will never return. The third way that the conflict has impacted the economic environment is that it has made civil administration nearly impossible. Since there still does not exist a legitimate government and so many people have been driven from their homes into neighboring countries, legitimate elections are very unlikely in the near future. Although no reliable GNP data is available, these three factors have contributed to what is suspected to be several years of negative growth in their GNP, extremely high inflation, 50% by some estimates, and bleak prospects for the future.

One area of the economy that remains strong, however, is the international shipping registry. Because it is still a flag of convenience for shipping companies to fly on their vessels, over 1,600 ships now fly a Liberian flag. Of these 1,600, nearly 50% come from four countries, Germany, the United States, Norway and Japan.

2. Current Issue: Corrupt Government

Although in 1997 Liberians elected Charles Taylor as president of the country, conditions for the 2.4 million residents have not improved. Economic conditions continue to worsen as warring factions refuse to recognize Taylor's authority as a legitimate government. Taylor is responsible for most of the mounting economic instability and has allowed and even endorsed an environment where corruption and illegal activities are flourishing. He was the key figure in the murder of many of his political opponents, and he has amassed a great deal of his ill-gotten wealth by defrauding the very government he is supposedly in charge of (Africa News Service 2). It is rumored that Taylor continues to embezzle hundreds of thousands of dollars in customs revenues. In addition, he has allowed several of his friends' companies to operate in Liberia tax-free. One such company, which epitomizes the way Taylor's government runs things, is a company called the Greater Diamond Company. Corrupt South African businessmen run the company with known connections to crime in both South Africa and Italy. The company acted with the help of Taylor's government officials to "secure customs and tax exemptions reserved only for relief organizations to import donated equipment and supplies" (Africa News Service 3). The Greater Diamond company has imported over 3,000 pieces of earth moving material to mine diamonds and has not paid import tax on any piece of the equipment. In addition, Taylor lets them take resources out of the country freely, a policy that is referred to by opponents as nothing short of pure exploitation (Africa News Service 3). Other disreputable figures have also surfaced in Liberia. Individuals from South Africa are rumored to be running a money laundering operation out of a bank that was established with Taylor's endorsement, and some of Taylor's associates are reportedly running a gun smuggling operation out of Monrovia.

Recently there has been a great deal of disruption in Liberia. There has been growing support for Charles Johnson, a fierce opponent of Taylor, and this has exposed just how deep the corruption and violence in the Taylor government run. Taylor's forces have acted to squash any political rallies in support of Johnson, and these actions resulted in fifty-two deaths recently. Taylor's government has also acted to squash any publicity that Johnson may get by shutting down a radio station loyal to him and forbidding the posting of relevant news on the Internet (Africa News Service 4). The corruption and instability has now gotten to the point that the U.S. ordered a travel warning for Liberia, shut down the embassy, and positioned military forces off of Liberia's coast. The shipping registry, however, continues to thrive.

3. Current Issue: Human Rights Abuses

3.1. Political and Extrajudicial Killings

The civil strife has also resulted in numerous human rights abuses to the people of Liberia. As previously mentioned, the death toll for the war has ranged anywhere from 150,000 - 200,000 people, and as many as 1.5 million require humanitarian assistance just to survive. Further, recent events point to several more years of bloodshed. Some of the more significant events that signal that the conflict is nowhere near over are as follows:

- September 16, 1996: fourteen civilians were killed and the hometown of a State Councilwoman, Kango Town, was burned to the ground.
- September 16, 1996: sixteen civilians were murdered in Kango Town.
- September 23, 1996: seventeen civilians were murdered in Dia Town.
- September 28, 1996: fourteen civilians were killed in Sinje.
- September 1998: fifty-two civilians were killed.
- September 19, 1998: 300 women and children were massacred in Monrovia.

Of these events, very little effort was put into investigating who was responsible, and little effort was made to bring the culprits to justice.

3.2. Disappearance of Political Enemies of Charles Taylor

Many of Taylor's opponents have been reported missing over the past years. These include non-governmental organization workers, nuns, and children of enemies. It has also been reported that the children were used to illegally tap rubber trees, to perform timber operations, to harvest gold, and to mine for diamonds (U.S. State Department).

3.3. Torture and Other Inhumane Treatment

According to the Human Rights report on Liberia, all of the political factions engage in torture and other inhumane, degrading treatment (U.S. State Department). This has included rape, live burnings, starvation and unjust jailings. The Red Cross estimates that over 90% of the residents of the jails in Liberia have been jailed for as long as a year without even being charged. These jails, which are operated by the government, have deplorable living conditions, and law officials often take bribes to jail political opponents of different factions (U.S. State Department). On top of these crimes, none of the prisoners has been given a fair and public trial. All of this occurs in a judicial system that was supposedly modeled after the system in the United States.

3.4. Freedom of Free Speech and Press

As previously mentioned, the government is still controlling the media, to a great extent deciding what can and cannot be reported. Citizens, justifiably, have also been showing self restraint as to what they are reporting due to fear of possible retribution.

3.5. Governmental Processes

Although Charles Taylor claimed victory in the most recent elections, initial reports are that the election was far from being corruption free. In a country of 2.3 million people, where 1.2 million people have been internally displaced, and another 750,000 are refugees in neighboring countries, Taylor's political party claimed that nearly 700,000 voted.

3.6. Treatment of Children

Of the 60,000 combatants who have participated in the most recent strife of the civil war, the Red Cross has estimated that nearly 50% are under the age of nineteen. In addition, it has also been estimated that 50% of the women under the age of eighteen have undergone genital mutilation (U.S. State Department).

The government has done very little to correct any of the violations, and they are widely suspected to endorse them.

4. The Benefits of the Liberian Ship Registry

Liberia began open registration of ships in 1949 and grew to be the largest registry of ships in the world by 1993 (Flags of Convenience). Although Liberia lost the title of the largest ship registry to Panama because of the civil war, it remains the second largest registry still today with over 60 million gross tons flying under the Liberian flag (International Registries, Inc. 1998).

This ranking as a world leader in ship registry is the result of a favorable business regulatory environment. Although some countries have duplicated the open business environment, Liberia's favorable reputation due to stringent safety regulations allows banks and creditors a high level of assurance on their investment, something not readily available through other countries. Banks are less hesitant to loan money to shipping companies registered in Liberia and to provide financing for the ships registered there because the ships are subject to higher safety requirements and consequently are less risky than ships registered in other countries with lower standards. Liberian-registered ships have a five-year loss ratio of .22 compared to the rest of the world's shipping industry of .30 during the period from 1990 to 1994 (International Registries, Inc. 1998).

The ships registered in Liberia are subject to mandatory annual inspections that are based on international standards. Liberia maintains a worldwide network of nautical inspectors who conduct in-port inspections. These inspections serve not only to ensure safety of ship, crew and cargo, but they also ensure that operations can continue quickly if a particular port authority decides to attempt to hold up a ship. This reassures lending institutions which are dependent on the company's ability to generate continuing cash flow.

Liberian safety requirements also include officer certification. The certifications include educational and physical standards, professional examinations, as well as experience. The certifications expire after five years, and each officer must be re-certified upon expiration.

Not only are there requirements for the officers, but each seaman must hold a valid identification issued by Liberia. This identification tracks the individual's record of service and states the areas in which he is qualified to work. In order to get the Liberian identification, the individual must have a letter documenting his employment with the specified vessel. These safety regulations have greatly contributed to the continuing role that Liberia plays in the registration of shipping.

As previously mentioned, there are several business advantages to registering a ship in Liberia. The first of these is that Liberia allows substantial flexibility for international operations. While many countries of registry, such as Panama, place limits on the location of corporations and on foreign ownership and control of the corporations, Liberia is different. Corporate offices and operations can be anywhere in the world, and there is no requirement that any facet of the organization be located in Liberia. In addition, no restrictions are placed upon the composition of the Board of Directors or the shareholdership; they may be of any nationality and located anywhere in the world.

The second advantage to the Liberian registry is that there are no restrictions placed on the conduct of business, specifically on location. A Liberian-based corporation is free to conduct business anywhere in the world. This allows shipping companies to take advantage of the tax and regulatory benefits without moving the companies' headquarters or changing executives. This advantage of the Liberian registry allows existing companies the ability to set up shipping companies registered in Liberia while maintaining existing operations. This means that companies can register in Liberia and realize substantial cost savings. The lack of taxation and less stringent reporting requirements allow companies to spend less on tax and administrative costs. Registering in Liberia also allows the shipping company to hire less expensive labor because it does not necessarily have to come from the expensive U.S. labor market. This is in contrast to ships registered in the U.S. which are required to have a crew consisting of at least three-quarters U.S. citizens. Because the U.S. labor force is unionized, it is very expensive compared to other countries' labor forces. The Liberian-based ships can draw cheaper labor from places such as China and Singapore and substantially reduce costs.

A third reason companies find it favorable to register ships in Liberia is that there is substantial privacy regarding ownership and operation of the shipping company in comparison to other countries. This is evident when compared to the United States, where shipping corporations are required to report annually to Federal and local governments. In addition, U.S. companies are required to release a great deal of information when they file various forms of tax information on an annual basis. Liberian regulations do not have these requirements. There is no requirement to list ownership or to list corporate officers during the taxation process because there is no taxation.

Another reason why companies register in Liberia is that the law covering capital structure is not restrictive. There is no minimum amount of capital required, and there is no reporting requirement for issuing shares. The corporation can even issue bearer stock. Bearer stock is more liquid and less traceable because it does not require the owner of the stock to be recorded. Whoever may have possession of the stock is the owner and is entitled to the benefits of ownership.

Some of the benefits discussed are common among other popular ship registry countries such as Panama or Belize. A unique characteristic that sets Liberia apart, however, is its legal structure. Because the legal system of Liberia is based on the United States' structure, it is very well defined. This provides a stable and less risky legal environment in which the corporations operate, and, although the civil war has damaged the stability of the government, the legal structure affecting the shipping registry has remained virtually unaffected.

5. An Ethical Evaluation

While it may be beneficial for shipping companies to register their ships in Liberia, it is clear, with the current political and human rights situation in that country, that doing so represents a poor ethical choice. This becomes evident when the choice for the flag of convenience is examined in accordance with the ten guidelines for a multinational set forth by Richard De George in his book *Competing with Integrity in International Business* (1993). In the following section, the choice to register ships is examined using those guidelines that can be applied to the situation.

5.1. Guideline 1: Multinationals Should Do No Intentional Direct Harm (to or in the Host Country)

When examining the ethical status of the decision to fly the flag of Liberia on a vessel, this is actually the most damning of De George's guidelines for the corporation. Beyond what the guideline states, De George believes that a company should look past the direct dealings they may have with a country and consider the impact their actions may have on any associated third parties. This means that shipping companies need to examine the government of Liberia because when they register their ship under the Liberian flag, it is the government of Liberia that they are offering support to, both monetarily and morally. De George states, "If the regime with which one deals is known to be corrupt, the difficulty (corruption) is exacerbated and the possibility of harming innocent third parties is increased" (De George 1993:46). What this means, in applying it to the shipping registry, is that in providing support to the government through the fees paid for registration, the companies are providing the corrupt and inhumane government of Charles Taylor a portion of the support it needs to continue to operate. In this manner they are indirectly harming a third party, the people of Liberia, who have repeatedly been abused at the hands of Taylor. It may not be a direct harm to the people, but it is certainly intentional, as the abuses and events in Liberia are no secret to the rest of the world.

This guideline goes even further to stipulate that if a "government cares not for the interest of its people but only the aggrandizement or government officials," then the MNC should provide the people what the government is not providing (De George 1993:46). However, this is not a realistic course of action for the shipping companies since they have no physical presence in the country of Liberia and certainly would not be able to afford to replace or replenish the legitimate government that Liberia has been missing for ten years. Yet, since the registration of ships supports a corrupt government, it does represent an unethical behavior. Even though the contribution for each ship may be small, it is still providing the resources to allow the continuance of a corrupt regime, thus indirectly harming the people of Liberia. To avoid doing harm or contributing the harm that already exists, companies have to consider factors in addition to the fact that they may be saving some money. Since the registration of ships in Liberia is unethical by the standards of this first guideline, then to act in an ethical manner would be to discontinue the registration of ships. In other words, the only way to do the ethically correct thing is to avoid acting unethically, which means registering ships in a country in which the proceeds will not be used to harm indirectly a third party.

5.2. Guideline 2: Multinationals Should Produce More Good Than Harm in the Host Country

This second guideline builds upon the premise of the first guideline, but goes one step further to require that a company's actions and behavior in a host country "must not only benefit it, but also the host country" (De George 1993:47). This means that for the registration of ships to be classified as an ethical behavior, it must in some way benefit the country of Liberia. While the registry may benefit the leaders of Liberia, these are an elite few, and the "good of the country is not the same as the good of an oppressive elite of the country" (De George 1993:49). Applying this guideline to the ship registration means that companies' actions must benefit the oppressed refugees who have had family members killed, raped or maimed. Unfortunately, the registry does no such thing. Not only does it not do enough good to overcome the damaging regime it is contributing to, but the registration of ships does not even go beyond contributing to a wealthy minority. The wealth, and in turn the registry, is controlled by an elite ruling party that only uses funds to continue their reign of terror. In effect, the registry is doing more harm than good for the country of Liberia as a whole. With this in mind, De George's second guideline defines the registration of ships as an ethically unjustifiable action.

5.3. Guideline 3: Multinationals Should Contribute by Their Activity to the Host Country's Development

This third guideline stipulates that the multinational should contribute to a country's development through the transfer of knowledge, technology or methods. This idea could be applicable to a country such as Liberia whose infrastructure is in a state of shambles after years of war. Particular areas in which the shipping community may be able to offer assistance to Liberia are the construction of port facilities and the reconstruction of the main roadways and railways. Because these are transportation related, they would not only help Liberia but may be able to help speed up some of the shipping times for the companies. Activities such as these would also help to justify morally the presence of so many in the shipping registry. In other words, it would provide a form of compensation to the residents of Liberia for the use of their flag on numerous ships. Unfortunately, the registration of ships in the registries in Liberia fails to meet the standard imposed by this guideline as well. Because nothing is required of the companies that register their ships in Liberia, including no physical presence, no tax contribution, they do nothing to assist in the development of the country. This lack of action coupled with the dire need of the country and its people represents the third reason why the shipping registry is an unethical practice and fails De George's third guideline for multinationals.

5.4. Guideline 6: Multinationals Should Pay Their Fair Share of Taxes

The sixth guideline listed by De George, that multinationals should pay their fair share of taxes, is in direct contradiction to one of the primary benefits of registering ships in Liberia. Because of the absence of a tax structure, shipping companies pay no tax at all for the registration of ships. Liberia has no annual filing requirement and no annual tax liability on ships registered there. The shipping companies are not actively avoiding the payment of taxes since they are merely taking advantage of the incentives offered by the Liberian government, but they still should be required to contribute in some form to the well being of a country and its people for the use of their national symbol. This is particularly true in a country that has seen such an incredible amount of devastation and human rights violations. While not required by written law to pay taxes to the government of Liberia, some form of compensation beyond the annual fees is required by social law demonstrating what De George calls "an ethically mandatory social responsibility" (De George 1993:83). The favorable tax code and the minimal payments required of the shipping companies results in pure exploitation of a poor and less-developed country. Because of this, the shipping registry fails the sixth guideline of De George, and therefore is not an ethically justifiable action.

5.5. Guideline 7: Multinationals Should Cooperate With the Local Government in Developing and Enforcing Just Background Institutions

The reason for this guideline is that De George believes multinationals have a duty to work with less developed countries to establish background institutions that will oversee the development and fair treatment of the population. When involved in a less developed country, multinationals should try to help the country eliminate violations of human rights, promote fair competition, and guard against the exploitation of the country's scarce resources.

Based on these standards, most companies registering ships in Liberia are acting unethically. Most are registering their ships to take advantage of the benefits and have no interest in developing the infrastructure of Liberia. Over the course of the past ten years, companies with ships registered there have not attempted to stabilize the government nor have they removed their ships from the registry as a form of protest against the events in Liberia. There was a slow down in the registering of new ships since the start of the civil war but due to the uncertainty caused by the war and not because of ethical considerations.

Most of the companies that register ships there do not have any presence in the country at all, and very few have corporate offices located in

Liberia. In addition, a vast majority of the owners of the ships do not reside in the country. They merely pay a small annual registration fee that is largely used to finance the war effort, not build effective government or institutions.

6. Conclusions

As a result of the failure of the registering of ships to meet even one of the applicable guidelines for multinationals in a satisfactory manner, it can be classified as an unethical practice. While companies that register ships under Liberia's flag of convenience may not be directly contributing to the events there, the shipping companies are providing support to the government that is responsible for the atrocities that are occurring on an ongoing basis.

The companies have not attempted to provide benefits to the country in terms of developing and enforcing strong background institutions to protect the citizens. The companies are not paying any taxes and are not trying to stabilize the political upheaval. The companies are registering their ships in Liberia simply for economic benefits without regard for the harm being done to the citizens. In this fashion, they are acting in an unethical manner, all to save some money. Their lack of concern or even attention to the conditions in Liberia is a gross injustice.

To correct this problem, companies must act with moral courage. They can do this by paying the extra funds either to support a legitimate government or to make changes in the existing government in Liberia. If companies are not willing to develop the necessary background institutions, then they should stop registering their ships in Liberia and cease doing business in the country.

References

Africa News Service 1. http://www.africanews.org/usaf/liberia.
Africa News Service 2. http://www.africanews.org/west/liberia/stories/19981006_feat3.
Africa News Service 3. http://www.africanews.org/west/liberia/stories/19981006.
Africa News Service 4. http://www.africanews.org/west/liberia/stories/19981027.
Conciliation Resources 1. http://www.c-r.org/cr/accord/actors.
Conciliation Resources 2. http://www.c-r.org/cr/accord/chrono.
Conciliation Resources 3. http://www.c-r.org/cr/accord/sesay.
De George, R. T. 1993. *Competing with Integrity in International Business*. New York: Oxford University Press.
Flags of Convenience. http://www.flagsofconvience.com/liberia.html.
International Registries, Inc. 1998. http://www.register-iri.com/Liberia.html.

Kramer, R. 1995. "Liberia: A Casualty of the Cold War." *The Africa News Service*. http:/
/www.africanews.org/usaf/liberia.html.
One World News Service. http://www.oneworld.org/ips2/jul/Liberia.
The World Fact Book. 1998. http://www.odci.gov/cia/publications/factbook/li.html.
U.S. State Department. http://www.state.gov/www/global/human_rights/1996_hrp_report.
West-Africa.Com. http://www.west-africa.com/Liberia/Liberia.html.

Advertising – the Art of Manipulation. Cultural Determinants in Effectiveness of Advertising, Polish and American Cases

Monika Dębicka
Collegium Invisibile
Warsaw, Poland

You can fool some of the people
all the time and you can fool
all of the people some of the time.
But you can never fool
all of the people all of the time

Abraham Lincoln

There are many ways to look at advertising – as a business, as a creative process, as a social phenomenon and as a fundamental ingredient of everyday life. Unfortunately, most often, advertising is mistakenly taken at its face value, its influence over individuals undermined and its role in society taken for granted. Colorful pictures and clever slogans are just the surface, the tip of the iceberg, which – although most noticeable – is only a small part of the whole. What is most important about advertising is not visible in newspapers or on TV. It is the power of advertising to govern human behavior. Thus, I choose to look at advertising as the art of manipulation, an art sometimes beautiful – selling us our dreams and fulfilling our deepest needs – but sometimes an art that is harmful and dangerous.

For those reasons selling a product cannot be viewed as the ultimate, harmless function of advertising. It would not reveal the complexity and sophistication of the advertising phenomenon. For even this obvious function of advertising – selling things – involves a "meaning" process; that is, advertisements take into account not only the qualities and attributes of the product that they are trying to sell but also the way in which they can make those properties mean something to people, the way in which they can most effectively manipulate people.

To do so, advertisements have to translate statements from the world of things into a form that means something in terms of people. Ordinary things must be given a humanly symbolic "exchange-value." For example, a Parker pen is not just a pen; it is beauty, professionalism, sexiness, perfection, etc. For one person it may mean something different than for another. The advertisement invites people to read their individual desires into the product. People buy products for what the products mean, not only for what they can do, and that meaning is created by advertising. This idea was expressed by Thorstein Veblen, who suggested that many people engage in "conspicuous consumption" (Cateroa 1990:143); they purchase things they do not need, just to show off their wealth, position, etc. A great number of advertisements are based on that theory, where products are presented not in a context of their functionality but as symbols of success, social position, etc. People buy these products not because they need them, but because they want to show themselves off. For the same reason women in California buy fur coats, though it will never be cold enough to justify wearing one. Through advertising products acquire meaning. They become symbols telling others who their users are, what they have achieved, what their social class is.

Summing up, people do not need to know only how to use a product and what it can do. They want to see what it means to them. The price a customer is willing to pay for a product depends more on the product's image rather than its real value. They want to buy "the steak" but pay for "the sizzle." Advertising adds "psychic" value to a product in a consumer's mind. That's why people pay more for products featured in TV commercials or printed ads than for an unadvertised brand – even though most of them are functionally the same. Dr. Ernest Dichter, a psychologist known as the father of motivational research, concluded that even though an ad may say nothing about the product's quality, the positive image conveyed by advertising may denote quality, may make the product more desirable to the consumer, and thereby add value to the product (Arens 1994:29).

Subsequent studies supported the view that a product's *image,* which is created in a great degree by advertising, becomes an *inherent feature of the product itself.* The image that a product has in consumers' minds results from all the impressions they receive from advertisements. It relates to the fundamental satisfaction, both practical and symbolic, which individuals seek. It is a vision that is conjured up by an individual when he thinks of the product. For example, some consumers may consider a motor boat a means of conveyance over water with a specified load capacity and the power and speed necessary to perform its function. Other consumers think of the same boat as a means of exciting the interest, admiration, and even the envy of people they wish to impress. They may be more interested in the "status symbol effect" than in its technical qualities. Some consumers receive more satisfaction from owning such a boat than they do from using it. The image of a product depends on the way a consumer perceives a given advertisement. Different consumers perceive the same ad in different ways. It relates to the configuration of ideas, feelings, and meanings which consumers attach to presented symbols and messages.

In advertising, a message is a combination of words and symbols transmitted to an audience. Many messages use symbolism and try to relate safety, social acceptance, or sexual appeal to a product. For example, in commercials, life insurance provides safety for family members; clothing styles offer acceptance by peers; toothpaste brightens teeth and makes a person more sexually attractive. However, the message, in order to be properly understood, must be well constructed or encoded. It is not enough to translate an idea into words and symbols; for symbols to work, sender and receiver must agree on their meaning. Sometimes this basic rule is ignored by an advertiser. A good example is a Polish campaign for Silkcut cigarettes, where advertisements presented nothing but cut sheet of silk. It might have been understood in the U.S. but never in Poland. The advertising did not convey any message to a Polish respondent; the picture did not have any meaning, simply because the sign and the message did not correspond in Poles' minds.

Another important factor, the way the message is decoded – interpreted by the receiver – is only partially determined by the words and the medium used. Most important are the unique characteristics of the receivers, the manner in which they interpret various stimuli, that is, the perception of the stimuli. Perception is one of the major influences that affects the way people receive and respond to messages and how they behave as consumers. Perception has been defined as the process by which an individual becomes aware of the environment and interprets it so that it fits into a frame of reference (Cundiff 1996:197). Although so significant, it has very little in common with reality. What people perceive is what their culture taught them to perceive rather than what is actually there.

Advertisements are artifacts of material culture and they play a very important role in building and changing it. Similarly, culture is a powerful component of advertising. It affects the effectiveness of every single ad or commercial, and determines their success or failure. For example, a few years ago Procter & Gamble, one of the most successful global marketers, experienced some problems entering the Polish market with the issue of culture and its values. Its candid campaign for the Always sanitary tampon proved to be too controversial and shocking for conservative and predominantly Catholic Poland. Conversely, Johnson & Johnson, after analyzing Polish cultural values, adapted its commercial of its baby-care products to include shots of a husband holding an infant and sharing household tasks. The advertisements turned out to be a great success as they appealed to Poland's Catholic family traditions.

The significance of culture in understanding advertising's capability to influence and manipulate is that, although all customers may be biologically similar, their views of the world, what they are responsive to and what affects them differ according to their cultural backgrounds. That's why Americans' purchase decisions are influenced by different stimuli than Poles' and vice versa. Both nationalities value different things, and while shopping they look for them in the products. If low price is important, they respond well to advertising emphasizing 'money saving' rather than luxury or status. Even nowadays, where the world is often viewed as a "global village" these differences are very distinct. For example, while Americans find "healthy" and "environment friendly" attributes extremely important, Poles place the greatest emphasis on practicality, origin (foreign or domestic), and technical excellence. FIGURE 1 illustrates the described differences.

FIGURE 1

Differences in Product Attributes Valued by Americans and Poles

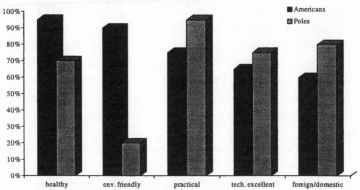

Source: Americans : "Loudon, Consumer Behavior", p. 143.

Americans place a lot of value on health and fitness issues. Compared to Poles, they drink more bottled water and fewer alcoholic beverages, buy more low-salt, low-fat, and low-cholesterol substitutes, smoke less and eat less sugar. They are more environment- conscious, buying products that are ozone-friendly and reduce pollution. Thus, American marketers quite often try to appeal to these values. In Poland, such an approach would not be successful. As a nation, Poles are more interested in acquiring the goods they need rather than the effect of these goods on the environment. Thus, advertising such a product, marketers are emphasizing rather qualities of the product. For such reasons, marketing strategies that work in the United States often cannot be directly applied in Poland.

Unfortunately, many American companies entering the Polish market use their standardized marketing mix, with minimal modifications. In such a way, they try to save money and take advantage of economies of scale. They use the same TV ads, the same visual images. The only modification is translation of the copy into Polish language. Some of it works, some does not. A global advertising approach sometimes may be appropriate for products that have universal appeal, such as Coca Cola, Levi's jeans or cosmetics. To some degree, consumers' tastes converged and cultural differences eroded. In Poland, one can find successful ads taken straight from American magazines. For example, a Marlboro cigarette advertisement placed in Polish media could easily appeal to the same values as it would in America. However, "Marlboro Man" is one of only a few exceptions. In most cases, advertisements that force themselves across the ocean end up being either misunderstood or resented. Differences in tastes, habits, and life styles have proved to be a big obstacle to global advertising. For example, the big campaign for two-in-one shampoo/conditioners was to many Poles meaningless, as hair conditioners alone were still quite a new product. Americans advertising a 'new improved' version of a product did not take into account the fact that Polish consumers did not have the time yet to get used to the old one.

The above-described situation is by no means exceptional. Very frequently advertisers think that the beliefs, values, and symbols of their own culture apply everywhere and they try to sell "the same in the same way in different places." About ten years ago, in 1989, a lot of American advertising agencies began to flood the Polish market with their products. And although they had by then gotten some insight into Polish culture and reality, many of them were still failing to get it right. Cultural gaffes were commonplace, as were glamorous, Western-style ads that were either irrelevant to the everyday struggles of Polish consumers or meaningless. A good example is a campaign for IBM computers, where in every ad and commercial the company was symbolized by a big blue rose, or a big bunch of blue roses. Average Poles found blue flowers rather strange and wondered what was the message behind it. They did not connote, what an average American would do automatically, that 'Big Blue' means IBM. For a country where advertising for a long time was virtually nonexistent, advertisers demanded a very high level of sophistication from consumers. A similar situation took place when Ever Ready Battery Co. was introducing Energizer batteries into the Polish market. In a TV commercial, it used its famous pink Energizer bunny, an advertising icon to American viewers. But again the commercial confused Polish consumers, who thought the ad was touting a toy bunny, not a battery. As a result, consumers became frustrated when they could not find the toy on store shelves.

The role of culture in decoding messages is so great that it often requires advertisers to acquire widely varying approaches to the message. When a promotional message is written, symbols recognizable and meaningful to the given culture must be used. When designing an ad, its appearance must be made culturally acceptable if it is to be operative and meaningful. Of course, there are world renowned and respected companies that ignore these facts, such as Benetton, with its ads showing human genitals, death, animal intercourse, etc. However, such ads intend to shock and be remembered rather then accepted and not too many companies can afford doing so. In most cases, whenever advertisers violate cultural canons, the advertisements are rejected by society and fail to influence/manipulate consumers.

Advertisers' efforts are judged in a cultural context for acceptance, resistance, or rejection. However, without comprehensive cultural studies, it is very difficult to foresee what is admissible and what is not in a given society. For example, a very popular subject of social advertisements in America – the use of condoms – in Poland turned out to stir up a lot of controversies. In July 1997, Poles were taken aback by very blunt safe-sex billboards with a condom on a thumb. The ads carried the message "Stay cool. It's O.K. Condoms prevent AIDS." The spot was placed on 400 Outdoor Billboard Promotion's billboards across Poland. The company ran the advertisement free of charge. Intended as a public service campaign against AIDS, the advertisements drew fire from some quarters, especially in smaller towns. Zbigniew Kaczmarek, Outdoor's sales manager, in one of many interviews said, "we created the ad to make people aware, not to offend anyone's feelings." Still, many resented the advertisement arguing that it encourages young people to engage in immoral and indecent behavior. Those against the ads used economic pressure to fight them, enlisting property owners who lease sites to Outdoor to demand that the ads come down.

What is considered perfectly acceptable in one culture may be offensive to another. That is why advertising messages must be closely related with cultural values, standards, etc. To be effective, the emotional appeals, symbols, persuasive approaches and other characteristics of an advertisement must coincide with cultural norms. Only then are advertisements able to influence a consumer's mind and stimulate a decision about wants and needs.

Over the years, advertisements have become an inevitable part of everyone's lives and a powerful factor molding the culture of a society. Present in all the media, advertising forms an enormously influential superstructure. Over 50% of the surveyed Poles admitted that the choices they make are affected by advertisements (FIGURE 2).

FIGURE 2

Purchase motivants

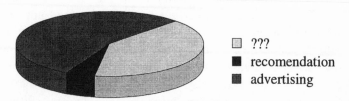

□ ???
■ recomendation
▩ advertising

Source: Own Research.

Modern marketers are well aware of the power a little ad may have over a consumer's mind. Thus, printed advertisements, radio spots or TV commercials are masterpieces thoughtfully created and placed in order to influence consumers. They stimulate emotions, change attitudes and tamper with our minds. To do so, advertising employs many sophisticated techniques to achieve its goal, which very often violate the balance between efficiency and ethics. A good example is excessive usage of sex and nudity in advertisements. Quite often it can be observed that many advertisements' goal is simply to flash some nude scene and shock the audience hoping that breaking cultural norms will cause people to take notice of this advertisement. People may not remember what it was supposed to advertise but they will remember the ad. There is some truth and logic in that statement. Generally, such ads do have a greater potential for being remembered. This occurs because material with sexual or shocking themes is least affected by the interference process of forgetting. What is more, according to Freud's theory, they appeal to the inborn drives of human beings. Thus, many companies reach for such approaches and themes for their messages. A good example is Benetton, which based a whole advertising strategy around shocking, sexual and surprising themes, having very little to do with the company's products. Benetton, selling comfortable clothes all over the world, decided to shock and make sure that the very controversial advertising campaign will be remembered, and – what is more – will get a lot of publicity, rather than take the risk of being ignored and melting with all the other advertisements.

Benetton, although not always in good taste, is at least genuine in its ideas, which cannot be said about many Polish companies trying to win the battle for customer attention by using sexual themes in all their ads.

Unfortunately, most of them do not even aspire to be creative or subtle while employing the nudity and sex in their campaigns. Probably the best illustration of the problem is an advertisement published in a local newspaper showing a vending machine and a very attractive blond woman sitting on it, with the tag line "If you put it in, now take it out." Very suggestive and vulgar was also Peugeot presenting a woman with a big cleavage assuring that if we "look inside" – the cleavage?, the car? – we will be nicely surprised, because "it is bigger than we think."

Although there are so many of these ads in the Polish media, Poles do not really like them. Only 5% of the respondents expressed their unconditional approval of using sex in nudity in advertising. The majority (78%) accept them but only in advertising of grooming and personal hygiene products.

FIGURE 3

Poles Feelings towards Sex and Nudity in Advertising

What do you think about using sex and nudity in advertising?	
I don't like it regardless what type of products is advertised	*17%*
I don't mind, but only if the advertised products are cosmetics, Underwear, etc.	***78%***
I like it regardless of type of products	*5%*

■ Don't like it
■ Like it
▦ Depends

Source: Own Research.

Where nudity is relevant to the product, people are less likely to regard it as obscene or offensive. However, in a very conservative country like Poland, even in such instances it evokes controversies, as it happened in July 1996 with a commercial for Denim Kult after-shave. The commercial showed a young woman sliding her hand into a man's jeans after he has used the after-shave. The use of a sexually attractive model and sexually suggestive theme was too "immoral" for Poles, who decided that the commercial "violates the right to privacy and people's dignity."

As it was described above, marketers go to great lengths to capture the customer. Sometimes however, they go very far – to the subconscious level of people's minds. They create ads that appeal to stimuli that are below the level needed to reach conscious awareness. In other words, people receive messages without being aware of the communication.

The subliminal perception controversy was raised with the publication of such books as "Subliminal Seduction" by Wilson Bryan Key and "The Hidden Persuaders" by Vance Packard. The first one, subtitled "Here Are the Secret Ways Ad Men Arouse Your Desires to Sell Their Products," includes numerous examples of what the author believes are sexual symbols and pornographic pictures buried in the otherwise bland content of various ads. In his publication, Key accuses advertising people of planting hidden sexual messages in print ads and concludes that such "hidden persuaders" are carefully contrived just to seduce consumers and manipulate them at a subliminal level. The fear that consumers may be trapped into buying through appeals made to "unconscious" buying motives was also strongly expressed in Vance Packard's work. Packard strongly implied that advertisers manipulate people to the commercial advantage of product manufacturers.

After publication of the above mentioned books, many people begun to look for, and as a result find, symptoms of subliminal advertising. Such interest, on a small scale, could have been observed also in Poland. In May 1996 the president of the Committee of Culture and Mass Media claimed that a commercial for Wella shampoo watched at slow pace contained the logo of one of the private TV stations, POLSAT (Warsaw Business Journal, May 1996). The logo, although not registered consciously by the audience, was supposed to have a big impact on the rapidly increasing popularity of POLSAT, especially that the supposedly subliminal messages were emitted on competing channels. Although the accusation was very formal and publicly stated, Poles have not taken it seriously. In Poland, subliminal advertising is still underestimated. As research proved, many of the respondents (48%) believe that the problem does not exist and only 13% believe that it happens in Poland.

FIGURE 4

Opinions on the Problem of Subliminal Advertising

What do you think about subliminal advertising?	
The problem does not exist	48?
The problem exists, but not in Poland	**37%**
The problem does exist in Poland	13%
No opinion	2%

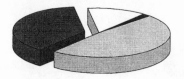

☐ problem doesn't exist
☐ it exists, but not in Poland
■ it exists in Poland
■ ???

Source: Own Research.

It should be mentioned though, that Poles seem to be more accepting of being manipulated in this way. Over half of them, 64%, accept the fact that advertisements are manipulative and only 23% believe it is unethical.

FIGURE 5

Opinions on Hidden Advertisements in Movies

What would you think if it turned out that you bought a product just because you have been influenced by a hidden advertisement in a movie?	
it's unethical	23%
it's OK, advertising is meant to be manipulative anyway	**64%**
no opinion	13%

■ It's OK
☐ It's unethical
■ No opinion

Source: Own Research.

At the same time, Poles seem to be cautious to trust advertisements. Over 60% feel a need to double check the information given in an ad, as is illustrated in FIGURE 6.

FIGURE 6

Poles Reliance on Information in Advertisements

Do you double check the information about an advertised product in some other source?

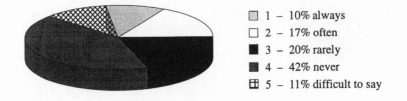

▨	1 – 10% always
☐	2 – 17% often
■	3 – 20% rarely
▧	4 – 42% never
⊞	5 – 11% difficult to say

Source: CBOS: "Polacy o reklamie" (Poles On Advertising), December 1996.

As is presented above, people are not so helpless and naive when it comes to evaluating advertising messages. Whatever their reaction or attitude toward advertising, it cannot be said that people just accept it and let it manipulate their lives. Very often they resent an advertising message and filter it out of their cognitive memory. It should be remembered that it is a consumer, not a page in a magazine, not commercials or posters, who makes the final decision. Advertising may sway the buyer into one direction or another, yet it is the consumer who decides. People are not docile, brainless creatures. As recent research proves, customers do not take ads thoughtlessly. They question, criticize, or get to like them. In each case it is a conscious decision.

References

Arens, W. F. 1994. *Contemporary Advertising*. Boston: Irwin.
Cateora, P. R. 1990. *International Marketing*. Boston: Irwin.
Cundiff, E. W. 1996. *Basic Marketing: Concepts, Environment, and Decisions*. New Jersey: Prentice-Hall.

The Grameen Bank:
Lessons to Be Learned

Lawrence Pineda
John Walusis
University of Notre Dame
South Bend, Indiana, USA

1. Introduction

Bangladesh is one of the most impoverished nations in the world. The living conditions in many of the villages are almost unbearable. Food is scarce, adequate housing is not widely available, healthcare is substandard and disease is rampant. In addition to these problems, women in Bangladesh historically have faced oppression in the name of religion, by the male dominated Islamic culture. In a country such as this, with an ever increasing population, an average life span of only fifty-six years, a literacy rate below 35%, and where the majority of the population is under the age of sixteen, should multinational companies play a role in the country's development (Bangladesh)? If they should indeed play a role in this development, how can they do so without having a significantly negative impact on the financial performance of the firm? These are two of the primary questions we will address in this paper. Other ethical issues we will focus on are the empowerment of women in developing countries, the idea that access to credit is a basic human right and the international implications of the Grameen Bank lending model.

2. Striking Contrast Between Two Villages in Bangladesh

In July 1996 I (John Walusis) traveled through the countryside and visited several small villages in rural Bangladesh. I was shocked by conditions in the first village that I saw. There were few houses that looked habitable. Homes in rural Bangladesh are made from a combination of mud and sticks. Most of the homes in this village were only half standing. The recent floods brought on by the monsoons had washed away a good portion of the walls and foundations. A typical structure that was about twelve feet square housed as many as eight people at a time. The children, whose stomachs were bloated from malnutrition, ran around without any clothing. Most of the men and women had only one set of clothing per person. I stopped at one home to speak to whomever was inside. As I stuck my head in the door to ask if I could speak with anyone, two veiled women simply turned away and would not speak with me. On the way out of the village I observed that the water source there was also being used for bathing and for the animals' drinking supply. After we had left the village, I asked our guide, named Bachu, if this was typical of the conditions in all of the villages. Bachu said, "No. There is no Grameen Bank presence in this village. You will see a difference in other villages."

As we approached the second village, I noticed an immediate difference. There were several women standing around and talking outside of the homes. They did not seem to be disturbed by my presence at all. The homes looked sturdy and intact. Even though the homes were made of essentially the same materials as the ones in the other village, these had smooth mud walls and were larger, and some even had metal roofing. I approached one home where there were a couple of women standing. Using Bachu as my translator, I spoke with the women. There was the smell of fresh fish and rice coming from the house. I asked a woman why the homes did not appear to be damaged by the monsoon rains. She replied that they were able to afford to make repairs, and the metal roofing limited damage. As I was speaking with her, two of her young daughters were approaching, wearing school uniforms and carrying books. I spoke with one of the men in the village, and he invited us to stay for dinner. He said that they had plenty of food, and we were welcome there. I also noticed that everyone seemed to be well clothed, and the children were keeping busy playing soccer in a clearing. A group of about forty villagers followed me with curiosity as I wandered through the village.

This was definitely a sharp contrast from the previous village that we had visited. Bachu explained to me that one of the main reasons for the good conditions in the village was that the Grameen Bank had a strong presence in the area. The bank loaned money to women in the area to start businesses for themselves and provide additional income for the families. Their economic contributions also gave the women in the village more freedom and courage to be outspoken. The Grameen Bank certainly appeared to have made a positive impact on the lives of these people. I thought that there was a good lesson to be learned here for companies that are conducting business in Bangladesh.

3. Core Idea and Successful Development of the Grameen Bank

The Grameen Bank was established in 1976 by Professor Muhammad Yunus in an effort to help develop poor villages of Bangladesh as well as empower women in these same communities. The single greatest obstacle Professor Yunus saw in improving the living conditions and the standing that women had in the home was the lack of employment opportunities for women in Bangladesh. Mainly due to cultural norms in Islamic nations, the rights of women in Bangladesh were limited in the eyes of this male-dominated culture. Professor Yunus believed this cultural way of thinking could be changed by providing an opportunity for women in Bangladesh to contribute to the financial wellbeing of the family through employment opportunities. He believed that even in this male-dominated culture, the attitudes of men towards their wives would change if they saw the women of Bangladesh contributing to the household income. In a country as underdeveloped as Bangladesh with high unemployment among its people, this would be no easy task. At the same time, however, Bangladesh could begin making progress in developing itself into a more healthy and productive nation. As a means to accomplish this, the Grameen Bank was born (Grameen: Banking for the Poor).

The Grameen Bank operates a system of loaning to people who own under half an acre of land and mainly focuses on loaning to women. The idea is that empowering the poor to be self-employed will allow them to generate income and eventually pay back their loans. Once a person has demonstrated her ability to repay her loan, further loans can be made to further expand the business. The bank prudently evaluates whether it believes businesses will succeed and in some cases will not loan individuals money unless they choose another business idea. The Grameen Bank has been successful because it lends money to groups of individuals and then holds the group responsible to repay loans that any of its members do not repay. This leads to a system of self-monitoring and relies on peer pressure to encourage members to succeed in each of their businesses. Another reason for the success is the strong work ethic of the Bangladesh people and their desire to achieve success in their business and more adequately provide for their families. These two factors combined have resulted in huge success for the Grameen Bank and ultimately have established a benchmark for similar programs in other countries (Bornstein 1996).

Our research into the Grameen Bank has shown that this type of banking institution can be financially profitable and therefore is not charity. Since this project has weathered the test of time, it should be seen by other organizations as a method not only to provide opportunities but also to do so in a manner that can be a profitable enterprise. Since the Grameen Bank has been operating under a profit, these 'profits' have been used to establish other funds to help the local villagers. Funds such as the Group Fund Loan, Emergency Fund, Children's Welfare Fund, Special Savings Account/Joint Enterprises, House Loans as well as several other programs help to alleviate much of the poverty in some rural villages of Bangladesh. They have been used to increase the health, education and overall living standards of the Bangladesh villagers.

In the twenty-two years of existence of the Grameen Bank, the bank has loaned over $2.5 billion to 2,357,000 people. The number of houses built with Grameen funding exceeds 448,000. The repayment rate has been a phenomenal 98%, which is better than many large, private banks throughout the world (Grameen: Banking for the Poor). Programs established by the Grameen Bank have reduced illiteracy, provided the infrastructure in villages to provide tubewell water, provided healthcare and improved the way women are viewed in many rural villages of Bangladesh by their husbands. Historically, women in Bangladesh have not been given the same rights as men due to a cultural belief that goes back many centuries and is a reflection of the Islamic faith. Many husbands treat women who have succeeded under the Grameen Bank, more fairly since the women are able to contribute to the economic health of the household. Although this may not be seen as much of an ethical dilemma by some, it is viewed by many within the Bangladesh villages as a positive step.

4. Learning from the Grameen Bank

The ethical challenges for nations such as Bangladesh are many. The challenge we want to focus on is the issue of providing the most basic human rights by not just governments of these countries but also private organizations who come in contact with these villagers and the country overall. We are not suggesting that any company that does business in these countries should establish a banking system similar to the Grameen Bank, but they should have some responsibility to research ways of positively impacting the living conditions of the local citizens. Richard T. De George points out, in his book *Competing with Integrity in International Business* (1993), "that multinationals should contribute by their activity to the host country's development" (De George 1993:49 f.). We agree with this but also believe that it should not be left entirely up to multinational companies. If left entirely up to multinationals, then we could possibly see the consequence of organizations only worrying about the growth and not the development of its people. David Bornstein, in his book *The Price of a Dream* (1996), states that growth and development are two entirely different aspects that need to be clarified. Growth is only concerned with the amount of resources that are provided to the poor in these countries and not how these resources are most effectively used in empowering these people. Various organizations need to take an active role for true development to occur, or societies will not obtain the most benefit from resources that are available.

The model of social arrangement in civil society is effective to show that the government, corporations and private groups all need to work together to effectively implement any similar type of plan to tackle the issue of allowing all individuals their basic human rights (see Enderle 1997, Enderle and Peters 1998). Private groups are important since providing growth opportunities does not necessarily mean development. Most would agree that private groups are very effective in monitoring government spending or corporate spending since allowing only one group to make the decisions that affect all stakeholders may have a negative impact. Giving this authority to only one organization may result in that organization acting in its own self-interest. Since corporations are more accustomed to operating at a profit, their knowledge can complement a government that has more resources than the corporation. The Grameen bank was subsidized by the government in its early stages but was operated to generate a profit. This method is necessary to implement similar lending programs in other countries. In addition, corporations have developed a better understanding of capitalistic markets than have governments and can be valuable in lending this knowledge to organizations interested in establishing social causes. We believe this knowledge has come directly from interaction with the same groups of individuals that require assistance at times. We believe the acquisition of knowledge necessitates some reciprocation of knowledge so that different socioeconomic groups can benefit from it.

Empowering individuals in underdeveloped areas can best achieve the objective of development rather than growth. The most obvious ways of empowering people are through education and allowing individuals the opportunity of self-employment, as the Grameen Bank is doing. Development is the means that allows the poor of these nations to sustain their improved living conditions over the long-term and not just as a temporary solution until the resources dry up. If groups other than multinationals do not take the responsibility to oversee this development, then long-term benefits are not going to be sustained. Our contention is that organizations that do business in underdeveloped countries should work in conjunction with private groups to achieve sustainability. Again, expertise from corporations can be shared with private groups interested in meeting their objectives of establishing successful programs designed to allow citizens to obtain their basic human rights. We believe that corporations not sharing their knowledge are not acting in an ethically responsible manner.

Another ethical challenge facing Bangladesh is the treatment of the women in this country and how private groups should bear some of the responsibility in correcting this situation. Statistics show that the Grameen Bank has had a powerful influence on the empowerment of women in Bangladesh and has had a dramatic impact on increasing the living conditions in villages that have a branch of the Grameen Bank. Throughout the history of United States, women have slowly become more empowered and have begun to contribute to the economic welfare of U.S. families. This appears to be the trend developing in Bangladesh and is happening out of necessity to provide better lives for people in rural areas of Bangladesh. Without the establishment of the Grameen Bank, it is possible that many villages in Bangladesh would be even less developed than they are today. Not allowing women the same opportunities to employment as men is denying women their basic human rights. The Grameen Bank has been instrumental in correcting this injustice in parts of Bangladesh.

In a country with limited employment opportunities and financial resources, self-employment begins with the access to credit. Professor Yunus makes the argument that the access to credit is a fundamental human right. Since credit is based on having collateral and since the poor do not have access to this, there is no basis on which to lend to them. Yunus wrote,

> There is nothing inherent in the nature of credit that keeps it away from the poor. Nonetheless, the poor have no access to credit institutions. The logic behind this practice has always been considered infallible: Since the poor cannot provide collateral, the argument goes, there is no basis for lending to them (Mizan 1994).

Yunus goes on to state that those who are unable to accept this are likely to turn credit into charity to prove that credit will not help the poor. This is why Yunus believes it is so essential that his project succeed. It will demonstrate that credit will allow the poor to create employment opportunities for themselves. This theory of banking is consistent with the belief that instead of giving fish to a poor person, it is better to teach that person to fish.

5. Implications for Corporations

We believe that corporations could get involved with the poor of these nations without having to directly set up credit institutions such as the Grameen Bank. As the villagers of Bangladesh have shown, they are a hard working people who have not defaulted on many of the loans that have been provided to them. Corporations should get involved in funding the initial stages of these programs and let private organizations run the lending institution. The possibility exists for these corporations to have the start-up money returned to them with profits similar to those generated by the Grameen Bank. The Grameen Bank has shown that this program does not have to result in sunk cost; there is the possibility of implementing such a plan without having a negative impact on the bottom line of the company.

Corporations could also contribute without having to fund the project themselves but instead act as a cosigner by guaranteeing some loans. If new programs are as effective as the Grameen Bank, this may be done at a minimal cost. We are not suggesting that corporations guarantee every loan, but only a percentage over a threshold that would be covered by the profits from a newly established Grameen-style bank. We believe these two ideas would give more access to credit to the poor. This would serve the purpose of allowing the poor to have access to collateral indirectly and possibly eliminate the injustice of the poor not having access to credit. The ability to provide collateral does not directly predict how effectively a person can run a business so this alone should not be the sole factor for denying credit to an individual. The Grameen Bank provides an excellent example of how corporations can fulfill an ethical responsibility to help provide basic human rights to individuals. It can be done at a lower cost than previously thought.

The reason we believe corporations should bear some responsibility for developing these areas in third world countries is derived from simple logic. Businesses exist because society allows them to exist. Society allows and encourages business because society can benefit from businesses. Therefore, businesses have a responsibility to answer not only to their shareholders and owners but to society as a whole. If our society deems it necessary that businesses contribute to the development of society, then they must do so. We believe that corporations should concentrate some of their resources into looking into ways they can improve living conditions of the poor in nations where they do business even if the poor are not the people buying their products. Corporations should have some interest in what the individuals who are buying their products think is the social responsibility of those corporations. Since these are the people who are sustaining the existence of the corporations, then the corporations should have a moral obligation to do some things its customers feel are important. If it is helping to improve the living conditions of some of its citizens, then this is what corporations should be researching. The Grameen Bank has demonstrated that tackling such a challenge does not necessarily have to be a cost to the company, but rather can be done in a profitable way. This is not to say that all corporations should add this type of lending institution to their lines of business. Rather, if they choose this approach, they can find creative ways of doing it at a lower cost than previously thought. This approach can be encouraged by the argument that helping to develop new markets for their products can help the long-run success of companies. By increasing the living standards and income of individuals, those individuals may in turn become customers. This is another way in which involving corporations can assist in the development of individuals rather than just increasing the amount of resources available.

6. International Reach

The international implications of the Grameen Bank are clear since many similar lending organizations have been established in other developing areas throughout the world using the Grameen-style lending as a model. In Honduras there is the Goat Milk Program which loans villagers goats to produce milk. The income generated from the sale of the milk is used to pay for the original goats and subsequently to purchase additional goats and other animals to generate more income. Also in Honduras, the Program for Rural Reconstruction (PRP) was established to aid in development of the poor. The Women's Self-Employment Project in Chicago (WSEP) was based on the Grameen model in a large inner city context (Todd 1996). These are a few examples of programs that have had some success and demonstrate how the Grameen idea applies worldwide. The willingness of organizations throughout the world to attempt to duplicate the Grameen-style of lending is a testament to its validity and effectiveness in Bangladesh. Just as in Bangladesh, governments have been instrumental in assisting in the establishment of these programs during their infancy. Corporations can have a dramatic impact on the success of these programs either by lending their resources or their knowledge to develop similar programs in their communities.

7. Conclusion

In conclusion, we believe companies should play a role in developing areas of the world in which they operate. The model of social arrangements in civil society demonstrates this. This is also true because businesses have a responsibility to help in the improvement of human rights and the development of society. The Grameen Bank has proven that these responsibilities can be addressed while making a profit at the same time. In addition, the Grameen Bank has shown that collateral is not necessary for providing loans to people. Now that this concept has been proven, the basic human right of access to credit can be granted on a wider scale. Professor Yunus has addressed the issue of the oppression of women in an effective manner as well. When women gain access to credit, they have been able to gain economic freedom. This economic freedom has allowed women to contribute financially to the family and, as a result, overall freedom and education of women has improved. The lending style model implemented by Professor Yunus through the Grameen Bank can be used on a global basis to aid in the development of depressed areas. This is evident from the numerous organizations wordwide that have been successful in implementing Grameen-style lending.

References

Bangladesh. http://parallel.park.org/Japan/TokyoNet/aip/country/bangladesh/

Bornstein, D. 1996. *The Price of a Dream*. New York: Simon & Schuster.

De George, Richard T. 1993. *Competing with Integrity in International Business*. New York: Oxford University Press.

Enderle, G. 1997. The Role of Corporate Ethics in a Market Economy and Civil Society. In *Civil Society in a Chinese Context,* ed. Wang Miaoyang, Yu Xuanmen and Manuel B. Dy, 203–30. Washington, D.C.: The Council for Research in Values and Philosophy.

Enderle, G. and Peters, G. 1998. *A Strange Affair? The Emerging Relationship Between NGOs and Transnational Companies*. London: PriceWaterhouse. Also: http://www.pwcglobal.com/uk/eng/ins-sol/survey-rep/ngoreview_allsalliukeng.html.

Grameen: Banking for the Poor. http://www.grameen.com.

Mizan, A.N. 1994. *In Quest of Empowerment*. Bangladesh: University Press Limited.

Todd, H. 1996. *Women at the Center, Grameen Bank Borrowers After One Decade*. Boulder: Westview Press.

The Fall of Barings: An Analysis of Ethical Issues and Contributing Factors

Sue Cooper
Imperial College
University of London
London, England (U.K.)

1. Introduction

On 27 February 1995, newspapers announced the collapse of Barings, a merchant bank with over 230 years of successful trading behind it. Barings was subsequently sold to ING for £1. Barings bondholders lost investments worth £90 million. Barings executives lost their jobs, and both the management of Barings and the Bank of England came in for severe criticism, shaking confidence in the regulatory system which is a necessary factor in London' pre-eminence as a financial centre.

The cause of all the chaos was a loss of around £600 million on an unauthorised options position held by one of Barings traders in Singapore, Nick Leeson, who was given a six year prison sentence in Singapore. Nick Leeson had for some time been covering up errors made by himself and his team by making entries in an 'error account' (account number 88888) whose existence he kept secret from his managers in London. He then sold futures and options tied to the Nikkei index to cover the errors, gambling on the market remaining stable. Unfortunately the market moved against him (following a devastating earthquake and a 2% drop in the dollar against the yen) and the losses multiplied.

Particularly with the benefit of hindsight, it is very easy to describe Nick Leeson's actions as wrong. From a deontological perspective, taking and concealing unauthorised options positions breaches the principle of honesty which appears in most moral codes. From a utilitarian perspective, the amount of harm caused – to Nick Leeson himself, to his colleagues in Barings, and to Barings' investors – easily outweighs any temporary pleasure which accrued to Mr. Leeson from his ability to keep drawing his salary (which would have been compromised by revealing the losses his unauthorised position was designed to conceal).

A closer analysis, however, reveals some interesting moral questions:
(a) How wrong were Nick Leeson's actions from both deontological and utilitarian perspectives? What moral principles can be used to assess his actions, and what weighting should be given to those principles he breached as opposed to those he may have acted by?
(b) Were the actions, or lack of actions, of other parties contributing factors? If so, what blame is attached to them?

2. Moral Perspectives

Before attempting to make any kind of moral judgement about Nick Leeson's actions, it is necessary to consider his motives. According to his biography, Nick Leeson first opened the notorious error account number 88888, to which his unauthorised positions were posted, as a means of concealing a mistake made by a new and junior member of his staff, who would – according to Nick Leeson – have lost her job if the mistake had been reported. Nick Leeson says (1996:42):

> It wouldn't be easy for her to find another job on SIMEX with just one week at Barings on her CV. And if she lived with her parents, she'd be bringing in money which they needed...

He is clearly here appealing to the "good Samaritan" principle – helping others as a justification for breaching the principle that honesty is a good thing.

Later, unauthorised options positions were similarly taken to conceal losses made by another colleague, and it was some months after the error account was first opened that Nick Leeson started to use it to cover up losses for which he was personally responsible. These losses, it should be stressed, arose in the normal course of trading by himself and by his team. They were thus not morally culpable in themselves – but they would have adversely affected the team's bonus position. As discovery neared, Nick Leeson invented stories, and forged documents, in attempts to prevent the auditors discovering the account.

From a deontological perspective, we need to consider whether Nick Leeson's actions were intrinsically wrong according to the principles of a moral code. The primary exponent of deontology (the doctrine that the moral worth of an action is independent of its consequences) was Immanuel Kant. Kant attempted to define a universal rule for determining whether actions were "moral:" "act only in ways that you would want all others to act." From this rule he derived certain "categorical imperatives" against which courses of action could be judged. Whether something is in accordance with a categorical imperative can be determined by considering what would happen if it were universalized. On this view, killing people is wrong because if everyone did it there would be a general loss of welfare to society. Helping people, on the other hand, must be right because if everyone helps each other the world is a better place.

If one were to adopt Kant's view, Nick Leeson's actions would have to be condemned outright as they involved deceit and breach of trust, which would be regarded as wrong (because if universalized they would undermine the fabric of society). Kant's view was that:

> Truthfulness in statements which cannot be avoided is the formal duty of an individual to everyone, however great may be the disadvantage accruing to himself or to another. (Kant, "On a Supposed Right to Lie," quoted in Bok 1978:38.)

Many commentators, however, adopt a more teleological view, taking into account the outcome of an action rather than taking an absolutist view of its intrinsic moral quality. Often quoted is the example of a lie told to hide from a murderer the whereabouts of his intended victim. Many regard such a lie as justifiable, because its object is to avert harm. Indeed, a utilitarian view (which assesses actions according to their capacity to increase pleasure or utility) would be that in these circumstances it would be more moral to lie (which would bring about the greater good of preserving life) than to tell the truth (which would bring harm to another).

The issues in the Barings case are not quite so clear cut for the utilitarian as the extreme example where a lie is told to save life. Nick Leeson deceived his employer, not to save lives, but to protect himself and his team from the consequences of his employer discovering mistakes –

a lesser, and also a more legitimate, threat than murder. With hindsight, it is easy to condemn his actions from a utilitarian perspective, given the amount of harm they caused. But the question is, need they have caused that degree of harm? If there had been no earthquake, and the market had remained stable instead of falling at the crucial point, Nick Leeson might have been able to close out the position and reverse the losses. Barings would not then have suffered by his actions, and Nick Leeson and his team would have profited by retaining their jobs and earning bonuses. On this view, the main criticism of Nick Leeson will be that he failed to give sufficient weight to the risk that the market would move against him – arguably an error of judgement rather than of simple morality (although it could be argued that the way in which one assesses risk to others when it is balanced against the prospect of immediate gain for oneself does have a moral dimension).

The dilemma facing any commentator wishing to make a moral assessment of Leeson's actions is neatly summarised by viewing the entire episode through a rule utilitarian and a strict consequentialist (act utilitarian) perspective. An act utilitarian or strict consequentialist would look at the probable consequences of Leeson's actions in isolation. Given Leeson's success in making profits from market fluctuations in the normal course of his job, it would have been difficult to predict with any degree of certainty that adverse consequences would follow from his unauthorised actions, while the short term benefits (retention of job security) were, in contrast, highly probable. On this view, his actions look considerably less morally culpable than when viewed from a deontological perspective.

The rule utilitarian, however, holds that you draw in certain deontological tenets in order to temper the stricter act utilitarianism which looks only at the outcome of an individual action. A rule utilitarian might assert that *in general* deceit, and breach of an employer's trust, can lead to an unhappy state in the long term – and so it should have been avoided by Leeson. The question then arises whether the circumstances were extreme enough to justify a breach of the general rule, given that the team would face lawful dismissal by an employer, rather than murder. Different answers to this question are possible, depending on the view taken of the legitimacy of the threat of dismissal for errors. But the presupposition must be that an action involving deceit and breach of trust should be avoided if at all possible.

Milton Friedman advocated a teleological view of morality under which actions have to be assessed according to whether or not they further the objectives of the owners of the business. He argued that the only outcome towards which business should work was the increase of its profits:

> There is one and only one social responsibility of business – to use its resources and engage in activities designed to increase its profits so long as it stays within the rules of the game, which is to say, engages in open and free competition without deception or fraud (Friedman, *Capitalism and Freedom*, quoted in Friedman 1970:82).

It follows from this view, according to Friedman, that the primary responsibility of the company's executives, as agents of the company, is to conduct the business in such a way as to make as much money as possible for the owners, and that it would be wrong for them to pursue other ends, no matter how socially worthwhile those ends are. On this view all Leeson's actions would be regarded as wrong because they did not directly further the company's aims, no matter how altruistic his motives may have been at the outset. The "utilitarian calculus" here involves taking into account only possible gains to the company, and not possible gains to others. Friedman's justification for this is that anything which interferes with the free operation of the market adversely affects welfare generally – therefore it is unreasonable for companies, or their executives, to put concern for individuals before the profit making motive in determining courses of action.

It can be said, then, that from a strict act-utiltarian point of view the position is not entirely clear cut, in that Leeson's actions need not have led to an unhappy outcome for anyone. But from a deontological (universalist) point of view, and from those teleological perspectives which bring in deontological tenets as general rules (to be broken only in extreme circumstances), Leeson's actions would generally be regarded as wrong.

3. Other Factors

Reports by the Bank of England and the Singapore International Monetary Exchange (SIMEX) criticised the supervisory and management failures of Barings as contributing factors. Barings should not have put Nick Leeson in the position where he was running both front and back offices and therefore in a position to cover up mistakes. Having done so, they should have put in place proper management controls. The

Report of the Board of Banking Supervision Inquiry into the circum-stances of the collapse of Barings (The Bank of England Report 1995), concluded (paragraph 13.4) that:
(a) the losses were incurred by reason of unauthorised and concealed trading activities within BFS [Barings Futures Singapore];
(b) the true position was not noticed earlier by reasons of a serious fail-ure of controls and managerial confusion within Barings;
(c) the true position had not been detected prior to the collapse by the external auditors, supervisors, or regulators of Barings.

The report by the Singapore authorities put the blame even more squarely on Barings:

> In our view the Barings group's management either knew or should have known about the existence of account 88888 and of the losses incurred from transac-tions booked in this account. Barings London settlements, knew, or should have known, that the margin feed constituted a complete breakdown of the margin calls that were being made by BFS on its clients. Yet Barings London settle-ments claimed that it never used the margin feed, a simple one-page document, to resolve the unreconciled balance (Singaporean Report into the collapse of Barings, p. 5, quoted in Leeson 1996:260–1).

Barings' supervisory failures however, constituted sins of omission rather than of commission. Misplaced trust may be unwise, but is not necessarily morally culpable (although one could take the view that the failure to protect shareholders' interests in itself represented a breach of trust).

What is more interesting is to speculate on the extent to which the culture created by Barings put pressures on Nick Leeson which led him to conceal mistakes rather than own up to them. The climate of the trad-ing floor was highly competitive. Success was rewarded by huge bo-nuses; failure by ignominious dismissal. Not being seen to make mis-takes was essential for survival. Since not making mistakes in the hothouse environment of an open outcry trading floor is impossible, the pressure to conceal them must have been intense.

The pressure to succeed is likely to have affected not only Nick Leeson, but also those above him in the management chain who should have found the problems earlier. Since their bonuses depended on his suc-cess, there must have been a very strong temptation to believe in that success, and not to probe too deeply into any doubts.

Lynn Sharp Paine puts forward the view that organisations must take some responsibility for putting pressures on employees that adversely affect their judgement. She describes (Paine 1994:106) how Sears' CEO Edward Brennan acknowledged "management's responsibility for putting in place compensation and goal-setting systems that "created an environment in which mistakes did occur." (Sears' employees had been selling customers unnecessary parts in an attempt to meet their sales targets.) She concludes that errors of judgement often "reveal a culture that is insensitive or indifferent to ethical considerations or one that lacks effective organizational systems." The parallels with Barings are immediately obvious.

Added to this pressure, the kind of financial duplicity practised by Nick Leeson seems – while it is successful – like a victimless crime. If the market had remained stable instead of falling, no-one need ever have known about account 88888, and arguably nobody would have been any worse off. (The counterparties to the real trades posted to account 88888 traded because they wanted to do so: what Nick Leeson was doing in terms of buying and selling securities was no different in kind from what he, or any authorised trader, was paid to do in the normal course of business.) The culpability was not in the intrinsic nature of the transactions, but in the fact that they were unauthorised and concealed – and large.

Nick Leeson, in his autobiography, accepts that despite contributing factors, the responsibility for his actions was his alone.

> This was the full catalogue of my crimes. Set out in black and white, they looked appalling. I tried to remember the pressure I'd been under to perform and produce profits, but then I realised that this was just looking for excuses. These were my crimes... (Lesson 1996:249).

But nonetheless Barings must bear some blame for the pressures they created to "perform and produce profits," and for putting Nick Leeson in a position where he controlled both the front and back offices – thus providing both the motive and the opportunity for the unauthorised account. And both Barings and the Bank of England failed in their fiduciary duty to investors to carry out adequate checks on unauthorised positions and unorthodox requests to transfer funds.

4. Conclusions

From a deontological perspective, Nick Leeson's actions were clearly wrong insofar as they involved deceit and breach of trust. It is easy to see, however, how – given the apparently "victimless" nature of the transactions – the process was initiated, initially to hide the mistakes of his team, for more altruistic reasons.

From a strict "act utilitarian" perspective, the actions were clearly wrong with hindsight – but without hindsight, and given the possibility of a different outcome, the issue may become one of misjudgement of risks rather than of morality. And the culture within which Nick Leeson was operating, the failure of Barings management to exercise proper controls, and the supervisory failures of the Bank of England, were all contributing factors.

Certainly regulators around the world were very quick to accept responsibility for tightening the regulatory environment to lessen the risk of recurrence. In May 1995, futures and options market regulators from 16 countries met in Windsor and agreed a programme of work, set out in the "Windsor Declaration," designed to address the regulatory concerns raised by Barings. This work was taken forward at a global level by a number of bodies such as the IOSCO[1] Technical Committee, the Futures Industry Association Global Task Force on Financial Integrity, and the Group of Thirty, a private sector group whose members were drawn from leading banking and securities firms. The *Final Report from the Co-Chairmen of the May 1995 Windsor Committee to the Technical Committee of IOSCO*, published in 1996, concluded that valuable progress had been made in providing for market authorities to share information which would help identify high-risk exposures, in establishing procedures for dealing with market crises, and in increasing the transparency of default procedures to provide increased investor protection:

> Significant concrete steps have been taken in a remarkably short period of time relevant to key areas identified above, including large exposures, procedures in a market crisis, enhanced transparency of market protection and procedures, client asset protection and minimizing the systemic effects of a market disruption. These developments have the potential to reduce systemic risk and enhance regulatory safeguards in an increasingly global financial market place (Windsor Committee 1996, Conclusion).

Within the UK, the Bank of England report of 18 May 1995 highlighted errors of judgement and supervisory failures within the Bank (and to a lesser extent within the SFA[2]), as well as failings in Barings' management and control systems. The report's recommendations included improved risk analysis procedures (including monitoring of large exposures and review of internal control systems as well as results), revised procedures for the approval of solo consolidation (whereby the aggregation of the results of a number of entities can obscure the risks run by each), and closer working with other regulatory bodies. A subsequent report announced a reorganisation of the Bank's surveillance functions, a projected increase of up to 25% in total annual spending on supervision, the setting up of a Quality Assurance function, and the development of a systematic model of risk assessment.

Work on improving regulation and minimising risk has continued: in the last eighteen months the publications of the Basle Committee on Banking Supervision have included, inter alia, reports on Core Principles for Effective Banking Supervision (1998), and on a Framework for the Evaluation of Internal Control Systems (1997). The merger in the U.K. of nine regulatory bodies into a single Financial Services Authority (the FSA) in 1997 was intended to provide improved co-ordination of regulatory functions, envisaging that, in the words of Howard Davies, its first Chairman, "it will be possible, within such a framework, to achieve significant improvements in operating efficiencies, in consumer responsiveness, and in sensitivity to the market."

However, as the Co-Chairmen of the May 1995 Windsor Meeting pointed out in the conclusion of their report to the Technical Committee of IOSCO, "despite their best efforts, supervisory authorities cannot alone ensure that a major market event will not again occur" (Windsor Committee 1996, Conclusion). The need for internal controls is widely recognized as a key factor in preventing recurrence, but this aspect is not easy to regulate for. As early as 1992, the Cadbury report on Corporate Governance recognised the importance of internal controls, recommending that company reports should include a statement on the effectiveness of internal controls (Cadbury 1992:par. 4.32). In January 1998, the Hampel report noted that this recommendation had not been widely complied with, apparently due to concern that "directors or auditors who confirmed the effctiveness of a company's control system may be exposed to legal liability if unintentional misstatement or loss of any kind is found to have occurred" (Hampel 1998:par. 6.11). Hampel suggested that directors should simply be encouraged to report on the system, without commenting on effectiveness – which sits a little uneasily with the statement that "we fully endorse the Cadbury comment that internal control is a key aspect of efficient management" (Hampel 1998:par. 6.13).

Still harder, perhaps, to regulate for are the cultural aspects that created the pressure on Nick Leeson to be seen to succeed; large bonuses remain a feature of life in the financial world. And pressure to deliver can take other, less obvious forms: the U.K. Office for National Statistics have recently been criticised for publishing data which they knew to be flawed, presumably because the pressure to deliver (notwithstanding the probable absence of large bonuses as a factor) outweighed the ethical considerations which might have stopped publication pending review (Financial Times 1999).

However, it is perhaps by addressing the cultural and ethical issues, subjective though they may be compared to regulatory requirements, that firms can most effectively seek to minimise risk. Organizations should attempt to outline a clear code of conduct which puts a high premium on integrity, and allows some tolerance of mistakes while making it clear that there will be zero tolerance of attempts to conceal mistakes. Senior managers can do much to send appropriate signals to employees about the need to uphold such a code – not least by ensuring that the reward system takes account of integrity as well as of results. And even within existing reward frameworks, good management can endeavour to create a more supportive, team based culture than was in existence at Barings, to reduce the sort of pressures which helped tempt Nick Leeson to cover up his mistakes.

Endnotes

1. International Organization of Securities Commissions.
2. The Securities and Futures Authority, which subsequently became part of the Financial Services Authority (the FSA).

References

Bank of England Press Release. 1996. 24 July. Available online: http://www.coi.gov.uk/coi/depts/GBE//coi0832c.ok. [Accessed 27 February 1999].

Bank of England Report. 1995. *Report of the Board of Banking Supervision Inquiry into the circumstances of the collapse of Barings, 18 July 1995.* London: HMSO. Available online: http://www.numa.com/derivs/ref/barings/bar00.htm [Accessed 27 February 1999].

Basle Committee on Banking Supervision. 1997. *Core Principles for Effective Banking Supervision.* Committees at the Bank for International Settlements. September 1997. Available online: http://risk.ifci.ch/138190.htm [Accessed 27 February 1999].

Basle Committee on Banking Supervision. 1998. *Framework for the Evaluation of Internal Control Systems.* Committees at the Bank for International Settlements (BIS). January 1998. Available online: http://risk.ifci.ch/142380.htm [Accessed 27 February 1999].

Bok, S. 1978. *Lying: Moral Choice in Public and Private Life.* Hassocks: Harvester Press.

Boylan, M. (ed.) 1995. ed. *Ethical Issues in Business*. Fort Worth, Texas; London: Harcourt Brace College Publishers.

Cadbury Report. 1992. *Report of the Committee on the Financial Aspects of Corporate Governance 1 December 1992*. London: Gee.

Financial Times. 1999. 3 March.

FSA Press Release. 1997. 28 October. Available on line: http://www.sib.co.uk/pressrel/ prcover.htm [Accessed 8 March 1999].

Friedman, M. 1970. "The Social Responsibility of Business Is to Increase Its Profits," *The New York Times Sunday Magazine* 13 September 13, 1970. Reprinted in Boylan 1995:76–83.

Hampel Report. 1998. *Committee on Corporate Governance, Final Report January 1998*. London: Gee.

Leeson, N. (1996) *Rogue Trader*. London: Little, Brown and Co.

Paine, L.S. 1994. "Managing for Organizational Integrity." *Harvard Business Review* (March–April).

Windsor Committee Report. 1996. Final Report from the Co-Chairmen of the May 1995 Windsor Committee to the Technical Committee of IOSCO. International Organization of Securities Commissions (IOSCO), No. 44: IOSCO/SIB/CFTC. September 1996. Available online at: http://risk.ifci.ch/140340.htm [Accessed 27 February 1999].

Shell in Nigeria

Simon Bernstein
Imperial College
University of London
London, England (U.K.)

1. Introduction

Through its oil operations in Nigeria, Shell stands accused of causing environmental destruction to Ogoniland in the Niger Delta and of supporting a repressive military dictatorship that has met the protests of the Ogoni people with violence. Criticism of the Nigerian government and Shell reached a peak in November 1995 when Ken Saro-Wiwa, leader of MOSOP, the Ogoni protest movement, was hanged with eight others following months of torture and a trial described by John Major, then British Prime Minister, as "Judicial murder" (*The Independent*, 13 November 1995). A number of pressure groups including Greenpeace and Amnesty International urged Shell to assert its influence on the Nigerian government to intervene on the prisoners' behalf. They also called for a consumer boycott of Shell and demanded the company cease its operations in the country.

Shell disputed the causes of environmental damage and argued that it was a matter of policy not to intervene in political affairs. It also claimed that money had been re-invested in the community through a series of socially beneficial projects. At the time of writing this essay Shell intended to go ahead with a £2.28 billion gas project in Ogoniland and had renewed its contract to operate oil pipelines in the region.

This case provides an interesting opportunity to examine the dilemmas facing a multinational company. Although there are ethical issues surrounding the behaviour of the Nigerian government, and indeed foreign powers, this assignment is focused on the dilemmas facing Shell. As such, an analysis of Shell's position will be presented along with an examination of the company's response to their critics. An attempt will then be made to suggest steps Shell could take to avoid such criticisms in the future.

2. Background

The Anglo/Dutch oil giant Shell is one of the most powerful corporations in the world. It is Europe's top profit-maker and in 1992, its sales exceeded the GNP of all but twenty-three countries worldwide (*The Ethical Consumer*, Issue 34). Shell has been operating in Nigeria since 1937 with oil production beginning in 1958. By 1995 there were ninety-four oilfields spread over 31,000 square kilometres of the Niger Delta. The company employs 5,000 staff directly and over 20,000 via contracts. The Shell Petroleum Development Company (SPDC) is the largest of the six oil majors active in Nigeria and operates as a venture on behalf of the Nigerian National Petroleum Corporation (55%), Shell (30%), Elf (10%), and Agip (5%) (Shell Briefing 1995).

Perhaps the most significant fact is the massive financial contribution the venture makes towards Nigeria:
- More than 90% of net revenues from each barrel of oil go to the Nigerian government;
- Oil provides 90% of Nigerian exports;
- Oil makes up 80% of government revenues (*The Financial Times*, 26 July 1995).

Nigeria is run by a military regime that annulled the democratic elections in 1993 and imprisoned the president-elect, Chief Moshood Abiola. The government has a reputation for human rights abuse and is also the subject of an arms embargo by many Western governments, including the U.K. Ogoniland is a densely populated oil-rich region in southeast Nigeria where 500,000 people live mainly by fishing and farming. The Ogoni people have numerous grievances about the way Shell has operated in the area, not least that they have received virtually nothing from the exploitation of their land. Few Ogoni households have electricity; there is only one doctor per 70,000 people and one hospital for the whole region; unemployment is 85%; only 20% of the population is literate; there is no piped water; and the average life expectancy is fifty-one – three years lower than the Nigerian average (*Guardian Weekly*, 15 January 1995).

In 1993, an environmental report on Ogoniland found badly-maintained and leaking oil pipelines, polluted water, fountains of emulsified oil pouring into villagers' fields, blowouts, air pollution, canals driven through farmland causing flooding and disruption of fresh water supplies, footpaths blocked by pipelines, drainage problems, polluted wells, delays in repairing faults and continuous noise (Ashton-Jones 1995). In addition, many of Shell's gas flares are situated close to villages, causing thick soot deposits and soil pollution, making farming impossible. Greenpeace research also found Shell spilt 1.6 million gallons of oil there between 1982 and 1992 – 40% of its total spills world-wide (Greenpeace 1994).

In 1993, 300,000 people participated in a peaceful protest against what they claimed was the devastation of their land, water and air by primarily, Shell (*Guardian Weekly*, 15 January 1995). A few weeks later, Shell suspended its operations in Ogoniland due to the alleged intimidation of its workforce. The Nigerian government sealed off the region and waged a military campaign against MOSOP. Amnesty estimates that more than 1,800 people have been killed and has evidence of the destruction of villages, rape and theft by soldiers.

3. Arguments Supporting Shell

Shell defends its position in Nigeria by arguing:
- the company makes a substantial contribution to the Nigerian economy;
- environmental damage is due to factors beyond their control;
- "quiet diplomacy" is more effective than confrontation in dealing with the Nigerian government;
- a complete withdrawal from Nigeria would not serve anyone's best interests.

Shell claims to contribute significantly to the Nigerian economy through the sale of oil – it states the company shares only $1 per barrel with Elf and Agip, that 90% of net revenues go to Nigeria, benefiting its people through the building of schools, roads and universities. The company admits more money could have gone back to the six million inhabitants of Nigeria's oil-producing areas, although it claims to have influenced the government's decision to increase the proportion of revenues given to these areas from 1.5% to 3% in 1992. In 1995, the government stated the amount would rise further to 13% (Shell Briefing 1995).

Besides employing thousands in Ogoniland, Shell has contributed directly to the local economy in the Delta region. Not only has the oil industry advanced economic progress apace, but also Shell spent $25 million on a community aid programme in 1994. It can cite agricultural assistance schemes, hospitals, schools, roads and water projects as examples of local social benefits.

Shell argues it has transferred a significant amount of technical know-how to Nigeria providing training, overseas assignments for eighty Nigerians, introducing the latest techniques such as horizontal drilling and setting itself up as a model of anti-corruption whilst striving for long-term objectives over short-term profits.

Environmentally, Shell admits gas flaring is a problem. However, it claims saboteurs are responsible for much oil pollution and the environment is being destroyed by factors beyond its control – such as over-population, deforestation, poor agricultural practices and over-fishing. It has sent 3,000 staff on community and environmental awareness courses and in 1995 initiated a $4.5 million Niger Delta Environmental Survey.

Shell argues gas flaring can only be targeted if it is allowed to undertake its liquefaction operation. This will provide more employment and allow Nigeria to diversify away from being a crude oil economy when dividends begin to flow to the government around 2007. To cancel would be to deny the obvious benefits to the Nigerian people (Shell Briefing 1995).

Shell has a clear policy in relation to political affairs: it should not get involved. It claims its tactics of quiet diplomacy led to the peaceful resolution of a strike by SPDC workers in 1994. Top managers are involved in the Nigerian Economic Summit, providing advice to the government on economic and social issues. In fact, Shell says a number of favourable initiatives in the 1995 budget arose from suggestions by the group (Shell Briefing 1995). An approach favoured over confrontation.

Finally, Shell can justifiably claim any rival would simply take over operations if they left. In addition, it could not simply pack up production facilities and its objective is to provide maximum profits for shareholders. Oil projects take years to plan and complete and it can be decades before a return on investment is seen. In this climate, short-term political demonstrations are simply not an option.

4. Arguments Against Shell

Shell can be criticised on a number of fronts. Firstly, the Ogoni people claim the company has spent only $200,000 on its community assistance programme – a mere 0.000007% of the value of the oil extracted (*The Ethical Consumer*, Issue 34).

The Guardian (20 September 1995) states that the projects mentioned did not receive anything, only corrupt officials benefited, and refutes Shell's assertion that it spent more. In addition, social conditions described above (see Background A) indicate that in Ogoniland, at least, the life of inhabitants has barely improved.

On the environment, Shell is also open to accusations of hypocrisy and double standards. Whilst the company makes great play of its «greener» image in «developed» countries, even basing a television commercial on the invisibility of its pipeline in a beautiful Welsh valley, its environmental record in Nigeria is very different. Whilst Shell blames sabotage for 60% of oil spillage, the Nigerian Ministry of Petroleum puts the figure at nearer 18% and attributes 38% to equipment malfunction (*The Ethical Consumer*, Issue 34). Indeed, Shell itself admits its facilities are in need of upgrade and renewal (Shell Briefing 1995).

The claim that the company wishes to reduce the environmental impact of its operations by, for example, ceasing gas flaring and investing in a liquefied natural gas project also seems to ring hollow: a cynic might observe gas flaring results from an excess of oil and thus wasted potential profits; the gas project would enable Shell to realise this income in the long term. One can also argue that a commitment to clean up the massive damage already done is a case of too little too late.

Perhaps the most serious charge is Shell's refusal to intercede with the Nigerian government on behalf of both the nine Ogonis facing the death sentence and the wider Delta community. By employing Friedman's maxim "business is the business of business", Shell state it is not their role to take such action (Shell Briefing 1995). However, as The Economist (on 2 December 1995) alleges, politics can be viewed as part of the company's daily business. Multinational firms can (and in the case of Shell have) alter a country's geography and ecology or change the balance of wealth between its regions. Shell's entanglement in Nigerian politics was perhaps inevitable.

By Shell's own admission it has tried to influence the government to invest more money in Ogoniland – it advises on economic and social issues and claims to have affected changes to the 1995 national budget (see above). Shell has also used Nigerian security forces to protect its installations. One document shows a Shell manager writing to the regional governor for the "usual assistance to enable the project to proceed". This assistance was known by Shell to involve the use of violence, especially given the public pronouncements of the extremist security forces leader (*The Financial Times*, 16 December 1995). Finally, under increasing pressure, Shell changed its line only days before Saro-Wiwa's execution by writing to General Abacha requesting clemency on humanitarian grounds (*The Financial Times*, 11 November 1995). This of all their actions perhaps represents the greatest hypocrisy. By continuing its operations, Shell has been accused of supporting a repressive regime. It could be argued that disinvestment by one multinational makes the position of others less tenable and thus political change more likely. On this basis Shell should pull out of Nigeria.

5. Evaluation of Shell's Response

Despite campaigns from Greenpeace, Friends of the Earth, Amnesty and the Body Shop, plus protests at a shareholders' meeting in London, Shell decided to press ahead with the natural gas project. Certainly from an environmental perspective this makes sense: liquefaction will reduce the pollution caused by gas flaring. Shell's shareholders and the Nigerian government will also benefit financially from around 2007. Perhaps by this time Nigeria may have a more liberal government.

In response to the many criticisms, Shell put its PR machine into overdrive. It appears the company learnt from the Brent Spar affair that PR is important in winning a public argument. The Shell Briefing used as a source here was clearly produced and distributed to the media with this in mind. Protest groups were attacked for using an old photograph of gas flaring that Shell claimed was taken three years previously (*The Financial Times*, 24 November 1995).

In addition, a series of press advertisements was taken to put forward the company's case. However, Shell's advertising campaign itself misfired when the daughter of the imprisoned president complained that parts of her interview on BBC Television's "Newsnight" were quoted out of context and permission to use her name and words in the advert was not sought (*The Guardian*, 20 November 1995).

It is interesting to note how Shell dealt with the Nigerian affair compared to Brent Spar given that each was handled by different parts of the organisation's complex structure. The latter was very painful for Shell because it created a division between the U.K. arm and the group overlords in The Hague. Finally, The Hague overruled the U.K. arm's decision. In Nigeria meanwhile, The Hague had sole responsibility – resulting in a more consistent business line being pursued (*The Financial Times*, 15 Novermber 1995).

Shell has faced previous dilemmas – including oil leaks and spillage in the Mersey in 1989 and 1990, their withdrawal from Burma in 1992 and the manufacture of pesticides near Denver on a site previously used by the U.S. army for making nerve gas. Perhaps the best known case, however, is that of South Africa where the company ignored world opinion and remained because, it argued, it was good for business and South Africa's black population. Shell could argue this strategy paid off as it now holds a strong position there. In addition, recent events in Libya, Iran and Iraq seem to indicate sanctions are not always effective if aimed at removing repressive governments. Nigeria demonstrates a certain consistency with South Africa, although Shell's departure from Burma was attributed by many to the autocratic regime and its poor human rights record – not the "commercial reasons" cited by the company (*The Independent*, 14 November 1995).

At the time of writing this essay it was unclear whether Shell had a code or set of rules on ethical matters. Undoubtedly it has developed a reputation for long-term scenario planning and considers its impact on the environment (Johnson and Scholes 1993:86–87) but how far these very high level plans are put into practice is not known. It appears from the above cases that Shell tends to be reactive rather than proactive in its approach to ethical issues – hence the change of policy over Brent Spar and the SaroWiwa letter to the Nigerian government.

The ethical issues of openness and honesty also arise. Should Shell have attempted to conceal its use of Nigerian security forces to protect its operations? It knew violence was being used against the Ogoni people (*The Financial Times*, 16 December 1995). Aside from the moral dilemma, it was possible evidence of both its own requests for assistance and that the ensuing brutality would be discovered. Should Shell have raised its hand and expressed "deep regret" in advance or taken a chance on not being exposed later?

It is clear multinationals are in a unique position as they operate across different cultures and belief systems. Moral relativity therefore plays a complicating role in the decisions faced by such companies. Moreover, oil companies are involved in projects which can take decades before any return on investment is realised – so they cannot make and break contracts at the drop of an executioner's axe.

Oil companies, however, are often more deeply involved with governments than other companies because their business involves extracting and exploiting a country's natural resources through joint ventures. Thus they have greater power and influence than other companies. They also have greater responsibility when it comes to poor environmental social and humanitarian standards set by governments, which leaves us with the proposition of world government by business. Would we be happy if Shell were found to be interfering in the internal political affairs of the U.K.? It is a tricky dilemma.

6. Recommendations for the Future

Many guidelines have been suggested for companies to adopt to help carry out business ethically – whether on an individual dimension or organisationally. Individually, these include internal training programmes, self and peer perception and more focused selection procedures. Organisationally, it includes having an established Code of Ethics and Rules of Ethics, an Ethical Policy Statement, ethical management, an Ethics Committee and where possible an ethical ombudsman (Drummond and Bain 1995). These are methods Shell should be using to give them clearer direction as an organisation, and for their individual employees to follow an ethical organisational culture. In addition, the establishment of an international standardised ethical code for the big oil companies would help to avoid double standards worldwide and set out clearer guidelines on ethical behaviour.

Shell must illustrate its commitment and performance by consulting more effectively with its stakeholders, delivering a balanced assessment of critical situations that should then be externally validated to rebuild the credibility of information supplied by Shell. Shell needs to ensure its auditing and reporting activity address *all* three questions of economic prosperity, environmental protection and social equity (*The Financial Times*, 18 December 1995). In addition, they must remember who the stakeholders are – not just their shareholders and the Nigerian government, but also the people who live in the areas they are allegedly destroying.

Is it feasible for Shell to develop higher environmental standards worldwide to gain competitive advantage – aiming for long-term over short-term profits by raising brand value rather than degrading it? Improved environmental standards and direct reinvestment into areas in which they are present would certainly be advantageous to Shell in fighting off the threat of consumer boycotts (such as during the Brent Spar issue when sales in Germany fell by 30%), improving their public image and avoiding future conflicts.

With regard to political intervention, is it not up to governments to deal with such complex situations? Shell was left in a highly vulnerable situation with no lead given by any government during this crisis. Should Shell set a precedent that they only obey embargoes introduced by home/powerful governments? This would certainly tighten public pressure on Shell in situations such as this and force governments to act more forcefully.

As with many other firms Shell needs to adopt a solid framework of ideas, promote employee awareness and implement institutional supports for evaluating their ethics. They must be aware not only of constant and current ethical issues, but also of emerging issues, and should look at what similar firms are doing, thus adopting compliance and benchmarking measures for their behaviour.

7. Conclusions

Business Ethics is "The study of those decisions of managers and corporate management which involve moral decisions" (Gandz and Hayes 1988) and is of growing importance in today's business environment. Corporations are becoming more and more powerful (IBM's sales are ten times the GNP of Ethiopia) as they grow and governments politically retreat, but the general population is also becoming more powerful. Due to improved communications and public awareness, people are more discerning about what they buy and how they invest their disposable income. As such, corporations have to be more aware of their responsibilities to their stakeholders, which includes their shareholders and employees, but also environmentalist groups, local communities' etc. So, where should firms draw the line? The Shell case has highlighted the importance of firms having very clear ethical standards and knowing exactly where their obligations lie, and to what extent they should enforce them.

In analysing this case, one needs to base ones ethical evaluation on factual information as well as moral judgement. The facts as they have been imparted by Shell and various interested groups have been presented, so how does one morally judge Shell? There are those, such as Friedman who believe "[t]he social responsibility of business is to increase its profits", and others such as Evan and Freeman who uphold the stakeholder theory. Individuals have different perceptions about right and wrong, and thus have different ethical standards, but there are a number of ethical theories that help people draw different conclusions (Beauchamp and Bowie 1983).

- The utilitarian or teleological approach of "The greatest good for the greatest number" where human welfare is promoted by minimising harms and maximising benefits. This theory implies that Shell should have acted for the good of the majority, but how does one define "good" and who is this majority – the general population in Nigeria or Shell's wider stakeholders?

- The universalist or deontological approach where tenets state that the "moral worth of an action is independent of the consequences," suggests that people should be treated as ends in themselves, rather than as a means to an end. What were Shell's motives in their treatment of the Ogoni people and their lands? Were they treated as a means to an end – the end simply being profit, or did Shell believe their actions would benefit the population as a whole?

- The rights based approach based on the Universal Declaration of Human Rights, the U.S. Constitution and the European Convention on Human Rights. Did Shell follow the Universal Declaration of Human Rights? Did they do all they could to protect the Ogoni lands and people, and was it their duty to fight for Ken Saro-Wiwa?

- The justice approach is based on the principle: "equals ought to be treated equally and unequals unequally" – like cases should be treated alike. Taking this further, "distributive justice" refers to the distribution of social goods and social burdens. However, how can Shell decide what is "equal" and how these goods and burdens should be distributed?

- The natural law's golden rule is "Do unto others as you would have others do unto you." If the situations were reversed, would Shell's management like to be treated in the same manner as they have treated the Ogoni people? Can they truly justify the environmental destruction of Ogoniland, their dealings with the Nigerian government and their non-intervention on behalf of Ken Saro-Wiwa?

Whichever view one does take, it is clear that Shell adopted double standards over the environment and was hypocritical in their dealings with the government. It is, however, important to note that they were in a very delicate position due to the political regime in Nigeria where they were contributing vast amounts to the economy. However, whilst it is difficult to judge Shell on their political involvement, it is clear that they should have consulted more thoroughly with their stakeholders and held a clearer line, taking all the facts into consideration.

In conclusion, one can only hope that Shell has learnt a major lesson in business ethics and will be more ready to cope with and, more importantly, avoid international crises in the future – that they will adopt a proactive rather than reactive ethical stance for the future.

8. Update – 1999

In April 1998, Shell became the first mainstream multinational to publish an ethics report (The Shell Report 1998; Profits and Principles – does there have to be a choice?). It included a bold statement of principle on the company's responsibility to society:

> To conduct business as responsible members of society, to observe the laws of the countries in which they operate, to express support for fundamental human rights in line with the legitimate role of business and to give proper regard to health, safety and the environment consistent with their commitment to contribute to sustainable development (Shell Report 1998:14).

The report was the first real evidence that the traumatic events of Brent Spar and Nigeria had brought home to Shell's bosses the need to change its perceived culture of secrecy and arrogance. It was also a reflection of the growing awareness among business leaders of the need to adhere to the triple bottom line of social, environmental and financial objectives – that a company's reputation is based, in part, on how governments and peoples at home and abroad assess its behaviour (*The Guardian*, 18 March 1999). What has happened to Shell in Nigeria since 1996 and what are perceptions of the company since they published their ethics report?

It would appear from press coverage that Shell's operations in Nigeria have continued to be dogged both by local unrest and criticism and condemnation from overseas. In September 1998, Shell was losing 800,000 barrels a day of production in Nigeria due to a combination of leaks and sabotage (*The Times*, 2 September 1999). Inhabitants of the Niger delta are still restive over the lack of development in a region that produces most of the country's wealth. In Ogoniland, Shell has started to pay for more schools, but has done little to provide water and electricity or employ local people (*The Guardian*, 26 February 1999). Meanwhile, the Ogoni people were not consulted about pipelines that passed within metres of their homes and peaceful demonstrators have been met with force by the Nigerian military (*The Big Issue*, 19 February 1999). Shell has threatened to pull out of a £6 billion joint venture if Nigeria fails to improve its human rights record, saying they will monitor the situation closely when the new government is installed in spring 1999 (*The Express FT*, 12 February 1999).

In February 1999, Shell announced its worst set of results in history, blaming a 33% fall in oil prices (*The Financial Times*, 12 February 1999). It also announced it would be shifting its focus from high-cost operations, such as those in North America, to low-cost sites including Nigeria. Chairman, Mark Moody-Stuart, said the key to surviving the price squeeze was access to low-cost oil. Challenged on the company's controversial presence in Nigeria, he said while Shell would encourage the Nigerian government to use its quarter-share of oil revenues in a constructive way, the company could not lay down the law (*The Guardian*, 12 February 1999). Shell thus plans to invest $8.5 billion in oil and gas projects in Nigeria, leading to a potential 25% increase in the country's oil output over the next five years. Such investment would entrench Shell's presence in Nigeria. Significantly however, the key elements of the investment are four offshore reserves that should offer Shell brighter prospects away from the community disturbances (*The Times*, 9 February 1999).

It is difficult to check Shell's performance against their emerging economic, social and environmental performance indicators. Shell has set up an internal Social Accountability Team and is working with Arthur D. Little and SustainAbility to develop a range of "total net value added" measures to improve its triple bottom line accounting, auditing, reporting and benchmarking (Elkington 1998:47). Chairman, Mark Moody-Stuart, has declared: "We won't achieve our business goals unless we are listening to and learning from the full range of our stakeholders in society" (*The Guardian*, 18 March 1999). It promises its next audit, published in April 1999, will be "more balanced" including comments from six independent assessors. Press reports indicate Shell is pumping £25 million into a publicity campaign (including a series of stakeholder forums) tied to the launch of its next report to convince the world it is serious about issues such as human rights, sustainable development, business honesty, care for the environment and safe working (*The Independent*, 15 March 1999).

Kaptein and Wempe, who were involved in the verification of the first Shell report, believe an ethics report must provide a realistic picture of a company's operations: problems must not be disguised; differences of opinion and insight must not be papered over so that the report can be used to inform company decision-making in the future. They warn that if such reports are used for PR purposes, they will not make good tools for debate between and with stakeholders – to feel confident their contributions will be listened to and acted upon, stakeholders must believe the company sees itself as vulnerable and willing to improve, not merely proud of the changes it has made to date (Kaptein and Wempe 1998:138).

Has Shell merely jumped on the bandwagon of ethical auditing to silence its critics or is there a genuine desire to change? The evidence three years on is that the company has adopted a more proactive ethical stance as we indicated it should, but little appears to have changed in its behaviour towards the Ogoni people of Nigeria. Listening to its stakeholders' criticisms is one thing, but acting on them is quite another. If Shell uses its latest ethics report simply as a PR tool to manage bad news and doesn't deliver on its promises, it risks alienating its customers and investors. Hopefully, Shell's future ethics reports will be issued for the right reasons.

References

Ashton-Jones, N. 1995. "Pro-Natura." Reported in *The Guardian* 15 January.
Beauchamp, T. L. & Bowie N.E. 1988. *Ethical Theory and Business*.
Drummond, J. & Bain, B. 1994. *Managing Business Ethics*.
Elkington, J. 1998. *Contributing to Society. The Shell Report*.
Gandz, J. & Hayes, N. 1988. "Teaching of Business Ethics." *Journal of Business Ethics* vol. 7: 657–69.
Greenpeace. 1994. *Shell-Shocked* (July).
Johnson, G. & Scholes, K. 1993. *Exploring Corporate Strategy*. Prentice Hall.
Kaptein, M. & Wempe, J. "The Ethics Report: A Means of Sharing Responsibility." *Business Ethics: A European Review* 7 (July).
A Question of Values Conference. 1989. Cambridge, U.K.
Shell Briefing. 1995. *Shell in Nigeria* December.
The Shell Report. 1998.

Notes about the Authors and Editors

Michelle Amestoy, a U.S. citizen, holds a Bachelor of Arts degree in Political Science from the University of California, Berkeley. She received her CPA certificate in 1994 and worked for a public accounting firm where she specialized in providing executives with personal financial planning services. Ms. Amestoy graduated with a Master of Business Administration from the University of Notre Dame in May 1999. After graduation she is pursuing a career working in the finance field. During her MBA course on international business ethics in fall 1998 she read an article in the *Wall Street Journal* that focused on the child labor problems in the orange juice industry. This article also prompted her interest in learning more about the complex issues facing the orange juice industry specifically in Brazil and that interest lead to this research paper with Melissa Crosbie.

Simon Bernstein, Director of Communications and Fundraising, Friends of the Earth, London, U.K. earned his BA (Hons) in History from the University of Warwich and received his MBA from the Full-time Management Program at Imperial College in 1996. This essay was originally composed as a group presentation within the Business Ethics MBA module. He has further developed the chapter including providing an update on recent Shell activities in Nigeria. Mr. Bernstein has worked in Marketing for various U.K. Local Authorities including five years in communications for the National Society for Precention of Cruelty to Children (NSPCC) as well as a consultancy role with the Royal National Institute for the Blind (NRIB).

Marvin T. Brown teaches in the Philosophy Department and in the College of Professional Studies, University of San Francisco where he was 1989 Teacher of the Year, and the California School of Professional Psychology in Orinda, California. Dr. Brown holds a MDiv in Practical Theology and a Ph.D. in Theology and Rhetoric. He is the author of *Working Ethics: Strategies for Decision Making and Organizational Responsibility* (San Francisco: Jossey-Bass, 1990) and *The Ethical Press: An Approach to Controversial Issues* (New York: Prentice-Hall, 1998). He has been a consultant and has conducted workshops in the ethics of decision making in the U.S.A. and abroad as well as Facilitator in the Diversity and Ethics Program, Levi Strauss and Company, San Francisco.

Sue Cooper graduated with a first in English Language and Literature from Glasgow University in 1981 with studies in General Philosophy and received a M.Litt. from Balliol College, Oxford in 1982. From 1983–1997 she joined the U.K. Inland Revenue working first as a tax inspector responsible for reviewing financial aspects of domestic and multinational companies. She then served on a small team responsible for recommending new legislation and advising Government Ministers on Tax Policies related to financial markets and foreign exchange. This updated essay was first written while enrolled in the Executive MBA Module in Business Ethics. Ms. Cooper completed her Executive MBA at Imperial College, University of London in 1998. Presently she is an Assistant Director of a U.K. investment bank based in London.

Melissa Crosbie, a U.S. citizen, holds a Bachelor of Science, summa cum laude, in Accounting from Wilkes University and received her CPA license in 1994. She graduated with a Master of Business Administration from the University of Notre Dame in May 1999 and accepted a position as a Senior consultant with Deloitte and Touche Solutions in Chicago, Illinois and commenced employment after graduation. In her MBA course on international business ethics in fall 1998 Ms. Crosbie became interested in researching the topic of Brazilian child labor and the orange juice industry after reading an article in the *Wall Street Journal*. She was especially curious to learn how widespread child labor is within Brazil and what actions have and are currently being undertaken to help solve this problem.

George Cui, a Chinese citizen, holds a Bachelor of Art in English Literature from Shanghai International Studies University. His education exposed him to a cross cultural environment and aroused his interest in exploring the differences and their possible explanations. Such early experience was enhanced later in his career. As administrator for China operations of AMSCO, he was involved in negotiations for setting up joint ventures. His second job was similar in nature when he helped establish a China/U.S. joint venture, Shanghai Lomason Automotive Seating Systems Co., Ltd. and later became the assistant to president in that company. The experience in joint venture negotiations provided Mr. Cui with vivid examples concerning issues of business ethics and argument from both sides of the table. It has become the basis of this paper written in the MBA course on business ethics in April 1998. From 1997 to 1998 he studied in the MBA program at the China Europe International Business School (CEIBS) in Shanghai and then at the Darden Business School of the University of Virginia as an exchange student. He is working as the program manager in Shanghai Lomason, exporting scat assembly to the U.S.A. He enjoys being a communication bridge for the cross cultural management team in his company.

Monika Dębicka was born in Augustów, Poland in 1972. Since 1996, she has been employed by Potamkin International Poland Ltd., the exclusive licensee of the American company Office Depot in Poland, where she is the Director of Marketing. Ms. Dębicka is a 1998 honors graduate of the American Studies Center of Warsaw University, where she earned a master's degree in Business Ethics.

John Donaldson is an Honorary Visiting Fellow, International Centre for Law, Management and Industrial Relations, University of Leicester. Dr. Donaldson is the author of *Key Issues in Business Ethics* (London: Academic Press, 1989), *Business Ethics: A European Casebook* (London: Academic Press, 1992) and *Cooperative Management: A Philosophy for Business* (with Peter Davis) (Cheltenham: New Harmony Press, 1998). He is a graduate of Oxford University (Keble College) in Philosophy, Politics and Economics and also holds a Masters degree and diploma from Oxford.

Georges Enderle is Arthur and Mary O'Neil Professor of International Business Ethics at the University of Notre Dame, Indiana, and Vice President of the International Society of Business, Economics and Ethics (ISBEE). Before joining the faculty at Notre Dame in 1992, he was doing research and teaching in the field of business ethics in Europe over ten years and was co-founder of the European Business Ethics Network (EBEN). He also conducted a number of seminars on business ethics in companies like Ciba-Geigy and BMW. Since 1994 he has been involved in numerous research and teaching activities in China, particularly at the China Europe International Business School (CEIBS) in Shanghai. Hi has authored and edited many books and articles including *International Business Ethics: Challenges and Approaches* (Notre Dame 1999), *Region- and Country-Related Reports on Business Ethics* (*Journal of Business Ethics*, October 1997), *Handlungsorientierte Wirtschaftsethik* (Action-oriented Business Ethics, Bern 1993), *Lexikon der Wirtschaftsethik* (Encyclopedia of Business Ethics, Freiburg 1993), and *People in Corporations: Ethical Responsibilities and Corporate Effectiveness* (Dordrecht 1990). His research interests lie in understanding the ethical challenges of international business for corporate decision making, how they are to be analyzed in the context of global pluralism and lacking background institutions, how they can be met by ethical guidelines, corporate culture, and promoting background institutions.

Diane Flannery earned a doctorate in Organizational Psychology at the California School of Professional Psychology in 1997. Her area of research emphasized the relationships between business and society. She first undertook the topic of this paper while enrolled in a course in "Business Ethics" taught by Prof. Marvin Brown who was a Visiting Professor in her graduate program. Her dissertation was entitled: "Toward a Theory of Corporate Socially Responsible Images: Impression management and Corporate Social Performance." In 1994, Ms. Flannery founded and serves as CEO of Juma Ventures, a five year old, San Francisco based social-entrepreneurial organization. Juma Ventures uses business enterprises as the vehicle to provide employment and entrepreneurial training opportunities to low income young adults.

Pablo Flores, an Ecuadorian citizen born and raised in Quito, Ecuador, has always regarded the Amazon rainforest as a priceless natural resource in South America that should be preserved for the benefit of future generations. His research paper, written during his MBA course on international business ethics at the University of Notre Dame (October 1997), incorporates a valuable though often neglected ethical dimension that strengthens his position in favor of rainforest conservation. He holds a Bachelor of Arts, cum laude, in Management from Eckerd College, as well as a Master of Business Administration, cum laude, from the University of Notre Dame (May 1998). Presently, he works as New Project Coordinator for YPF Ecuador Inc., the largest private oil exploration and production corporation in Ecuador and Latin America.

Wojciech W. Gasparski is Professor of Humanities, Dr. S. is a Chairman of the Academic Board and a Professor of Humanities at the Logic of Language and Action Department in the Institute of Philosophy and Sociology of the Polish Academy of Sciences, Warsaw, Poland. In the Institute he heads the Research Group for Ethics in the Economy and Business. He serves as a Chairman of the Academy's Science Studies Committee. He teaches at the American Studies Center of the Warsaw University, Warsaw University of Technology, L. Koźmiński Academy of Entrepreneurship and Management in Warsaw, and Saybrook Graduate School in San Francisco, CA (U.S.A.). He was a Fulbright Senior Visiting Scholar at the State University of New York and visited universities in other countries and extensively contributed international conferences. He published several books and over two hundred and sixty articles and conference papers. He is Editor-in-Chief of series *Praxiology: The International Annual of Practical Philosophy and Methodology* (published in the U.S. by Transaction, New Brunswick, N.J. Publishers) and Polish journal *Prakseologia*. His recent books are: (1) W. W. Gasparski, D. Botham, eds., 1988, *Action Learning*, Transaction, New Brunswick, N.J.; (2) W. W. Gasparski, L. V. Ryan, C.S.V., eds., 1996, *Human Action in Business: Praxiological and Ethical Dimensions*, Transaction, New Brunswick, N.J.; (3) W. W. Gasparski, M. K. Mlicki and B. H. Banathy, eds., 1996, *Social Agency: Dilemmas and Education*, Transaction, New Brunswick, N.J.; (4) A. Collen, W. W. Gasparski, eds., *Design & Systems: General Applications of Methodology*, Transaction, New Brunswick, N.J.; (5) W. W. Gasparski, T. Airaksinen, eds., 1995, *Science in Society*, IFiS Publishers; (6) W. W. Gasparski, 1993, *A Philosophy of Practicality: A Treatise on the Philosophy of Tadeusz Kotarbiński*, Societas Philosophica Fennica, Helsinki. He was awarded a Polish Medal of National Education (1998).

Yan Guo, a Chinese citizen, has been working with the chemical industry ever since his graduation from Beijing University in 1988. His current job concerns many food ingredients including herbal products. He is currently the Shanghai office manager of the Dutch based Royal Pakhoed company. His education includes a BS and 20-month MBA (graduation in 1998) at the China Europe International Business School (CEIBS) in Shanghai. This article was based on a research paper for the business ethics course during the MBA program, and he is still very concerned in the industry.

Keven Joseph Kelleher, a U.S. citizen, grew up in the state of Con-
necticut, and since the time he was a young child, wanted to serve in the
Marine Corps. What drew young Keven to the Marines was their strong
sense of honor, courage and commitment, and the opportunites, responsibilities and challenges posed to their young officers. After graduating
from the University of Notre Dame with a Bachelor of Arts in English
and Economics, Mr. Kelleher entered the United States Marine Corps as
a Second Lieutenant and served six years in armor and then in the field
of logistics. He left the Marine Corps as a Captain to attend MBA school
full time. Mr. Kelleher wrote this paper during his MBA course on international business ethics in fall 1998. He graduated from the University
of Notre Dame's MBA school in May of 1999 and began his civilian
career as Senior Consultant for Deloitte and Touche's Solutions practice
in Cincinnati, Ohio, his wife's home town. Mr. Kelleher has two daughters, and for the immediate future, he plans on concentrating his efforts
on them and work.

William W. Kirkley, born in the U.S.A., emigrated with his family to
South Africa. He earned a degree in Industrial Sociology from the University of South Africa; later completing post-graduate studies in both
Labour Law and Management at the same university. Mr. Kirkley is
a Management Consultant providing specialist advice to New Zealand businesses in the areas of Organizational Transformation (OT), business
reconfiguration and strategy. He has consulted with multinational companies throughout the southern hemisphere primarily in the Human Resource
and Organizational development fields. He enrolled in the MA/LLM Program at University of Leicester, U.K. International Center for Law, Management and Industrial Relations. Mr. Kirkley completed his M.A. Dissertation, "Organizational Transformation and Strategic Success: The Role
of Values," by distance learning in 1999 under the direction of Dr. John
Donaldson, Visiting Fellow, Management Center, University of Leicester.

Elizabeth Klein graduated with first class honors in Genetics at the
University of Liverpool. She was employed by Zeneca Seeds as a Research Scientist before she entered the full time MBA Management Program at Imperial College. This updated essay was first written while
enrolled in the MBA Module in Business Ethics. Upon completing her
MBA in 1995, Ms. Klein worked at DE Shaw Securities International
trading equity linked derivatives. Currently, she is a Pharmaceutical and
Health Care Investment Analyst at Barclay Stockbrokers, London.

Krzysztof Klincewicz has studied management science at University of Warsaw, Philosophy at University of Helsinki, and Business Ethics at Collegium Invisibile, Warsaw. During his studies, he was co-founder and president of University Management Club – student association, part of Austrian-Polish managers union. He has worked as consultant for a British computer systems integrator ICL, and currently is holding a business development position at Team WARE Group, software division of Fujitsu Corporation, where he is taking care of Poland and other Eastern European markets. In his professional life, he is deeply involved in topics such as: process and knowledge management, and Customer Relationship Management (CRM), an information technology concept corresponding to the idea of relationship marketing. To his main interests belong business ethics (especially marketing ethics and relationship marketing), international business strategy, and business information systems. His publications on business ethics include the following articles: "Ethical Aspects of Sponsorship" (*Journal of Business Ethics*, Kluwer 1998), "Business Ethics According to Alasdair MacIntyre" (*Prakseologia*, 1998), "Ethical Leadership" (PWN 1999), "Postindustrial Perspectives for Business Ethics: A New Model for Client Relationship" (*Bulletin of the Polish Business Ethics Research Group*, 1999).

Bożena Kochman has a Master's Degree (1997) in American Business Ethics and Culture from the American Studies Center at the University of Warsaw and Bachelor's Degree (1996) in English from the University of Śląsk in Katowice. She works as an assistant at the English Studies in the Rzeszów Pedagogical Institute. During her studies and visits to the States and Canada she got interested in the American culture. However, her special field of interest includes ethical and cultural dilemmas in business in America and in Poland, what will be the subject of her Ph.D.

Kevin Lee Kreutner, a U.S. citizen, has been employed in the food industry since he was fourteen, working primarily in heavily Latino populated Southern California where he developed a concern for the plight of migrant laborers. That interest prompted this research study which he wrote during his Notre Dame MBA course on international business ethics in October 1997. Mr. Kreutner is Marketing Manager for the Doskocil Food Service Company in Hutchinson, Kansas, where he controls the company's brands of pizza products. He holds a Bachelor of Arts, cum laude, in marketing from the California State University at

Fullerton and a Master of Business Administration, magna cum laude, from the University of Notre Dame, from which he graduated in May 1998. Mr. Kreutner plans to further his academic interest at the doctoral level concentrating in business ethics and has considered researching the relationships between the corporate social mission and brand equity.

Hannah Lu, a Chinese citizen, after graduating from China Textile University in Shanghai with a Bachelor of Science, has spent most of her career years in foreign invested companies. Her first job, for less than a year, was in a Chinese state-owned enterprise working as a translator and technician. She then worked for Nestle Shuangcheng Ltd. as purchasing officer for three years. In 1997–1998 she pursued her MBA degree at the China Europe International Business School (CEIBS) in Shanghai. The experience in the joint venture raised some issues typical of multinational and multicultural management environment, which she later put into this research paper written in the MBA course on business ethics in April 1998. Ms. Lu is now working for Shanghai Henkel Kemeng Cosmetics Company Ltd. as a purchasing manager responsible for setting up management control systems and improving performance in this area by optimizing inventory and centralizing purchase. She certainly hopes to utilize her knowledge of business administration in her new job.

Christopher J. Moon is Senior Lecturer in Business and Organizational Ethics, Anglia Business School, Danbury and Cambridge, U.K. He earned his BA (Hons) at the University of Lancaster and a MSc in Applied Psychology at the University of Wales. He has been a Lecturer in Organizational Behavior, University of Greenwich and Visiting Lecturer in Business Ethics at the Management School, Imperial College, University of London, where he has completed requirements for the Ph.D. in Business Ethics. While at the Management School, Imperial College, he taught all the MBA modules in Business Ethics. From among those students, he selected the essays published in this volume. At Anglia, he has developed an MBA program in Organizational Ethics to be delivered via the Internet. Mr. Moon has published widely in the field of Business Ethics and presented papers at numerous national and international conferences. His Ph.D. thesis in Business Ethics is on Stakeholder Management and Community Relations. He is secretary of the European Business Ethics Network in the U.K. and a member of the organizing committee for the EBEN 2000 international conference held in Cambridge, U.K. on the theme of "Ethics: leadership and accountability." He is a member of the Institute of Social and Ethical Account Ability and has been trained as an ethical accountant and auditor. He is a Fellow of the Royal Society of Arts manufacturers and Commerce; a graduate member of the British Psychological Society; and President of Essex, Junior Chamber in the U.K.

Lawrence Pineda, a U.S. citizen, graduated from the University of New Mexico in Albuquerque in 1989. He spent six years working in public accounting and then worked for two years for a national healthcare firm. Mr. Pineda decided to enroll in the MBA program at the University of Notre Dame, from which he graduated in May 1999 with a finance concentration. He wrote this paper in the course on international business ethics. Upon graduation, he accepted a position with Delta Air Lines in Atlanta, Georgia. He has an interest in working internationally and hopes to, someday, use this experience to become involved in projects similar to the Grameen Bank in underdeveloped Latin American countries.

Agnieszka Ratajczyk-Zwierko graduated from the Teacher's Training College, Olsztyn in 1994 and started her job as a teacher of English in the Secondary School in Olsztyn. Since 1995 she studied at the American Studies Center at Warsaw University and specialized in American Business Culture. In 1997 she graduated from the American Studies Center. Her M.A. thesis titled "American and Polish Trademarks: the Culture and Ethics behind Them" is a comparative study of the cultural and ethical differences between the U.S. and Poland and their impact on the development and the present condition of the American and Polish trademarks.

Leo V. Ryan, C.S.V., Professor of Management, DePaul University (Chicago) and a Fellow, St. Edmund's College, Cambridge earned his Ph.D. in Management at Saint Louis University, an MBA in Marketing at DePaul and his Bachelor in Business Administration in General Business at Marquette University. Seton Hall University awarded him an honorary LLD in 1988. Illinois Benedictine University awarded an honorary DHL in 1997. In 1990 he received a Kościuszko Fellowship to study in Poland. Between 1991–1993 he was awarded five USIS Academic Specialist grants to lecture in Poland and from 1993–1995 he held a three year Fulbright appointment at Adam Mickiewicz University, Poznań. He received the DePaul Excellence in Teaching Award in 1995. Adam Mickiewicz University conferred on him their Medal of

Merit in 1995 for "distinguished contributions to the life of the University," and DePaul presented him their highest faculty honour, The Via Sapientiae Award 1999. Professor Ryan has also been Visiting Professor at the Poznań Academy of Economics, Polish-American Study Center, University of Łódź, the Higher School of Management and Banking (Poznań) and the Warsaw Higher School of Business and Law. He was elected a member of the Learned Society of Praxiology in 1994; named an Honorary Life Member and appointed to the International Advisory Board of the Society Annual in 1997. Professor Ryan is the former Wicklander Professor of Professional Ethics at DePaul and past-President, Society for Business Ethics (U.S.A.). He is the founder and member of the Advisory Board for the Institute of Business Ethics (DePaul), Institute of International Business Ethics (Thunderbird), and The University of Maryland, Management Education in Poland (MEP) Project. He serves on the Editorial Advisory Board for *Business Ethics Quarterly*, *European Business Journal*, *International Journal of Value-Based Management*, and *The Mid-Atlantic Journal of Business*. In 1996, he served as contributor and co-editor with Professor Wojciech W. Gasparski of *Human Action in Business: Praxiological and Ethical Dimensions* (International Annual of Practical Philosophy and Methodology, Vol. 5, Transaction Publishers, New Brunswick, N.J.). In 1997, he published with Professor Jacek Sojka, *Etyka biznesu; z klasyki współczesnej myśli amerykańskiej (Business Ethics: Classical American Texts from the Field)* (Poznań: W drodze). Professor Ryan received a research leave from DePaul in 1997 to accept an invitation as Guest Scholar, Helen Kellogg Institute for International Studies, University of Notre Dame to complete research and writing a book on Polish economic transformation and Polish privatization. *From Autarchy to Market: Polish Economics and Politics. 1945–1995* (Westport, Conn: Praeger, 1998) was co-authored with Professor Richard J. Hunter, Jr. Professor Ryan has also contributed chapters to numerous volumes in both Polish and English and published articles on ethics, economics, management, and privatization in professional journals in the U.S.A. and abroad.

Agnieszka Szumska earned her B.A. at the Teacher Training College, Rzeszów (1994) and her M.A. in American Business Culture at the University of Warsaw (1997). She completed her post-graduate studies in management at the Maria Curie-Skłodowska University, Rzeszów (1999). She has been teaching English at a high school level and giving instruction to the Teacher Training College students.

Barbara Szyszka, born in 1972, is a qualified teacher of English currently working for the Association of Entrepreneurship Promotion in Rzeszów, in the south-east of Poland. She received her M.A. in American Business Culture from American Studies Center, University of Warsaw, Poland in 1997.

Julia Tian, a Chinese citizen, graduated from Huazhong University of Science and Technology as an engineer in 1988. She then worked at Wanbao Electrical Appliance Group (Guangdong Province) for 7 years, where she was responsible for refrigeration system design. One of her group's designs was awarded a prize by the Ministry of Light Industry. Later, she acted as deputy manager for an entrepreneurial company for two years, where she was responsible for administrative and financial management. In 1997–1998 she attended the MBA program at the China Europe International Business School (CEIBS) in Shanghai and wrote this paper in the course of business ethics in April 1998. After graduation, Ms. Tian is now working with East Marketing Research Co., Ltd, a major market research company in south China. She manages research projects for various clients.

Victor Trujillo, a Venezuelan native, was first exposed to ethics while working towards his Public Accounting degree at the Universidad Católica Andrés Bello in Caracas, Venezuela. As a student representative, he was involved in discussions on how the university could better serve its country´s needs, including, and especially, working conditions and standards of living. Conclusions very often pointed to ethics. These discussions served him as inspiration for this research paper written in the MBA course on international business ethics (fall 1997) at the University of Notre Dame, from which he graduated in 1998. Mr. Trujillo is currently working as a Business Planning Analyst for Chevron's Latin American Headquarters in Caracas. He is involved in the company's strategic plan process as well as in mergers and acquisitions.

John Matthew Walusis, a U.S. citizen born and brought up in Dayton, Ohio, had never traveled to a developing country before he had the opportunity to visit Bangladesh in 1996 and again in 1997. There he learned a great deal about the Grameen Bank and its impact on Bangladesh. During his MBA course at the University of Notre Dame in international business ethics in the fall of 1998, John Walusis and Lawrence Pineda wrote this paper because they thought that businesses operating in countries like Bangladesh could learn something from the Grameen

Bank. Mr. Walusis holds a Bachelor of Science in Accountancy from Wright State University and graduated with a Master in Business Administration, cum laude, from the University of Notre Dame in May 1999. He is presently a consultant for SAP America, Inc. in Chicago, Illinois. His future plans include the continuing his education at the doctoral level.

Kerry Ward, a U.S. citizen, became interested in ethics while attending Wabash College where he majored in Psychology and Religion. After graduation, he began his professional career as a police officer with the Indianapolis Police Department where he earned two letters of commendation. Six years of experience as an inner city police officer reinforced his interest in ethics. While on the police department, Mr. Ward graduated magna cum laude from Indiana University with a degree in Business Administration. He passed the CPA exam and resigned from the police department to take a position in public accounting. During 1998–1999 he enrolled in the Notre Dame MBA program where he wrote this paper during his course on international business ethics. He completed his MBA in May 1999 and accepted a position with Deloitte and Touche LLP in Dallas, Texas.

Angela Xu, a Chinese citizen, majored in English for Science and Technology at Shanghai Jiaotong University in 1991. Afterwards she worked with Mitsubishi Corporation, a Japanese multi-national trading house, for five and half years. She first handled international trade and then acted as joint venture (JV) project co-ordinator for the majority of her time. Being a co-ordinator, she served as a bridge between foreign and Chinese partners, helped smoothing the negotiation process and successfully supported several JV's start-ups and implementation. In 1997–1998 Ms. Xu attended the MBA program at the China Europe International Business School (CEIBS) in Shanghai and wrote this paper in the course of business ethics in April 1998. After graduation, she is now working as project manager in an American non-for-profit organization, providing consultation to its membership companies.